CHARLEMAGNE
The Great Adventure

Donald Macpherson
7 Meikle Gardens
Westhill
Aberdeenshire

Dunblane 1st March 2015
Holidays

CHARLEMAGNE

The Great Adventure

Derek Wilson

HUTCHINSON
LONDON

944·014

First published in the United Kingdom by Hutchinson in 2005

1 3 5 7 9 10 8 6 4 2

Hutchinson
The Random House Group Limited
20 Vauxhall Bridge Road, London SW1V 2SA

Random House Australia (Pty) Limited
20 Alfred Street, Milsons Point, Sydney
New South Wales 2061, Australia

Random House New Zealand Limited
18 Poland Road, Glenfield
Auckland 10, New Zealand

Random House (Pty) Limited
Endulini, 5a Jubilee Road, Parktown 2193, South Africa

The Random House Group Limited Reg. No. 954009

www.randomhouse.co.uk

A CIP catalogue record for this book
is available from the British Library

Papers used by Random House are
natural, recyclable products made from wood grown in
sustainable forests. The manufacturing processes conform to
the environmental regulations of the country of origin

ISBN 0 0917 9461 7

Typeset by Palimpsest Book Production Limited,
Polmont, Stirlingshire
Printed and bound in Great Britain by
William Clowes Ltd, Beccles, Suffolk

Contents

Illustrations

1. Gothic Reliquary Bust of Charlemagne, IH163923. © Corbis Inc.

2. Charles Martel in the Battle of Tours, CS006426. © Corbis Inc.

3. Scenes from the lives of the Emperors: Coronation of Charlemagne. Paris, Bibliothèque de l'Arsenal © 1990 Photo Scala, Florence.

4. King Charlemagne Receiving an Oath of Fidelity from the *Chroniques de St Denis* Manuscript, AABR004570. © Corbis Inc.

5. Emperor Charlemagne (747–814) and his Army fighting the Saracens in Spain, 778 from the Story of Ogier (vellum) by Verard, Antoine (1450–1519), RVI101789 #175 Private Collection, Roger-Viollet, Paris. French, out of copyright.

6. Document signed by Emperor Charlemagne (742–814) with his monogram (vellum), ARH175033 #203 Centre Historique des Archives Nationales, Paris, France Archives Charmet, copyright unknown.

7. Gold Solidus of Empress Irene. © British Museum.

8. ALG172666 #203 Charlemagne (742–814) Placing the Relics of Christ in the Chapel of Aix-la-Chapelle (oil on canvas) by Orley, Bernard van (c.1488–1541) Galleria Sabauda, Turin, Italy Alinari Netherlandish, out of copyright.

21. The Emperor Charles V (1500–58) on Horseback in Muhlberg, 1548 (oil on canvas) by Titian (Tiziano Vecellio) (c.1488–1576), XJL23261 #203 Prado, Madrid, Spain, Italian, out of copyright.

22. Stage on the Large Pond representing the Isle of Alcine, third day of 'Les Plaisirs de l'Ile Enchantée', 9th May 1664 (engravi by Silvestre, Israel, the Younger (1621–91)', XIR154788 #189 Musée de la Ville de Paris, Musée Carnavalet, Paris, France. French, out of copyright.

23. *Napoleon at Charlemagne's Throne '98* by Henri Paul Motte, AALQ001558. © Corbis Inc.

24. Francois Guizot (1787–1874) after a painting by Paul Delaroche (1797–1856) c.1878 (oil on canvas) by Vibert, Jean or Jehan Georges (1840–1902) XIR158228 #235 Chateau de Versailles, France. Lauros / Giraudon. French, out of copyright.

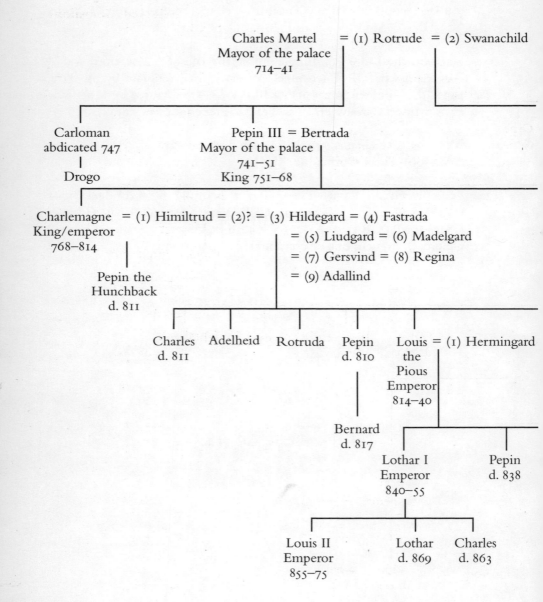

Charles Martel = (1) Rotrude = (2) Swanachild
Mayor of the palace
714–41

Carloman
abdicated 747

Drogo

Pepin III = Bertrada
Mayor of the palace
741–51
King 751–68

Charlemagne = (1) Himiltrud = (2)? = (3) Hildegard = (4) Fastrada
King/emperor = (5) Liudgard = (6) Madelgard
768–814 = (7) Gersvind = (8) Regina
= (9) Adallind

Pepin the
Hunchback
d. 811

Charles   Adelheid   Rotruda   Pepin   Louis = (1) Hermingard
d. 811   d. 810   the
                                             Pious
                                             Emperor
                                             814–40

Bernard
d. 817

Lothar I   Pepin
Emperor   d. 838
840–55

Louis II   Lothar   Charles
Emperor   d. 869   d. 863
855–75

Note: Charlemagne's numerous female partners cannot be divided simply
into 'wives' and 'concubines'. Frankish custom was far less rigid. This
enabled the king to choose whom he would elevate to the position
of official queen, thus legitimating their joint offspring.

The Carolingian Dynasty
Selected Genealogy

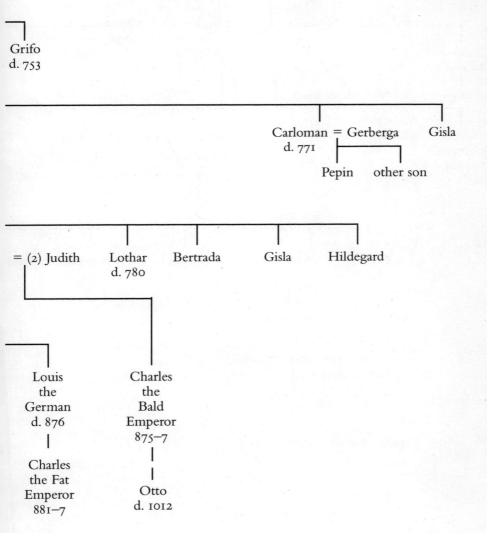

Grifo
d. 753

Carloman = Gerberga   Gisla
d. 771

Pepin   other son

= (2) Judith   Lothar   Bertrada   Gisla   Hildegard
d. 780

Louis
the
German
d. 876

Charles
the
Fat
Emperor
881–7

Charles
the
Bald
Emperor
875–7

Otto
d. 1012

Timeline
Rise and Fall of the Carolingian Empire

Date	Francia	Byzantine Empire
742	Birth of Charlemagne	Iconoclastic Controversy rages during reign of Constantine V (741–75)
743	Pepin III and Carloman install Childeric III as king	
747	Abdication of Carloman	
749		
750		
751	Pepin III crowned by Boniface	Aistulf captures Ravenna. End of Byzantine rule in northern Italy
752		
754	Stephen II asks for Pepin's aid against the Lombards. Pepin's first Italian campaign	
755		
756	Pepin's second Italian campaign	
757		
763		
767/8	Pepin completes conquest of Aquitania	

Western Christendom   **Islamic World**

Aistulf becomes King of the Lombards
and threatens Rome

                                           Overthrow of the Umayyads by
                                           the Abbasids everywhere except
                                           Spain

Death of Zacharias. Stephen II
becomes pope

Martyrdom of Boniface in Frisia

                                           'Abd-al-Rahman founds the
                                           caliphate of Cordoba

Death of Stephen II. Paul I becomes
pope. Death of Aistulf. Desiderius
becomes King of the Lombards

                                           Baghdad becomes the Abbasid
                                           capital

Death of Paul I. Conflict between
rival popes

Date	Francia	Byzantine Empire
768	Death of Pepin III. Charles and Carloman divide his kingdom	
769	Charlemagne suppresses revolt in Aquitania	
770	Birth of Pepin the Hunchback	
771	Death of Carloman. Charlemagne sole ruler	
772	Beginning of the Saxon Wars	
773/4	Charlemagne conquers Lombardy	
775		Death of Constantine V. Leo IV becomes emperor
778	Spanish campaign. Slaughter of the rearguard at Roncesvalles	
780		Death of Leo IV. Irene ruling as regent for Constantine VI. Renewal of the Iconoclastic Controversy
781	Italian campaign. Pepin and Louis crowned by the pope	
782	Massacre of 4,500 Saxons at Verden. Arrival of Alcuin at Charlemagne's court	
785	Baptism of Widukind. End of first phase of Saxon Wars	
786	Count Hardrad's abortive revolt	
787	Italian campaign. Defeat of Duke Arichis of Benevento Annexation of Bavaria to the Frankish Crown	Council of Nicaea endorses image worship

Western Christendom

Islamic World

Stephen III becomes pope

Death of Stephen III. Hadrian I becomes
pope. He appeals for Frankish help

Building of the Great Mosque
of Cordoba begins

Harun al-Raschid becomes
Abbasid caliph and inaugurates
a golden age of Islamic culture

Date	Francia	Byzantine Empire
788	State trial of Tassilo III	
789	Promulgation of the *Admonitio Generalis*	
790	Alcuin is principal of the 'court school'. Charlemagne issues the *Libri Carolini* against image worship	Constantine banishes his mother
792	Renewed Saxon war Revolt of Pepin the Hunchback	Irene regains power
794	Council of Frankfurt condemns image worship and Adoptionism	
795		
796	Conquest of the Avars. Beginning of major building campaign at Aachen. Alcuin leaves court for his abbey at Tours	
797		Irene deposes Constantine VI and, perhaps, contemplates marriage to Charlemagne
799		
800	Charlemagne crowned as emperor in Rome. First Viking raids on Frankish territory. Harun al-Raschid sends ambassadors to Charlemagne's court	
802	Council of Aachen imposes a general oath of loyalty to the emperor. Sporadic Viking raids along the North Sea and Channel coasts	Irene deposed by Nicephorus I. Diplomatic conflict with Charlemagne over the imperial title Beginnings of conflict with the Bulgars
804	Death of Alcuin	

Western Christendom	Islamic World
	Increasing Arab seaborne raids across the Mediterranean
Death of Hadrian I. Leo III becomes pope	
Leo III attacked and deposed. He goes to Paderborn to seek Charlemagne's aid	
Charlemagne restores Leo III	

Date	Francia	Byzantine Empire
805	End of Saxon Wars. The Doge of Venice pays homage to Charlemagne	
806	Charlemagne divides the empire between his three sons	
808	Danish invasion	
809	Pepin fails to suppress Venetian revolt	
810	Death of Prince Pepin. His son Bernard becomes King of Italy King Godfred of Denmark murdered. Peace between Denmark and Francia	Nicephorus I killed while fighting the Bulgars. Michael I Rhangabe becomes emperor. Peace concluded with Charlemagne
811	Death of Prince Charles and Pepin the Hunchback	
812		Michael I recognises Charlemagne's imperial title
813	Charlemagne crowns Prince Louis as joint-emperor	Michael I abdicates. Leo V becomes emperor
814	Death of Charlemagne. Louis the Pious succeeds as sole emperor	
816		
817	Louis divides the empire between his sons Rebellion of Bernard, who is killed by Louis	
820		Leo V assassinated. Michael II becomes emperor
824		

Western Christendom	Islamic World
	Death of Harun al–Raschid. Al–Amin becomes Abbasid caliph
	Death of Amin. Succeeded by his half-brother, Mamun, who becomes Abbasid caliph
Death of Leo III. Stephen IV becomes pope	
Death of Stephen. Paschal I becomes pope	
	Rapid dismemberment of the Abbasid caliphate due to religious divisions
Death of Paschal. Eugenius II becomes pope	

Date	Francia	Byzantine Empire
827	Arab conquest of Sicily and Sardinia	
829		Death of Michael II. Theophilus becomes emperor
833	Louis the Pious deposed by his sons	
835	Louis the Pious restored to the throne	
837	Empire divided between Louis the Pious and his son, Lothar	
838	Arabs invade southern Italy and Marseille	
840	Death of Louis the Pious. Lothar I becomes emperor	
841	War between Lothar I and his brothers Vikings sack Rouen and Paris	
843	Treaty of Verdun divides the empire between Lothar and his brothers. End of the united Frankish Empire	

Timeline

Western Christendom   **Islamic World**

Introduction

It is difficult for the British to understand the importance of Charlemagne. He seems to be a very 'continental' construct, and an obscure one at that. The 1,200-year-old legend and the historical figure who provides its basis are tightly woven into the self-identification of the French and German peoples. And not only them; Charles the Great features in the history books of schools throughout the nations that lie between the mouth of the Elbe and the Gulf of Otranto, the Danube basin and the Pyrenees – that territory over which the Frankish king held sway in a dim and distant past. In Aachen (Aix-la-Chapelle), the German city so nearly in Belgium or the Netherlands, thousands flock every year to pay homage at Charlemagne's shrine, and the civic authorities present an annual Charlemagne Prize to the statesman who has done most to promote the cause of European unity. On the other side of 'our' English Channel, the ancient emperor is spoken of regularly as the 'Father of Europe'. And that, surely, is the problem: Europe. We British are ambiguous about it. We are not sure whether we are part of it or not. When it comes down to it, we are not even clear what Europe actually *is*.

If there has to be a profound motive for writing this book, it is that I want to try to shed some light on this problem of identity. Clearly 'Europe' is not a geographical term: it has no obvious physical boundaries; it is simply a small part of the great Eurasian landmass. And, manifestly, it is not a political term, the area in question being made up of a number of nations, most of which have been in a state of intermittent warfare with each other for the best part of a millennium. Europe is a culture, a way of life shared by peoples who, while jealously guarding their own sovereignty, know that they belong to something bigger and, in some sense at least, more important:

> The European sense of superiority, of having been singled out, first by nature, then by God, to play a special role in the history of creation, derived from the conviction that only those who dwelt in the kind of law-governed, free urban communities of which 'Europe' was constituted would ever be likely to possess the capacity to harness nature to their purposes. The others, the 'barbarians' . . . remained forever in unenlightened herds. In Europe the arts were, in the full sense of the term 'liberal'. And if these . . . had begun in Asia, in Babylon and Egypt, it was only in Europe that their potential had been realised.[1]

Europeans have, over the centuries, unhesitatingly exported themselves, their technology and their beliefs to other lands in the unshakeable conviction that what worked for them − whether Christianity, or capitalism, or parliamentary democracy, or European art − would work for all peoples everywhere.

What has all that got to do with Charlemagne? Well, just about everything. As early as 799 an anonymous poet eulogised the Frankish leader as the 'King and Father of Europe'. What he was alluding to was Charles' creation of something very new: a political/religious/economic entity that had not existed before. Classical civilisation had been centred on the Mediterranean basin. Charlemagne had moved the focus to the Rhine. He had extended, and was still extending, his rule over a heterogeneous conglomeration of peoples north of the Alps (his hold on Italy would remain tenuous) and giving them a sense of cohesion that they were never to lose. The two most astonishing facts about Charlemagne's empire were its northernness and the survival of its core idea. The Mediterranean was still the economic heart of occidental life and would remain so for another seven centuries. There is very little evidence to suggest that a system of vibrant commercial towns situated on trade routes linking the North Sea and the Adriatic was an inevitable development. Charles extended the boundaries of his realm, while also giving it a large measure of internal stability, and it was this that allowed a network of peaceful trade routes to develop. But his grandsons tore his empire to pieces and, in doing so, showed themselves to be heirs of a long Germanic tradition, which, by insisting that a man's territorial possessions be divided among his sons, encouraged rivalry, anarchy, fratricide and the survival of the fittest. So, was Charlemagne's reign merely a brief interlude, a shaft of light in the 'Dark

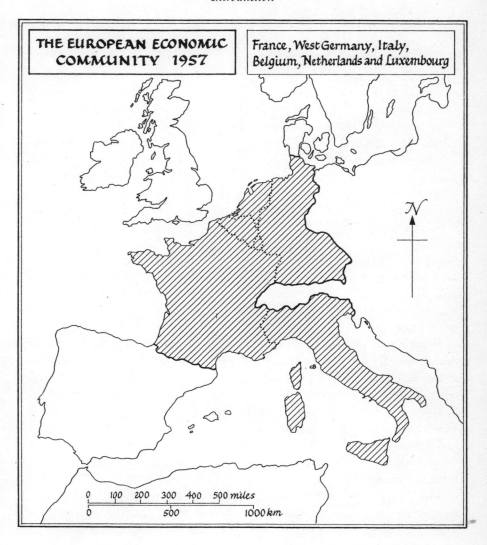

THE EUROPEAN ECONOMIC COMMUNITY 1957

France, West Germany, Italy, Belgium, Netherlands and Luxembourg

0 100 200 300 400 500 *miles*

0 500 1000 *km*

Ages'? It is because we have to answer this question with a firm 'No' that the story of this remarkable man and his legacy has become so fascinating down the centuries.

Something of what Charlemagne, his bishops, abbots and secular administrators created survived and, whether we like it or not, we have inherited it. That something is the core concept of 'Europe', which was for long years coterminous with Latin Christendom and which, even in the modern, secular age cannot be detached from its religious roots. Over and again, throughout all the centuries that followed – during which warrior-barons

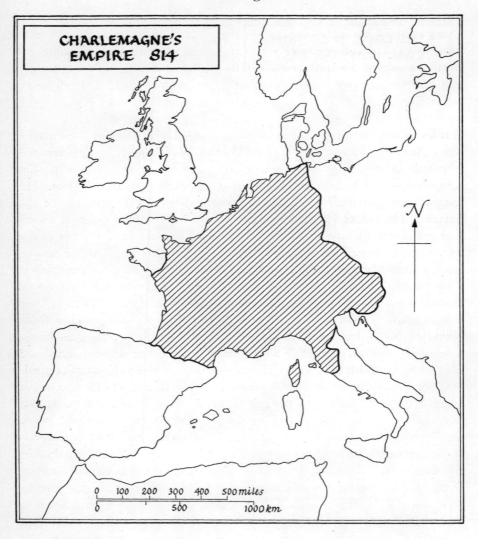

and the leaders of nation states who succeeded them fought to extend or defend their boundaries – bards, kings, political theorists and artists appealed to Charlemagne to justify their actions and support their ideals. A luxuriant myth grew out of the seed of ninth-century reality, putting out new shoots in every generation. Thousands of stories were added to the Charlemagne corpus. He became for different ages a saint, a crusader, the model of chivalry, a cultural icon, a champion of civilisation, an exemplar for absolutist monarchs but also an advocate of democracy, a focus of national pride but also the supreme internationalist. Charlemagne – man, monarch and myth – cannot be disentangled from the story of Europe. Every country has its heroes: men and women, part-fact, part-legend, who exist to explain and reinforce elements of the national psyche. None has been as powerful and influential as Charles the Great. In exploring his life and achievements we cannot help but discover more about what it means to be European.

But let us not get too po-faced about our subject. While the Charlemagne story illuminates some of the grand themes of our shared past, it remains essentially a *story*, and an adventure story at that. Here was a man who inherited – and had to live up to – a dynamic dynastic tradition. His magnificent grandfather, Charles Martel, had been the 'hammer' of the Saracens. His father, Pepin the Short, by a series of astute political moves had united the major tribal units of western Europe, ousted the last of the Merovingian rulers and grabbed the throne for himself. Whether he and his son would be able to hold on to power would depend on their continuing popularity with Francia's warrior-barons, who were more interested in their local power bases than in the creation of a 'greater Francia'. They would follow a man who was successful in war and could promise them abundant booty, but they felt no great loyalty to the Carolingian kings, who were, after all, usurpers. The tendency towards fissiparation, aided and abetted by Frankish inheritance laws, gave these nobles a means of controlling the development of strong centralised government. Since Germanic rulers tended to have a succession of royal wives in addition to several concubines, rivalry and feuding between jealous siblings were the norm rather than the exception – a state of affairs readily exploitable by aristocratic factions. Charlemagne had to face at least one rebellion launched in the name of an illegitimate son. Thus there was nothing inevitable, or even likely, about the emergence of a great European empire – quite the reverse.

It was only a stroke of luck that made it possible. On Pepin's death in 768, Charles found himself joint-ruler of Francia with his brother, Carloman, and there was an inevitable clash of interests and ambitions. But Carloman died at the age of twenty, leaving two infant sons to inherit his lands. Charles grabbed the opportunity to reveal himself as a determined and ruthless king. He proclaimed himself sole ruler and forced his brother's family into exile. Thus began the adventure and, as with all good adventure stories, the hero found himself faced with all manner of dangers and seemingly insurmountable problems. There were enemies within and without his realm and he would spend almost all the ensuing forty-two years fighting them.

What appears on historical textbook maps as 'Francia' was in reality no more than a conglomeration of semi-autonomous kingdoms, dukedoms and tributary states, which had emerged from the encounter of Germanic tribes with the declining Roman Empire. By far the fiercest of the barbarian settlers were the Franks – tall, red-headed warriors who struck terror into the hearts of Romano-Gauls and rival invaders alike. They established their mastery in two main areas, the 'East Kingdom' of Austrasia between the middle Rhine and the Moselle, and the 'West Kingdom' of Neustria, which stretched southwards from the Rhine estuary to the Loire valley. The two regions were culturally, ethnically and linguistically distinct. Austrasia's peoples were exclusively Germanic and here the Franks were in the majority. Neustria was the heartland of the old Roman province of Gaul. Much of the population spoke Latin and preserved many of the old institutions and laws. Further from the centre lay other political entities that had come under Frankish suzerainty – Burgundy, Aquitania, Gascony and Provence. Here effective Carolingian control was at best intermittent. It is scarcely surprising that Charles, like his forebears, had to be continually on the move simply to hold his patrimony together. Any concept of a Carolingian 'empire' governed from a 'capital' is anachronistic.

Its borders were constantly under threat. As recently as 732 the seemingly unstoppable Arab advance along the African littoral and northwards through Iberia had been brought to a halt at the Battle of Poitiers. The Muslims had been forced back beyond the Pyrenees but, although now bedevilled by internal divisions, they were still a force to be reckoned with. More pressing were the incursions from the east and north. Germanic migration continued as land- and booty-hungry Bavarians, Lombards, Alemanni and other tribes sought to emulate the successes of the Franks. Behind them came the Slavic hordes. Towards the end of his reign Charles had to face a new threat: seaborne invaders from Scandinavia who came in their sleek ships, first as raiders, but increasingly as settlers. The inhabitants of Charles' borderlands and the areas immediately beyond were being compressed against each other and were frequently forced to turn their aggression against their weaker neighbours. The majority of the campaigns Charles fought were defensive in nature, designed to secure his frontiers.

But that was not his only motivation. World-changing events depend on the merging of two kinds of power: military might and the force of an ideology. Constantine understood this when he grasped the significance of the mystical command *in hoc signo vinces* 'in this sign conquer'. Suleyman the Magnificent realised its importance when he took the title *Padishah-i-Islam*, 'Emperor of Islam'. Lenin dressed his regime in Marx's visionary garb of proletarian rule. Hitler's mesmerising speeches, mass rallies and torchlit processions encouraged the German people to lay hold on their destiny as the master race. Any leader who comes with armed support in the name of a compelling faith is sure of a following. The faith that underpinned Charlemagne's reign, and that would become the most powerful the world has ever seen, was militant Christianity.

Ever since King Clovis had converted to the religion of his Gaulish subjects in about 496 the Frankish kingdom had identified itself with Catholic Christianity and was opposed alike to paganism and Arianism (the heresy that had split the Church since the fourth century). The alliance of 'state' and 'Church' was, inevitably, disastrous for the cause of true religion. Institutionalism reigned: top ecclesiastical jobs went to members of Francia's elite families; monasteries and bishoprics grew rich and indolent on the offerings of the nobility; the Frankish Church lost its cutting edge as an agent for evangelism, education and moral reform. Enter the Celtic missionaries! Out to the west, in the islands of Britannia and Hibernia, constant pagan pressure, like the force exerted on carbon, had resulted in a hard, brilliant, diamond-like Christian spirituality. It was biblical; it was ascetic; it was scholarly; it was uncompromising; and it was evangelistic. Impelled by *peregrinatio*, a kind of divine wanderlust, pioneer missionaries such as Columban, Fursey, Willibrod and Boniface roamed the European mainland, converting pagans and tearing down their shrines, preaching affective religion to Christians, challenging monks and priests to live up to their vocations and establishing centres for contemplation and study. These puritanical and purifying missionaries exercised a profound influence on Charlemagne. He was stirred by their zeal and impressed by their scholarship, and it was a shared passion for the Gospel that provided the inspiration for his own mission. As the most powerful orthodox monarch in the world, he believed himself to be charged with a divine commission to bring pagans within the Christian fold and to ensure that everyone within that fold lived up to his profession. He was, in a word, the leader of Christendom.

But neither the pope in Rome nor the emperor in Constantinople could be expected to accept this view of the divine ordering of things. Each of them also claimed primacy. Every Easter the Byzantine ruler led the sacred ritual in the great Church of the Holy Wisdom. He appeared before the people apparelled in gem-studded robes and decked with gold, in living effigy of the resurrected Christ. There could be no more powerful symbol of his imperial priesthood, a priesthood which, he believed, was exercised over all Christian people throughout the Roman Empire. In reality, Latin West and Greek East were set on diverging cultural paths and, although Byzantium was able to exercise some influence in southern Italy through theoretically loyal dukes, any claim to sovereignty throughout the old empire was a fiction. In Rome, the ancient capital, imperial 'interference' was especially resented. The regime in Constantinople asserted its authority, but was unable to offer its subjects any protection. It was the pope who provided a figurehead for Christian civilisation. In the worst days of barbarian invasion, the pagan hordes had swilled like a sea around the rock of the papacy and failed to overwhelm it. Amidst the splendours of the classical past, a coterie of old patrician families clung to power and it was they who provided the Latin Church with most of its popes. By the end of the eighth century the Bishop of Rome headed an organisation that administered wide estates and claimed primacy over the whole Christian world in matters spiritual. This was universally accepted throughout the churches of the West – in theory. In fact, the ability of popes to intervene effectively in the affairs of kings and bishops in regions far from Rome was limited. Even in Italy their position was far from secure, for what they lacked was any military 'muscle', and to the north lay an ever-present threat – the Lombards. These Germanic people had ruled sub-alpine Italy since the mid-sixth century and were ambitious to extend their control southwards. By religion they had been Arians until the late seventh century, which meant that they bore no allegiance to the pope and were doubly abhorrent to Rome. Successive popes were obliged to look far afield for a protector from these heretics. What they needed was a loyal son of the Church who had the backing of a strong army. The only practicable candidate was the king of the tall, red-haired barbarians who ruled Gaul.

When that position fell, by inheritance and chance, to Charles, son of Pepin, the land that would eventually be known as Europe lacked cohesion. It was a Tower of Babel ethnically, religiously and politically, as well as linguistically. No one knew how long the new King of the Franks would reign, and no one expected him to change permanently the course of history. By the time he laid down his sceptre the world was profoundly, if indefinably, different. In one way Charles was just like all the other Germanic tribal leaders who had preceded him. He was a warrior chief who constantly had to assert his authority by force of arms: a rough-and-ready, unsophisticated *barbarian*. His greatness was built on the foundation of military success. But there was a broadness to his mind that elevated him from the rank of battle heroes to that of agents of civilisation. He was an idealist who valued men of religion, learning and culture, not just as officials who could help him run his empire, but for themselves. It is certainly true that the timing of his advent was fortuitous. But only a man of outstanding acumen and energy would have been able to take advantage of the opportunities fate had made available. Charlemagne became the pivot around which his contemporaries revolved. He dominated his world, inspiring devotion in his followers, fear in his foes and respect in everyone. If we had to propose one word to explain the impact he made, that word would be 'conviction'. Charlemagne believed passionately in his God, in his appointed task and in himself. Whether he was right or wrong, he pursued his objectives with unabated zeal. This made him a formidable military leader, a tenacious administrative reformer, a staunch friend and a terrifying enemy. So huge was his impact that when he left the land of the living his persona remained to infuse the centuries that followed with the ideals that had inspired him – or that men believed had inspired him. That is why the adventure he began has still not ended.

Notes

1 A. Pagden ed, *The Idea of Europe*, Cambridge, 2002, p.49

I

Charlemagne the Man

But though we know the names of famous men,
What know we of the men who carried them?
Boethius, On Fame

1

Inheritance

He pitched there a tent and was waiting in prayer the arrival of the new converts when, behold! instead of friends, a band of enraged infidels appeared on the plains all in arms and, coming up, rushed into his tent. The servants that were with the holy martyr were for defending his life by fighting; but he would not suffer it, declaring that the day he had long waited for was come, which was to bring him to the eternal joys of the Lord. He encouraged the rest to meet with cheerfulness and constancy a death which was to them the gate of everlasting life.[1]

That account of the death of Boniface, the 'Apostle of Germany', in June 754 is important because it marks a turning point in world history. It is also useful as a launchpad for this book because it may help us to get into the right frame of mind to approach the life and times of Charles the Great. Professor Barraclough succinctly observed, 'Without Boniface there could have been no Charles'[2] and that is a truth that we in the laid-back, agnostic, twenty-first century West should not lose sight of. If we find it difficult to understand the mentality of Islamic suicide bombers and tend to be dismissive of all fundamentalisms, then our imaginations need to be jolted so that we can place ourselves alongside the warriors, scholars and missionaries who created and led the first western empire. They were men who believed simply, felt passionately, saw complex issues in black and white, were aggressive in word and deed, and understood this world as but a shadow of a greater reality. And it was because they were the men they were – heroes in every sense of the word – that they turned the tide of events, took hold of a culture that seemed doomed to extermination by superior forces and forged the civilisation of which we are the heirs.

The Carolingian prince who would become Charlemagne was only twelve years old when the venerable English missionary, Boniface, went to his death in what is now Holland, but he knew Boniface and the septuagenarian's martyrdom will have made its impact on the boy. Boniface had been a very important figure in the life of Charlemagne's family, a bold, uncompromising religious hero and a Carolingian supporter who inspired gratitude and awe. This bustling, no-nonsense ecclesiastic towered over church life north of the Alps and it was he who legitimised the coup that established Charles' father as the progenitor of a new sovereign dynasty in Francia.

Frankish dominance in the area west of the Rhine had been established by Clovis in the fifth century, and his descendants of the Merovingian ruling house had pushed their boundaries ever further. But, in the way of hereditary dynasties, enjoyment of power gradually took the place of effective exercise of power. Successive rulers relied increasingly on their leading court officials, the mayors of the palace, to fight their wars and administer their lands. In 750, the reigning mayor, Pepin III (Pepin the Short), decided to bring this unsatisfactory situation to an end. But, instead of simply seizing power and disposing of Childeric III, the last Merovingian, he sought papal authentication for his usurpation. He sent Rome a message as brief as it was pregnant with significance: 'Is it wise to have kings who have no power or control?' Pope Zacharias, who had his own reasons for wishing to oblige Pepin, concluded that it was not wise. Armed with the permission of God's representative on earth, Pepin bundled Childeric off to a monastery where he lived out his days, while Pepin himself was anointed King of the Franks. The man deputed to officiate at this ceremony on Zacharias' behalf was Boniface. It was the forging of this unique bond between the spiritual and terrestrial powers that was to form the basis of what became the Holy Roman Empire. More importantly, the creation of a religious and civil infrastructure – neither theocracy nor secular state – made possible whatever it is that we call 'Europe'.

Only in the closing years of his reign did Charlemagne and his contemporaries begin to think of themselves as Europeans, and any notion they had of a newly emerging cultural entity was, at best, shadowy. They were too close to the political, religious and racial pressures that were forming this entity to be able to give it a name. We must, therefore, take a little time out to study the map of those lands where the slow but dramatic metamorphosis was taking place. The Roman world had been centred on the Mediterranean basin. As the triumphant armies of the Empire and the Republic extended their sway farther and farther from their homeland, they applied vague names to the hinterlands of those regions that remained largely outside their permanent control. To the south, beyond *Mare Nostrum*, lay Africa. Eastwards, over the Hellespont, was Asia. The land on the far side of the Alps bordered only by forbidding forest and the Atlantic world's edge was Europa. The appearance of Christianity as a world religion that replaced tribal and household gods gave the heterogeneous, over-extended Roman state what was no more than a semblance of cultural unity and greater political stability, even after Constantine converted to the faith of the crucified Jew.

Under pressure of the barbarian invasions of the fifth and sixth centuries, the Romano-Christian world contracted to the Mediterranean fringes and to scattered monastic outposts, where men and women of prayer kept the sacred flame of faith and learning flickering and planned the evangelisation of their pagan neighbours. Worse was to come in the shape of the Islamic explosion. After the death of Mohammed in 632, his followers, aflame with the zeal of their new faith and a passion for military conquest, surged in all directions from their Arabian heartland. Within a century the Mediterranean, once a Roman lake, was bordered by lands over which the crescent flag flew. From Palestine, along the African littoral, across the Straits of Gibraltar and on to the Pyrenees the champions of the new religion advanced with a speed and success that dwarfed the earlier achievements of Christianity. By the time that Charles, the eldest son of Pepin the Short, was born in 742, the followers of the Cross were everywhere under pressure. The once fiercely thriving North African Church had been obliterated. In the East, the Muslim advance had been halted at the Taurus Mountains, but this had not prevented military expeditions reaching the Bosphorus in 673 and 717. In the West, the seemingly inexorable triumph of Islamic arms had only been checked by Pepin's father, Charles Martel, at the Battle of Poitiers in 732. The Christianised transalpine tribes were between the hammer of an aggressive Islam and the anvil of disparate pagan communities to the east and north-east – Frisians, Saxons and Alemanni – who were themselves being harassed by the westward-thrusting Slavs.

As if that were not bad enough, the professional Church was in a parlous state. Ever since Constantine had moved his capital to the Golden Horn, a gulf had grown between the leaders of the Latin Church in Rome and the Greek patriarchs of Byzantium. Since both priestly houses claimed unifying authority, they effectively divided the Christian world.

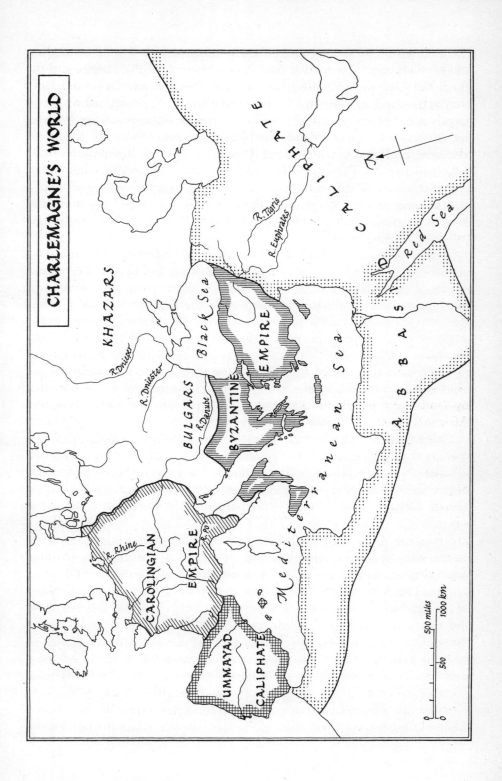

CHARLEMAGNE'S WORLD

KHAZARS

R.Dnieper

R.Dniester

BULGARS

R.Danube

Black Sea

BYZANTINE

EMPIRE

R.Tigris

R.Euphrates

CALIPHATE

Red Sea

Mediterranean Sea

A B B A S I D

CAROLINGIAN

R. Rhine

R. Po

EMPIRE

UMMAYAD

CALIPHATE

N

500 miles

500

1000 km

But that was only one of several tears in the seamless robe of Christ. Throughout the Latin half of the Church there was scant uniformity of either belief or practice. Wherever mass conversions were achieved, they usually involved an element of compromise with prevailing customs. Thus pagan and Christian symbols are often found side by side in ancient burials. Some Germanic tribes had actually embraced the old heresy of Arianism, outlawed at the Council of Nicaea in 325, to demonstrate their independence from the pope. In 664 it took a very acrimonious debate at the Synod of Whitby to induce the Celtic Church to celebrate Easter on the same date as the 'mother' Church in Rome. Even where ortho-doxy was impeccable, morality often was not. In a turbulent age the authority of the clergy depended almost entirely on their education and the purity of their lives. All too often they forfeited any influence they might have enjoyed by ignorant and unbridled behaviour. The peripatetic Boniface expended more effort in disciplining adulterous monks and clerical rapists than in bringing heathens to the baptismal font. A council at Aix-la-Chapelle in 836 denounced certain convents for practising infanticide in order to dispose of the evidence of their inmates' sexual activities. With all these internal weaknesses and external pressures, no betting man would have wagered on the emergence from this threat-ened culture of a world-conquering Christian civilisation. That such a civilisation did emerge is thanks to three types of men: Celtic mission-aries, Roman popes and Frankish kings.

Two religious currents – one from the north and one from the south – washed over Francia. Celtic spirituality was, and is, a very distinctive strain of religious experience. The conditions for its development and spread were restricted in both space and time. Like a diamond formed under intense pressure, it developed in a narrow cultural stratum sandwiched between the ancient rock of Celtic paganism and the new deposits of Anglo-Saxon paganism. The first native, British Christians built centres for the exercise of their highly disciplined routines of worship and medita-tion in the remoter parts of the remotest western province of what had been the Roman Empire. In the white heat of a spiritual commitment that refused to be obsessed with mere survival, they planned and launched ever more extensive evangelistic crusades. This, the first experience of Britain at the heart of Europe, was one of the most remarkable phases in the long history of Christian missionary endeavour, and its legends ring with the names of such heroes as Patrick, Columba, Aidan, Columban and Boniface. Most religious revivals peter out after a few decades. This one lasted in full vigour for an amazing four centuries, from the time when the last Roman conquerors departed to the moment when the first Viking invaders arrived. It would be impossible to overestimate the long-term effects of this religious explosion.

If we were to tease out from the multi-stranded life and teaching of these Celtic men and women (for women contemplatives always featured significantly within early British Christianity) a couple of features that help to explain their success, we might choose ones that seem, on the face of it, mutually contradictory. These saints manifested a strict puritanism allied with a flexibility towards pagan beliefs. On the one hand, they locked themselves in monastic 'fortresses' such as Iona and Lindisfarne, where they could practise their austerities undisturbed; on the other, they pledged themselves to *peregrinatio*, wandering among strangers and unbelievers, protected only by the 'breastplate' of faith, adumbrated by Patrick's famous hymn:

> Christ be with me, Christ within me,
> Christ behind me, Christ before me,
> Christ beside me, Christ to win me,
> Christ to comfort and restore me,
> Christ beneath me, Christ above me,
> Christ in quiet, Christ in danger,
> Christ in hearts of all that love me,
> Christ in mouth of friend and stranger.

Like itinerant holy men of all ages, the Celtic missionaries attracted curiosity and admiration. Numerous miracles were attributed to them. Yet in their preaching they did not exhort converts to commit themselves to the kind of renunciation and asceticism they followed themselves. They did not even demand unquestioning adherence to every tenet of Christian dogma and ethics.

One reason why Christianity has been the most successful of all world religions in crossing cultural boundaries is its adaptability. To be sure, this has not been manifested in all places and at all times. Some missionary endeavours have been based on the premise that any rival belief system is of the devil and must be totally obliterated. Contrariwise, there have been occasions when, for the sake of number-crunching, religious fundamentals have been sacrificed. On the whole, however, wise evangelists have understood not only that the Gospel may be garbed in a variety of national costumes, but that incorporating fresh customs and thought patterns actually enriches the life of new churches.

Celtic Christianity was itself an indigenous expression of 'the faith once given' and not a carbon copy of the church life of Rome. Some

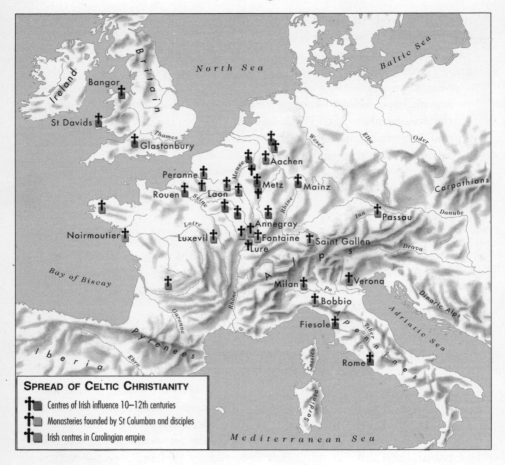

SPREAD OF CELTIC CHRISTIANITY

Centres of Irish influence 10–12th centuries

Monasteries founded by St Columban and disciples

Irish centres in Carolingian empire

of its customs were sharply at variance with what was culturally accept-able in Italy. It had married clergy and permitted women an active role in the liturgy – something anathema south of the Alps. Its organisation focused on monastic cells rather than territorial dioceses. In fact, 'organ-isation' was scarcely a word in the vocabulary of these Celtic monks. They were dynamic missionaries, pilgrimaging throughout this world on their way to heaven. They had little time or inclination for establishing power bases.

Evangelistic strategy motivated their interaction with the prevailing cultures. They had found ways to mediate Christianity in terms that were deeply meaningful to the nature-worshipping instincts of their own and other people. Their pagan ancestors had made offerings to the gods of mountain spring and oaken grove, had prayed to the spirits residing in the animals they hunted and the plants they gathered for their healing properties. Men of the new faith, like St Patrick, found ways to express their beliefs that were acceptable to a people living close to nature, without capitulating to pantheism:

> Our God is the God of all men, the God of heaven and earth, of sea and river, of sun and moon and stars, of the lofty mountain and the lowly valley . . . He has his dwelling around heaven and earth and sea and all that in them is. He inspires all, he quickens all, he dominates all, he sustains all . . .[3]

It was in the scriptoria of the Celtic monasteries that the old sagas were written down for the first time and preserved alongside the Christian Scriptures and the lives of the saints. And the most familiar of all expressions of Celtic art, the great stone crosses, were a continuation of an ancient custom of erecting standing monuments carved with the symbols of the old religion.

While sitting loose to power structures, the Celtic Christians could not avoid the realities of tribal government. Not only did they commend themselves to their own people and those of neighbouring tribes by empathising with their veneration of the mysteries of creation, but they taught that their God was also interested in politics:

> Tassilo, duke of the Bavarians . . . commended himself into vassalage with his lands, and swore innumerable oaths. Touching the relics of the saints, he promised fealty to King Pepin and his sons Charles and Carloman, behaving honestly and faithfully, in accordance with the law and as a vassal should to his lords. Tassilo thus swore on the bodies of St Dionysius, Rusticus, Eleutherius, St Germanus, and St Martin that he would remain faithful all his life . . .[4]

Just as the spirits, whether pagan or Christian, manifested themselves through the physical universe, so they also did through the ordering of society. The hierarchy, like Jacob's ladder, extended from earth to heaven. At its base were slaves and landless peasants. From them one ascended through the ranks of warriors, aristocrats and princes to the domain of the shining ones – heroes and ancestors or, in the Christian pantheon, saints and angels thronging the throne room of the triune God. Theologians, preachers and artists presented the court of Christ the King in terms of the splendour of earthly monarchs, and the splendour of earthly monarchs in terms of the court of Christ the King. There was a mysterium about human sovereignty which paralleled that of divine majesty. In ancient Celtic political theory, the king was charged by the gods with responsibility for the well-being of his people and endowed with magical powers to support his dignity and authority. Just as he received fealty from his vassals, so he paid homage to his spiritual superiors. This thinking was very easily Christianised. Thus, in those lands that fell under the influence of British missionaries, kings were conceived of as holding a divine mandate and being responsible to God alone for its execution.

In Francia the Celtic version of Christianity did not burst upon a people steeped in undiluted traditional animism. The pale Galilean had conquered the kingdom in the time of Clovis, who accepted the faith of the Gallo-Roman population he was in the process of overpowering. By the time of Charlemagne, 300 years later, there were 600 monasteries throughout the lands he ruled. Gallican Christianity, no less than Celtic, had its own characteristics, but it was closer to Rome and more under the influence of St Peter's successors, sporadically at least. And we must be very clear that with Roman Christianity we are dealing with a markedly different strand of politico-religious experience.

In the dying weeks of 753 Pope Stephen II set out on a historic journey. His stumbling horse made its hurried way along one of the crumbling Roman highways over the Alps in order to reach Frankish territory before winter set in. He was the first occupier of St Peter's chair to cross the mountains, and he did so only because the Church and the people for whom he was responsible faced a dire threat. North Italy had been a chaotic cockpit of war ever since 568 when one of the invading Germanic tribes, the Lombards, had crossed the Alps to fall upon a region of the Byzantine Empire rich in the production of wine and olive oil. The newcomers were doubly hateful to the occupants of the land; not only were they violent usurpers, but they had also adopted Arianism, a heretical version of Christianity. Yet even after their conversion to orthodoxy (largely for reasons of political expediency), they declined to live in peaceful coexistence with their neighbours. Their ambition was to rule the whole of the peninsula. The emperor's representative here, the Exarch of Ravenna, fought what proved to be an increasingly rearguard action against the barbarians. Decade after decade the invaders advanced ever closer to Rome. Little help came from Constantinople, and from time to time the exarch was obliged to look to the north for allies. In other words, he asked the formidable Franks for help.

To the leaders and the residents of papal territory the threat was even more pressing. The papacy was a strange, unique survival. The softer rock of classical paganism had been worn away by barbarian invasion and internal corruption, leaving a hard Christian core that controlled the religious and secular life of much of central Italy. The popes, as well as being patriarchs of the West, were Byzantine officials with lands to govern and a bureaucracy to help them do so. Their spiritual and political roles never sat easily together. Impressive church leaders who exhibited any holiness, and who possessed any vision for Christian mission throughout the portion of the old empire over which they claimed pastoral oversight, were rare birds indeed. Most popes were at best preoccupied with the governance of their Italian lands, and at worst interested only in enjoying their wealth and power. The means of obtaining that wealth and power had very little to do with the precepts of the Prince of Peace. Habitually the occupants of St Peter's chair gained or lost their position as a result of intrigue and bloodshed. During the two centuries following the death of Gregory the Great in 604 there were no fewer than thirty-two popes. Twenty-three of them were in office for less than five years, and twice the papacy was contended by popes and antipopes. By the late eighth century their main preoccupations were throwing off the yoke of Byzantine overlordship and protecting their lands from Lombard encroachment.

By 753 a state of crisis had emerged. The Lombard king, Aistulf, had captured Ravenna and direct Byzantine rule in Italy was at an end. Pope Stephen entered into frenzied negotiation with Aistulf, but he had little to bargain with and there was nothing to prevent the Lombards making Rome their capital. There was only one person who could head off total disaster, hence Stephen's hasty departure from Rome towards the end of the year. As he made his way over the Alps, he had plenty of time to work out his tactics. He was a subtle manipulator who had learned the art of intrigue in a hard school. There was no question of his throwing himself at Pepin's feet as a grovelling supplicant. His position might be weak and he would be asking the Frankish king for a major military commitment, but Stephen did hold certain strong cards. Pepin (who was, after all, merely a semi-educated barbarian) was a loyal son of the Church and it should be possible to overawe him with his sense of duty to protect the headquarters of Latin Christendom. There was also the fact that Pepin owed Rome a favour. Pope Zacharias had obliged the Frank by endorsing his seizure of the throne, and the king was therefore vulnerable to moral pressure to offer a quid pro quo. If pious suasion failed, Stephen still had one or two other tricks up his sleeve.

His objective was to be able to wield the threat of Frankish military might as a cudgel. He needed a barbarian protector who would be on hand when required, but who could otherwise be kept at a safe distance.

There was, after all, no sense in exchanging one over-mighty neighbour for another. Stephen soon discovered that Pepin was just as wily as himself and would not slip easily into the role Stephen had written for him. When the two men met at the abbey of Saint-Denis, near Paris, in January 754 they unwittingly inaugurated a long-running saga of negotiations and wars, which would not only determine the relations between Francia and the papacy, but, throughout the medieval centuries, those between pope and emperor, and thus determine the balance of spiritual and secular power in western Christendom.

One of the tools Stephen wielded to good effect was flattery. At their meeting, and in subsequent letters, he impressed upon Pepin the revelation that he had been raised up by God to fulfil a very special destiny. The Franks were, according to ancient legend, of noble ancestry, which put them on a par with – if not on a higher plane than – the Romans: for their descent could be traced back to the royal house of ancient Troy. Now, the moment of their greatness was come. They were to be the new Israel, and their leader, another David. Pepin would be the champion of the Church, rescuing it from its present danger and going on to bring other peoples under the Cross. To symbolise this high calling, the pope confirmed Boniface's earlier coronation by placing coronets on the heads of Pepin and his sons. In the words of Edward Gibbon, 'The royal unction of the kings of Israel was dextrously applied: the successor of St Peter assumed the character of a divine ambassador: a German chieftain was transformed into the Lord's anointed.'[5]

There is no doubt that Pepin was moved by all this impressive prophecy and ceremonial, but he was no one's fool. He had no intention of being at the pope's beck and call. Stephen had to find other arguments to convince the king that it was his sacred duty to come and split heads and shed blood on behalf of the Roman pontiff. It is very likely that Stephen had in his baggage a document impressive with the signs of age and authenticated by the seal of the Emperor Constantine. It told a dramatic tale of the emperor going as a leprosy-inflicted supplicant to Pope Sylvester I, receiving Christian baptism at his hands and being in the same instant miraculously healed. This story, based on the Old Testament account of the healing of Naaman (II Kings, 5), was a total fabrication. Constantine was not baptised until the very end of his life, in 337, two years after the death of Sylvester. But it was a good story and an impressive prologue to what followed. In gratitude, so the document claimed, Constantine made a spectacular gift of his own authority to Sylvester and his heirs for ever:

We decree that the sacred See of Blessed Peter shall be gloriously exalted even above our Empire and earthly throne . . . as over all churches of God in all the world . . . We convey to Sylvester, universal Pope, both our palace and likewise all provinces and palaces and districts of the city of Rome and Italy and of the regions of the west.[6]

In other words, papal territory had for centuries been an independent state and had never been part of the exarchate. The so-called *Donation of Constantine* was a thoroughgoing forgery, made for a specific purpose, at a particular place and time. It was the means chosen to achieve a specific end in a desperate situation, and it doubtless did not occur to the criminals who created it that it would be used to excuse a millennium of political intrigue, wars and carnage.

However, the *ideas* behind the *Donation* – a territorial basis to the expansion of western Christianity and the establishment of an ecclesiastical empire ruled from Rome – were not new. The Christianisation of the Roman Empire had inevitably led to the 'imperialisation' of Roman Christianity. The departure of the emperors to their eastern capital, Byzantium, left the bishops of Rome (usually members of old patrician families) as defenders, not only of the traditions of the apostles, but also of the traditions of classical thinkers and governors. Their heritage was an urbanised, *Christian* civilisation and when they turned their minds to foreign mission, they, like their nineteenth-century descendants who carried the Gospel to benighted 'heathen lands afar', did so in the conviction that they represented a superior, advanced culture. It followed that the liturgies, doctrinal assumptions and ecclesiastical organisation that defined the Church south of the Alps should make up the 'package' to be delivered to newly converted peoples in the territory beyond.

This had been the conviction of Pope Gregory I (590–604), the 'founder of the medieval papacy', who carried out sweeping reforms within the Church and initiated a new phase of Christian mission. It was Gregory who sent Augustine to preach to the pagan settlers of southern England and to bring the Celtic churches firmly under papal obedience. Gregory was a formidable champion of Roman supremacy, but he met his match in the Merovingian Clothar II, who insisted that the clergy were, first and foremost, his subjects.

This was essentially Pepin's understanding of the situation. Priests and monks were, above all, *his* subjects and it was his responsibility to discipline them, just as it lay within his remit to exercise authority over the lay people of his realm. Only by firm government could he hold together his heterogeneous empire. And there were strict protocols to be observed over launching the Francian war machine. The king never embarked on a military campaign without discussing it with his warrior-nobles. Thus, despite all Stephen's flattery and cajolery, it was only after several months and due consultation that Pepin decided to lead his army across the Alps and force the Lombards to make peace. When that peace broke down within months, Stephen sent urgent messages to his saviour, but Pepin was in no hurry to return. He had other priorities. Intervention in Italy was never high on the Carolingian agenda and only once more did he lead his forces down to the Lombard Plain.

Nevertheless, a major shift in political thinking had taken place. The concise royal annals provide matter-of-fact glimpses of the Frankish ruler's priorities:

> The Lord King Pepin then held a great council at Gentilly with Romans and Greeks about the Holy Trinity and the images of the saints. Afterward, he continued his march through Aquitaine into Narbonne and conquered Toulouse as well as Albi and Gevaudan. Returning home safely, he celebrated Easter at the city of Vienne.[7]

From this time on, Pepin's campaigns took on the character of crusades against the enemies of God. His warriors went into battle with their arms blessed by priests. Territorial and tribal conflict took on the character of holy war. His victories were the victories of the Lord of Hosts; his defeats the judgements of a holy God upon the sins of the nation. The integrity of the Church and the morality of the clergy were important to ensure the continued protection of God and the success of the warrior state. The fate of Francia was now watched over from Elysium, not only by the warrior ancestors, but also by the saints to whose relics Pepin and his people attributed magical properties.

Notes

1 A. Butler, *The Lives of the Fathers, Martyrs and Other Principal Saints*, 1949, II, p.604
2 G. Barraclough, *The Crucible of Europe: The Ninth and Tenth Centuries in European History*, 1976, p.28
3 I. Bradley, *The Celtic Way*, 1993, pp.36–7
4 *Carolingian Chronicles: Royal Frankish Annals and Nithard's Histories* (trs. B. W. Scholz with B. Rogers), Michigan, 1970, p.42
5 E. Gibbon, *Decline and Fall of the Roman Empire*, 1983 edn, VI, p.1168
6 The exact circumstances of the creation of the *Donation of Constantine*

are unknown, but it can be dated to the second half of the eighth century and, as the earliest extant copies were located in Francia, it is reasonable to suppose that it was used to impress the claims of Rome on Pepin and his son.

7 *Carolingian Chronicles,* p.46

2

Happy Families

Charlemagne was a bastard. To be more accurate, he was born out of wedlock. Not until some years after his birth in the early months of 742 did his father get around to marrying his mother, Bertrada.* Sexual mores among the Franks can best be described as 'relaxed'. This was not entirely an issue of loose morals as far as the upper echelons of society were concerned. Sexual liaisons were essentially about the procreation of healthy heirs, a chancy business at a time when the death rate from infantile diseases and childbirth complications was very high. It was not uncommon for a king to have a series of mistresses and to choose which of them he would marry on the basis of their suitability as breeding stock. In this case Pepin took his time about deciding which of his women to marry. What we know about Bertrada suggests that she was a formidable woman. She may have possessed a commanding presence. Charlemagne's first biographer, Einhard, wrote of Charles' appearance:

> He had a broad and strong body of unusual height, but well proportioned; for his height measured seven times his feet. His skull was round, the eyes were lively and rather large, the nose of more than average length, the hair grey but full, the face friendly and cheerful. Seated or standing, he thus made a dignified and stately impression, even though he had a thick, short neck and a belly that protruded somewhat.[1]

---

* There has never been agreement among all historians about the date of Charles' birth. The choice lies between 742 and 748, with rather better, though not conclusive, evidence for the former.

Since his father, Pepin III, was nicknamed 'The Short', it would appear that the genes governing Charles' basic physical appearance came from his mother.

There is something of the Macbeths about Pepin the Short and Bertrada. They were ambitious to establish their dynasty as unchallenged rulers of the whole of Francia – no easy task in a land whose boundaries were constantly fluctuating and whose regional rulers were always jockeying for power. If Charlemagne's parents achieved their goals through ruthlessness and violence, they were merely playing the game of Frankish politics according to the prevailing rules. For generations relationships between the rulers of Neustria, Austrasia, Aquitania and neighbouring regions had been decided by war, treachery and assassination. Changing allegiances, shifting alliances, broken promises and the emergence of king-makers and king-breakers were the stuff of political life. Pepin did no more than follow the aggressive pattern set by his father. Charles Martel had started out unpromisingly as a bastard son of Austrasia's mayor of the palace (the chief political and military leader of the state), but by sheer force and brilliance he asserted his authority over his father's true heirs, came to exert control over all the Frankish chiefs and established his own nominee on the throne. On his death, in 741, Charles divided his empire between his elder sons, Pepin and Carloman, and their half-brother, Grifo. The breath was scarcely out of their father's body before the heirs had fallen out. Pepin and Carloman ganged up on their sibling, whom they captured and locked away in 742. His mother was hustled off to a nunnery.

The two brothers worked together to bring under their sway all the chieftains who had grabbed the opportunity to assert their independence, and they set up their own tame Merovingian, Childeric III, whom they had to bring out of monastic seclusion, to add legitimacy to their proceedings. It is scarcely surprising that tensions soon appeared in the partnership. In 747, Carloman, perhaps under relentless pressure from his brother, elected to take the tonsure. There seems to have been an understanding that Pepin, who at the time had no legitimate heir, would nominate as his successor Carloman's son, Drogo. So Pepin took his nephew under his wing and Carloman travelled over the Alps to join the great Benedictine community at Monte Cassino. It is very doubtful that Pepin, with total power now in his grasp, had any intention of diverting it to his brother's posterity. Within months he showed his hand. In 748 he married his concubine, Bertrada and legitimised his son, Charles. Now Pepin precipitated a new round of family feuding by attempting to seize Drogo's territory. In the ensuing conflict everything did not go Pepin's way. His position became extremely precarious when his half-bother, Grifo, escaped from captivity and began stirring up trouble in Aquitania. Faced with war on two fronts, Pepin was obliged to come to terms with Grifo. Only after the latter was killed in battle in 753 was Pepin able to direct all his energies against his nephew. Within months he had Drogo safely under lock and key.

It was in the midst of these tumultuous events that Pepin decided that King Childeric was now surplus to requirements. The hapless monarch did not command the respect of the Frankish chieftains and was therefore no use as a focus of loyalty. Pepin planned to do away with the fiction of Merovingian rule and set up his own dynasty in its place. Where was he to find the authentication for such a move? There was only one man to whom the political nation would listen: the leader of the Church. As we have seen, Pepin pleaded Francia's need for stability and effective government and Pope Zacharias, who also needed a powerful ally, duly obliged by authorising Boniface to crown Pepin and his two sons in 751. Thus did some very fishy-smelling political manoeuvring acquire the odour of sanctity. From this point onwards the Roman and Frankish regimes stood or fell together.

It would be unduly cynical to dismiss Pepin's relations with the Church as governed entirely by pragmatic *raison d'état*. The teaching and preaching of Boniface and his predecessors were having a profound effect on society. Violent and licentious the lives of Francia's kings and nobles certainly were, but Christian standards were acknowledged and were steadily exerting their civilising influence. Pepin and Carloman were both educated in the already famous abbey school of Saint-Denis, Paris, where they came under the influence of Boniface's reform movement. Saint-Denis, where most of France's kings lie buried, was already closely associated with the ruling house. The abbey's status was vastly enhanced early in the seventh century by Dagobert I, who made lavish gifts of land and ornaments and ordained that he and his successors should be interred there. Saint-Denis became a prominent physical symbol of the interaction of Church and state, and several prominent royal servants were drawn from the ranks of its clergy. Carloman's decision to take up the contemplative life may have been very convenient for his brother, but there is no reason to doubt its sincerity.

If Pepin held his own teachers in high regard, valued religious education and wished to honour Saint-Denis (where he had decided that he would be buried), we might wonder why he did not put his own sons in the abbey school. Virtually no information has survived about the upbringing of Charles and his younger brother, Carloman, but monastic chroniclers would certainly have boasted of the great king's training by monks had that, indeed, formed a vital part of his nurturing. Charlemagne continued the practice of generous patronage to Saint-Denis, but he did not hold it in that affection that he would have done, had it been his *alma mater*. He famously created a new capital for himself at Aachen, where, in the fullness of time, he was laid to rest.

The reason for Pepin's decision not to send his sons away to school must, surely, lie in his own insecurity. He was deliberately founding a new dynasty and his supremacy was constantly being challenged. Like all dynasts, his Achilles heel was his children. They were vital to his whole scheme: he had to pass the symbols of sovereignty to heirs old enough and strong enough to continue the line. But there was always the risk that, before reaching maturity, they might be kidnapped or murdered. Worse still, they might fall under the influence of his enemies and become figureheads of rebellion. Sensitive about both the safety and the training of his heirs, Pepin had them educated at his own peripatetic court, along with the sons of his most trusted followers. What that meant was that, as soon as they were able to walk, they began learning how to ride a horse and their games would have been largely modelled on the martial arts. From about six years of age, military training began in earnest. There was no mollycoddled luxury existence for the sons of Pepin. They were, with increasing frequency, taken on campaign and experienced all the hardships of camp life – long marches in all weathers, frugal meals, orders driven home with the flat of a sword, and sleep in the open, huddled around camp fires.

It is doubtful whether such activity left much time for book learning. The Frankish warrior caste regarded literary pursuits as beneath them. However, Charles was taught his letters and grew up with a great respect for those who could understand ancient lore and set down new arguments. In later years he greatly regretted that he had not learned to write. He devoted much energy to educational reform and, though this was directed largely at the clergy, he also understood the importance of written communication in the administration of his expanding empire. He oversaw the setting down and rationalisation of the law codes. He had a grasp of theological niceties and could dispute knowledgeably with Church leaders. All this suggests that there was something contradictory in the upbringing of Pepin's sons. They were more familiar with the saddle than the desk, although they were made to understand that, as future rulers, they must be able not only to enforce the obedience of subjects at swordpoint, but to administer their lands wisely and efficiently.

Pepin took every opportunity to make his dynastic intentions very clear by involving his sons in public displays and in administrative activities. When Pope Stephen made his dramatic journey across the Alps in the closing days of 753, Pepin sent Charles as head of the welcoming party that met him on the road. Thus the boy performed his first important official function before he had reached his twelfth birthday. When the pope

TRIBAL AREAS OF FRANCIA AND
NEIGHBOURING LANDS c. 760

ATLANTIC

OCEAN

SAXONY

THURINGIA

AUSTRASIA

BRITTANY   NEUSTRIA

BURGUNDY   BAVARIA

ALAMANNIA

AQUITANIA

LOMBARDY

GASCONY   PROVENCE

UMMAYAD
CALIPHATE

Mediterranean Sea

```
0   100  200  300  400  500 miles
0            500           1000 km
```

consecrated Pepin at Saint-Denis the following summer, the two young
princes were included in the impressive ceremony. Amidst the chanting of
the monks and the cheering of the warrior throng, the boys had holy
hands laid upon them and were dedicated to the solemn responsibility of
ruling the Frankish Empire in succession to their father. It must have made
an enormous impression upon them. We next find Charles and Carloman
taking part in another elaborate ceremony at Auxerre in 755. This was the
transferring of the bones of the fifth-century St Germanus to a new and
more resplendent shrine, something that profoundly moved Charles, as he
admitted in later years.

By now Pepin had made his power felt from the Atlantic coast to the Danube. When Charles was fifteen and legally came of age, his father began to assign to him the overlordship of some of the Austrasian duchies, including a few whose loyalty was suspect. However, the king's major problem lay in Aquitania. The local dukes had, for twenty years, resisted Frankish overlordship and had been assisted by their neighbours, the Vascones (Basques), a staunchly independent people whose enclave had for centuries resisted a variety of invaders. Year after year Pepin campaigned vigorously in the south-west, knowing how vital it was to hand his heirs a united, or at least a subdued, Francia. Charles and Carloman took an increasingly prominent part in these military expeditions. Success came at last in June 768, when Duke Waiofar was assassinated by dissidents in his own ranks (perhaps encouraged by Carolingian gold). The elimination of the Aquitanian problem had come in the nick of time, for Pepin, worn out by his years of exertion, was a sick man. He managed to reach Saint-Denis in late summer and it was there that he made his provision for the succession. Having performed his last service for the dynasty, he died and was buried alongside his illustrious father.

Frankish law demanded that a man's estate be divided among his sons, so there was no question of the unitary empire being sustained. The exact details of Pepin's legacy are disputed in the records, but it seems that Neustria, Austrasia and Aquitania were each cut in two and the parts joined in such a way that Carloman received a solid block of land comprising the central and eastern parts of Francia, while Charles' allocation extended around it in a sweeping semicircle from the Pyrenees to the Elbe. Pepin must have hoped that Charles and Carloman would rule their respective territories effectively and live at peace with each other. His own experiences with family relationships might have warned him that this was wishful thinking.

Charles was in his mid-twenties and his brother eighteen, not of an age to submit meekly to arrangements made on their behalf by others. Neither was content with his portion, but Charles may have had the more justified cause to feel aggrieved. Both Saint-Denis and the old capital of Soissons lay in his brother's territory and Carloman's land also formed a barrier to Charles' direct contact with Rome. Charles celebrated his first independent Christmas in his modest villa at Aachen, enjoying the warm springs and brooding on his unfair treatment as elder son. By the following Easter he had an even stronger reason to be angry with his brother. Aquitania was, once again, in revolt. The new duke, Chunoald II, resolved to try the mettle of Pepin's young heirs. Charles lost no time in marching against him and called on Carloman for support. The brothers met near the modern town of Vienne, but instead of planning their strategy for the forthcoming campaign they fell to arguing. The outcome was that Carloman led his army back home. Charles' swift and easy victory over Chunoald did little to soothe his fury at his co-ruler's desertion.

Friction manifested itself again in 770, when both brothers became fathers. Carloman and his wife, Gerberga, were blessed with a baby boy. When the news reached Charles he found it disturbing, but much more infuriating was the information that the little prince had been given the name Pepin. Royal names were immensely important. Not only were they symbolic, but they were thought to convey – almost magically – the qualities of the ancestor they commemorated. The cognomen 'Pepin' carried resounding significance for the royal family. It had been borne not only by the brothers' father, but by the founder of their dynasty. In the baptism of his son Carloman was laying claim to the succession for his own line. Within months Charles' 'partner', Himiltrud, also gave birth to a boy. The name chosen for him? Pepin. Charles had taken up the dynastic challenge. However, the situation was not one of complete stalemate. All was not well with Charles' son. Einhard called him 'Pepin the Hunchback', and a deformity obvious in infancy would not have augured well for the future. This probably explains why Charles was in no hurry to marry the boy's mother. His failure to do so would create problems later.

There were two people who were particularly worried by the falling out between the royal brothers – their mother, Bertrada, and the new pope, Stephen III – and both now embarked on several months of remarkable diplomacy. Bertrada was concerned for the preservation of all that her husband had built up. Stephen's anxieties were more complex. Affairs at Rome were in an even more parlous state than usual. The death of Pope Paul I in 767 was followed by vicious faction fighting. One group placed their candidate, Constantine II, on the papal throne, whereupon King Desiderius of Lombardy had him removed and, for good measure, put out his eyes. Desiderius' nominee, Philip, lasted even less time and Desiderius' envoy was murdered. In the midst of this bloody confusion some semblance of a proper election was held and the lot fell to Stephen. Never had the papacy been in greater need of its Frankish ally. But who was that ally? Which of Pepin's sons was best placed to protect the legitimate pope?

Carloman's foot was in the door first. He had agents in the papal entourage and made use of them to strengthen his position in Rome. With the Church on his side, Carloman's standing within Francia would have been enormously enhanced. It was at this point that Bertrada intervened with a cynical effectiveness of which her husband would have approved. Her motivation was to encourage her sons to work together, but in

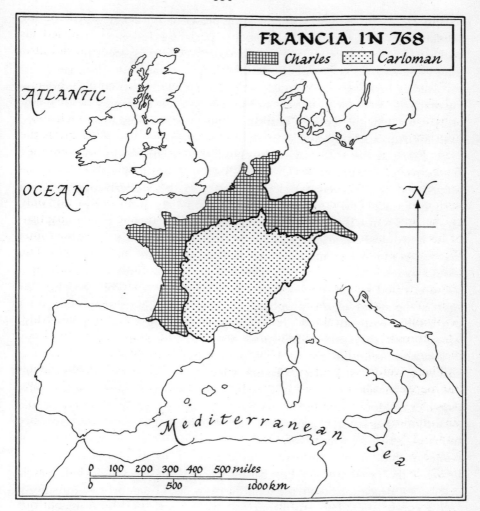

immediate, practical terms that meant counteracting Carloman's political advantage. Though she had officially retired to a nunnery, Bertrada emerged to make a long and arduous journey across the Alps. The first stage of her diplomatic pilgrimage was a visit to her younger son to urge him to stop intriguing in Rome against his brother. This approach having not proved wholly successful, Bertrada continued her travels and is next to be found in distant Bavaria, enlisting the support of her relatives. This mountainous, forested country marked the furthest extremity of the Celtic mission, as also of Frankish influence. Grifo had made the region his base in his struggle with Pepin and, on his overthrow, Pepin had installed his nephew,

33

Tassilo III, as duke. Tassilo might well prove to be a key player in any conflict between Charles and Carloman, especially as his wife was a daughter of Desiderius of Lombardy. The scheme that Bertrada developed as she jolted her way along crumbling Roman roads towards the Bavarian court involved a breathtaking political volte-face. Charles would set aside his current wife in order to marry another daughter of his family's old enemy, Desiderius. Having secured Tassilo's support for this design, she hastened over the Alps to Lombardy.

A glance at the map makes very clear the object of this policy. Under the terms of Pepin's will, Carloman had been granted a solid block of territory that effectively restricted Charles to the western and northern parts of Francia and blocked his contact with Italy and the eastern lands. By alliance with Bavaria and Lombardy, Charles would turn the tables. Now it would be Carloman's Francia that was ringed by territory under his brother's influence, and Carloman whose diplomatic and military activity would be restricted. The person who had just as much reason as Carloman to be alarmed by this extraordinary turn of events was Pope Stephen. As soon as he heard of the proposed marriage alliance he sent messengers northwards with an angry, desperate plea, warning Charles not to link himself with 'the faithless and most vile Lombard people'.

It was in her dealings with the pope that Bertrada displayed her cleverest and most subtle diplomacy. Having achieved her objective at Desiderius' court, she travelled on to Rome, where she presented herself as a dutiful daughter of Holy Church. She assured Stephen that, far from being directed against the papacy, the proposed arrangement had Rome's interests very much at heart. The terms of an alliance between Charles and Desiderius would include a comprehensive settlement of all the issues outstanding between the pope and the Lombard king. It would secure an honourable and lasting peace for Stephen and all his subjects. The pope was convinced, and Bertrada began her return journey satisfied with a job well done. In all likelihood she stopped off again in Lombardy to collect her son's intended bride. Carloman, meanwhile, was not inactive. He sent fresh envoys to Rome charged with making whatever promises were necessary to induce the pope to reverse his decision. Hearing this, Desiderius decided to back negotiation with force. Early in 771 Stephen was appalled to receive a flurry of disconcerting messages: the Lombard king was already on the road at the head of an army; factions within the city were locked in armed conflict; Carloman was about to bring his forces into Italy to break up Stephen's unholy alliance with the people he had so recently denounced as 'faithless and most vile'. The pope wavered, cursing the fraternal divisions in the Carolingian royal house that had placed him in such a perilous position. In fact, he had no real choice of action. Desiderius' force was the immediate threat and Stephen had to deal with it. He sent messages of welcome to the Lombards and let the Carloman faction within Rome know that they did not have his support. When Desiderius arrived, Stephen celebrated a Lenten mass for him. Meanwhile, on his orders, the leaders of the anti-Lombard faction were quietly put to death.

There followed an uneasy summer and autumn. Charles and Carloman refrained from military activity throughout the campaigning season. Each watched the other, anxious and ready to counter any hostile move. It seemed only a matter of time before the brothers would engage in a trial of strength. Throughout Francia the nobles considered their positions. Then, on 4 December 771, the twenty-year-old Carloman suddenly died. With that single event the destiny of Charles and the history of Europe were changed at a stroke.

Notes

1 *Einhard and Notker the Stammerer: Two Lives of Charlemagne* (trs. L. Thorpe), 1969, p.61

3

The Milk of a Male Tiger

Charles' new bride (so insignificant a cipher was she that we do not even know her name) was packed off back to her father. There was no longer any need for a Lombard alliance and so it was, without ceremony, set aside. This is a tiny intimation of the pragmatism – not to say ruthlessness – that underlay all Charlemagne's public dealings. In Shakespeare's play one of the characters says of the tyrant Coriolanus, 'There is no more mercy in him than there is milk in a male tiger.' Much the same could be said of the new sole ruler of Francia. At twenty-nine, Charles was a still-young warrior-king who had yet to prove that he was a worthy successor to Pepin the Short and Charles Martel (the Hammer). It was good fortune and not military or political brilliance that had won him his pre-eminent position. All the chief men of Francia and the leaders of tribute states were watching to see how he would handle himself. They soon discovered that their new master had inherited his father's determination and tireless industry, and had added to these traits a cold, crystal-clear rationalism. Charles would flinch from nothing that would secure his position and enhance his power, and the first ten years of his reign were spent almost entirely on stamping his will on all his subjects.

His central problem was, and always would be, ensuring the loyalty of his proto-feudal nobles. They constituted, at one and the same time, the main support of central government and the greatest potential threat to it. Charles' senior vassals were tied to him by land tenure. He needed them to keep the peace on their own estates and to provide him with warriors for his campaigns. As well as rewarding their faithful service with land grants and war booty, the king took them into his confidence, principally by conferring with them at the annual spring assemblies, which were called to discuss the forthcoming campaign season. But, like any absolute ruler, he was constantly on the watch for plots and plotters. Whenever possible he replaced local magnates, and particularly holders of hereditary dukedoms, with his own trusted servants. He appointed regional officers to preside over the law courts and administer royal demesne lands. He exacted oaths of loyalty and maintained a large corps of *missi*, royal agents who constantly rode throughout Francia conveying the king's will to his subjects. But the wealthy families who exercised real local power were, not unnaturally, jealous of their status and authority and intent on maintaining these from generation to generation. Thus political control in the expanding empire depended ultimately on power bargaining. And effective bargaining depended ultimately on the sheer strength of Charlemagne's personality.

We rely on the ninth-century writer, Einhard, for any description of the king's character, but although he was very close to Charles, Einhard knew him only during the latter part of his life. There is no reason, however, to modify the biographer's assessment of the main reason for Charles' earlier successes. This he attributes solely to his subject's indomitable will:

> Charlemagne was by far the most able and noble-spirited of all those who ruled over the nations in this time. He never withdrew from an enterprise which he had once begun and was determined to see through to the end, simply because of the labour involved; and danger never deterred him. Having learnt to endure and suffer each particular ineluctable circumstance, whatever its nature might be, he was never prepared to yield to adversity; and in times of prosperity he was never to be swayed by the false blandishments of fortune.[1]

While this is essentially true, it would be wrong to picture Charlemagne as a bull-headed tyrant who was impervious to reason and never considered the opinions of his advisers. He was energetic and impatient for success, the sort of man who carries others along with his own whirlwind enthusiasm. Yet, even as a young man, he was not foolishly headstrong. In 768 he inherited several problems that demanded some show of military strength and determination. Restless subordinates as well as aggressive occupants of the borderlands were ready to take advantage of his inexperience. He must have been tempted to show himself and his army in a number of locations in order to demonstrate his military might. However, throughout his thirty-eight-month-conflict with his brother he held himself in check, understanding well that family matters had to be settled and the loyalty of Francia's leading nobility ensured before he could risk long-distance campaigning. Once he was fully his own master he threw off the chains of constraint.

As soon as he heard of Carloman's death, Charles spurred to Laon where his brother's body lay. His motive was not to lead the mourning for his sibling, but to receive the homage of all who had sworn allegiance to him. Carloman left two infant sons and, by law, they should have inherited their father's lands, but their uncle was not to be balked by children of his opportunity to reunite all Pepin's territory. Queen Gerberga did not wait to discover her brother-in-law's intentions; she fled with her sons to Lombardy and placed them under the protection of Desiderius. The *Royal Frankish Annals* loyally observed that her panicked flight was 'needless',[2] but there can be little doubt what would have happened to the boys under Charles' 'protection'. Meanwhile, much hard bargaining was going on. Some of Carloman's henchmen readily transferred their allegiance, but others had to be wooed or bribed. In place of the two wives he had recently discarded, the king took Hildegard, of the ducal family of Alamannia, as a replacement. This secured the eastern region, and arrangements with other local leaders further strengthened Charles' position.

Internationally, the unforeseen turn of events had restored the situation to where it had stood before Pepin's death. The Lombards could no longer rely on a divided Francia to make life easier for them, and the papacy once more had a powerful protector. But of more immediate importance to Charles than the situation in Italy was the restoration of the old status quo along his northern border. Here he faced Francia's ancient enemy, the Saxons. These peoples, living between the Oder and the Elbe, had been regarded by the Romans as the ultimate barbarians. Accomplished raiders by land and sea, they were linguistically and culturally distinct from any of the tribes that had been brought within the civilising ambit of the Mediterranean world. They had long had a troubled relationship with the Franks. Population pressure and the inhospitable nature of their northern lands obliged the Saxons to be constantly seeking *Lebensraum* and that led inevitably to border clashes. There were frequent trials of military strength, but even when battles had been won and lost and terms had been agreed, peace seldom lasted long. This was in large measure due to the religious barrier. Solemn oaths sworn on the name of pagan gods carried little weight with Christian negotiators, and Saxon leaders were similarly unimpressed by vows made over relics of the saints. Franks and Saxons were, thus, locked into permanent confrontation. On several occasions Francia's rulers had imposed tributary status on their troublesome neighbours and had taken hostages to ensure compliance with the agreed terms, but as soon as either side detected a weakness in the other it sought to exploit it. Thus, in 747, the Saxons had given refuge to Grifo when he escaped from the captivity imposed by Pepin and Carloman.

It may be that they also took advantage of the discord between Pepin's sons and that Charles was unable to spring an attack upon them for fear of weakening his position at home. Only after his brother was dead did Charles launch a major onslaught across the northern border. However, it is equally possible that the campaign of 772 was largely unprovoked. It proved to be the curtain raiser to more than a decade of all-out war, which ceased only when the Saxons had been completely subjugated. It seems more than likely that Charles set out with the intention of putting an end to the 'Saxon problem' once and for all and, having so decided, pursued his goal with unremitting energy and efficiency.

In the spring of that year he held an assembly of all his nobles at Worms, a favourite Rhineland residence of the Carolingian kings, to discuss the forthcoming fighting season. From there, as the chronicle declares, he 'marched first into Saxony. Capturing the castle of Eresburg, he proceeded as far as the Irminsul, destroyed this idol, and carried away the gold and silver which he found.'[3]

That prosaic, unvarnished account veils two significant facts. The Saxon advance had for centuries been restricted to the area north of the Rhine tributary, the Lippe, along the valley of which the Romans had constructed a line of forts, roughly speaking between modern Wesel and Paderborn. Recently, however, the Saxons had crossed this line, and the Eresburg was a stronghold built on the banks of the Diemel, twenty kilometres farther south. The Irminsul was a vast, ancient tree trunk, elevated by the new-comers to the status of a shrine and believed by them to be one of the pillars of the heavens. Its location close by the Eresburg was thought to ensure the protection of the gods, whose support was sought by means of rich offerings. In territorial terms it was a statement of defiance, a tangible demonstration of the Saxons' determination not to be dislodged from this frontier region.

Charles' decision to strike at the castle and the holy place was an equally unambiguous declaration of intent that was both military and religious. He was making it clear that the Frankish army and the Frankish God were superior to those of their enemies. Charles, even at this early stage, seems to have been aware that paganism and Christianity were locked in a battle to the death and that he was the chosen leader of the *populus christianus*, the Christian world (or, at least, that part of it that did not fall under the dominion of the Eastern Emperor). His attack on the Irminsul is particularly significant because he was associating himself with what had hitherto been the activity of Christian professionals. Missionary bishops were frequently involved in the tearing down of pagan idols, but this is the first recorded instance of a political leader engaging in the same work. It received the unequivocal approval of the chronicler, who recorded that a divine miracle had endorsed the destruction. The region was afflicted by a drought, which obliged Charles to move his army on before the devastation was complete. However, at the last moment, a new spring gushed forth, enabling his men to drink their fill and return with fresh vigour to their anti-idolatry crusade.

'Crusade' is not too strong a word. State expansion always needs an ideological base. Those responsible for advancing imperial frontiers need to believe that what they are doing is for the benefit of the newly conquered peoples. Whether we are considering the legions of a caesar introducing barbarians to the advantages of the *pax Romana*, or Victorian pioneers spreading 'Christianity, commerce and civilisation', or modern US statesmen imposing 'freedom and democracy' on other cultures, the constant factor is one of belief: conviction that the conqueror knows what is best for the conquered, who will one day come to realise how much they have gained by throwing off their old ways and entering into the enlightenment of their new masters. Charles and his advisers regarded with loathing not only the beliefs of their pagan enemies, but also some of their 'barbaric' practices, which included human sacrifice, the burning alive of criminals and (apparently) cannibalism. There was no more doubt in Frankish minds that theirs was a superior culture than there was in the minds of Spanish conquistadore when confronted by Aztec religious rituals. The Franks were, in their own estimation, God's people. Their warriors were holy champions. Their arms were blessed by Christian priests. Their military feats were lauded by both preachers and bards. Their youthful king-general was divinely anointed to spread the faith.

The next year it was the old three-way conflict in Italy – between the papacy, Lombardy and Francia – that, once more, demanded Charles' attention. He tackled the situation with a new determination. Weary of the ongoing rivalries that had, over and again, intruded upon Francian politics, diverting the energies of his father and grandfather, Charles set his sights on a final solution. The situation in Rome had shifted with the death of Stephen and, with it, the collapse of his alliance with the Lombards. The new pope, Hadrian I, was made of sterner stuff than his predecessor and, when Desiderius resorted to bullying tactics, he sent an emissary to Rome's by now traditional saviour. Since the Lombards effectively blocked all the mountain routes, his messengers had to travel by sea to Marseille and thence via the Saône and Moselle valleys all the way to Thionville, near Luxembourg, where Charles had just set up his winter quarters.

This was in the autumn of 773 and the king responded with remarkable despatch. Instead of waiting for the next campaigning season, Charles made a bid to cross the Alps before the snows set in. He gathered a large army and divided it in two sections, one to advance via the Mont Cenis Pass and the other to take the Great St Bernard Pass. This shrewd move meant that Desiderius, commanding a smaller host, did not dare split his own army to resist the invasion and was obliged to fall back upon his capital of Pavia, an old Roman stronghold that he confidently believed to be impregnable. He cannot have been overly concerned when Charles camped close to the ancient walls and began a siege. Winter was approaching. The alpine blasts would do his work for him. The Frankish king would have to withdraw, as his father had once done before him. At the very worst, Desiderius would be obliged to agree a truce and make promises that he would have no intention of keeping.

But Desiderius was in for more shocks than one. Charles settled his men in for the winter. It was a prodigious psychological as well as logistical undertaking. His commanders and their men were not accustomed to being away from their homes throughout the darker, battle-free months, and it says much for the leadership qualities of their young king that he could maintain the loyalty and unity of his army. The Franks were still encamped on the banks of the Ticino when it was swelled by the melting snows of springtime 774. It was the inhabitants of Pavia who were suffering. Hunger and disease had begun to take a cruel toll. Still Desiderius held on. Not until midsummer did he sue for peace. He must have expected that Charles would demand a heavy tribute, then march his way back across the Alps. What the victor actually did was take for himself the Iron Crown of Lombardy (so named because of the supposed nail of the true Cross worked into the gem-encrusted golden circlet) and send Desiderius and his family into Francia as prisoners. He then received the homage of all the leading men of the nation, installed a powerful Frankish garrison in Pavia and finally set off for home. Charles, King of the Franks, was now also Charles, King of the Lombards. In less than two years he had conducted two monumentally successful campaigns. No one could now be in any doubt that Francia had a new kind of king.

He had also established his credentials as protector of the Church. He visited the new pope during his sojourn in Italy and was rapturously received. Well might Hadrian extend a warm welcome to the man who had permanently removed his arch-enemy and restored several confiscated properties to Rome. For his part, Charles always claimed to have an affectionate relationship with Hadrian and usually referred to him as his 'father'. The chroniclers eagerly embellished this closeness between the spiritual and temporal leaders of the *populus christianus*. However, there is in all this a large element of window-dressing, and everything was certainly not *couleur de rose* between king and pope. There is no doubting the sincerity of Charles' religious conviction, but he had his own reasons for playing up his friendship with Hadrian, especially in the early years of his reign. He needed the support of the Christian faithful throughout his territories. Many bishops and abbots had close connections, familial and otherwise, with the great Frankish noble clans. Charles kept his warrior-barons onside largely by fighting wars that united them against a common enemy and by offering the possibility of rich booty, but it also helped to have the enthusiastic endorsement of the nation's spiritual leaders.

What Charles was not prepared to do was yield to the pope any degree of political pre-eminence. He had responded as a dutiful son to the holy father's appeal. He had invested an enormous amount of energy and time in disposing once and for all of Rome's enemies. But he was determined to set his own agenda. He would not be dictated to by the pope, no matter what spiritual arm-twisting the latter might try to use. Having devoted more than nine months to the problems of Italy, Charles headed north to attend to more pressing business. Hadrian tried to restrain him. There was, he insisted, still work to be done: the Archbishop of Ravenna refused to acknowledge the pope's authority; illegal occupiers of papal lands were not giving them up; some Roman territory had actually been taken over by the Franks. All these matters demanded Charles' attention.

What lay behind these protests was Hadrian's fear that he might have exchanged one political master for another – and that, to a large extent, was what had actually happened. In this nascent Christian empire claims were already being made, and questions posed, about the balance of spiritual and temporal power. On the one side was the authority claimed by Hadrian and succeeding popes to dictate, in the name of God, even to kings and emperors. On the other was the divine sanction that Charlemagne and his heirs asserted as men exercising rule under God in all the affairs of their subjects. This rule extended to the clergy as well as laymen – the principle, later developed, of the 'two swords' entrusted to temporal rulers. The first round of this contest, which was destined to run for centuries, was clearly won by Charles.

Once again it was the Saxons who now demanded his attention. Charles realised that they posed a long-term threat and he committed himself to finding a long-term solution, just as he had done with Lombardy. Indeed, it may well be that his decisive action south of the Alps was in order to

This sumptuous, jewel-encrusted reliquary bust of Charlemagne brilliantly demonstrates the spendid myth that had developed by the 14th century.

Ice point mozut le prince pepin
le bref en lan de lincarnation de
noftre feigneur Bi. cens. La feig;

eftoit gouuernoit le royaulme fagement
elle et le roy Dagobert et Theodouault
fon nepueu qui en ce temps eftoit prince du

Charles Martel, Charlemagne's grandfather, halted the advance of the Moors at the
Battle of Tours (or Poitiers) in 732. Important though this victory was, it assumed legendary
importance in later centuries thanks to the ongoing conflict between Christianity and Islam.
This 8th century manuscript celebrates the event.

By the 15th century the crowning of Charlemagne by Leo III in 800 had become a cornerstone of papal claims to temporal as well as spiritual supremacy. In this version the Pope wears the triple tiara signifying his earthly authority.

One way Charlemagne maintained his authority over all the warrior-magnates of his empire was by imposing upon them an oath of personal loyalty. Here aristocrats line up to offer their allegiance.

From the 12th century onwards Charlemagne was regarded as the archetypical crusader and he was credited with a series of heroic but spurious exploits against the Saracens. Illustration from the 15th century *Story of St Ogier*.

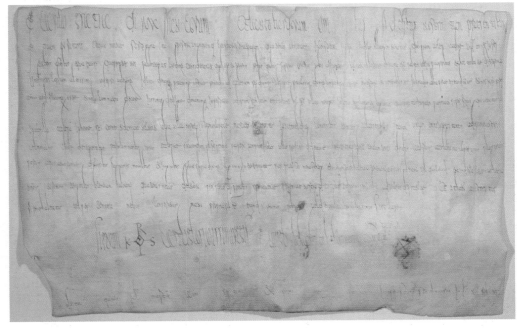

Document signed by Emperor Charlemagne with his monogram.

Gold Solidus of Irene, the ruthless ruler of Byzantium, who, according to one tradition, almost became Charlemagne's wife, thus uniting the two halves of Christendom.

The Renaissance revered Charlemagne as a cultural and religious leader. In this painting by Bernard van Orley he is depicted as placing relics of Christ in new chapel at Aachen.

13th century Venetian manuscript page depicting Charlemagne, with Roland, the hero of Roncesvalles.

A view of the Charlemagne chapel, now incorporated into the cathedral at Aachen.

The figure of Charlemagne on the new shrine made in 1215 to the order of Frederick II.

A page from a 9th century astrological treatise. Charlemagne was as fascinated by the study of the heavenly bodies as he was by the reading of the Bible and the church fathers.

dispose of this troublesome distraction, so that he could be free to devote himself entirely to getting rid of the Saxon menace. The basic problem confronting the Franks was that of war on several fronts and the concomitant drain it imposed on the nation's resources. This dilemma faces all empire-builders and, though Charles did not set himself on a career of territorial conquest, securing his borders inevitably led to pacifying the regions beyond the frontier and, thus, to further acquisitions. He was locked in conflict with his aggressive Saxon neighbours until 785 and his ultimate success stemmed from his determination to match their persistent violence. At first sight the king's campaigns may seem to be merely a continuance of the bloody border warfare in which his predecessors had been engaged, an expression of that tribal conflict and desperate competition for territory that marked the chaos of what was once known as the 'Dark Ages'. But Charlemagne was different. His success as a war leader rested on two foundations – his clear-sighted pursuance of well-identified objectives and his longevity. He was fortunate in that he lived long enough to achieve many of the goals he set himself.

The fortunes of war ebbed and flowed between 772 and 785. Charles would penetrate deep into Saxon territory, win some battles, enforce Christian baptism, demand tribute and take hostages. As soon as he had withdrawn into winter quarters, the enemy would renege on their agreement, counter-attack and regain much of the lost ground. But Charles was winning the war of attrition. Each season saw his secure border advance. Most years he did not leave the battle zone until he had established well-fortified garrisons in the conquered territory, and each castle, as well as being a military stronghold, was also staffed with clergy whose task was to spearhead religious advance.

Certain focus events during these campaigns are significant in giving us glimpses of Charlemagne's character and his development as a statesman-general. In 776 he began to build an impressive forward base at Paderborn, deep inside former Saxon territory. Unlike most Frankish population centres, Paderborn had no Roman origins and it is clear that Charles regarded the new town as having more than strategic value; it made a personal statement. He set his builders to construct a palace-church complex that was intended to overawe the local populace. It seems that his first intention was to make Paderborn his capital and to name it 'Karlsburg'. No northern ruler had ever conceived such a piece of permanent self-advertisement. Indeed, had Charles brought his plan to fruition, he would have joined a very select band of leaders whose names were perpetuated in this way, including Alexander, Constantine and Peter the Great. The following year he underscored the importance of Paderborn and demonstrated his determination to remain in control of the region by holding the spring assembly of his senior nobles and churchmen amidst the construction site for his new centre. Charles' prestige at this gathering was enhanced by the arrival of envoys from Muslim Spain who were seeking his assistance (see page 56). The King of Francia and Lombardy was emerging as an international statesman on a par with the emperor in Constantinople.

Such displays of power brought more submissions from the Saxons, often without the need for further fighting. However, there was never a lack of proud and brave Saxon warrior leaders prepared to continue resistance. The most formidable (or, at least, the most elusive) was a champion called Widukind. He proved to be a thorn in Charles' flesh for several years, attacking weak points in Frankish defences, then retreating into the forests and marshes of his homeland or slipping across the border into Frisia or Denmark. The military impact of this national hero was slight, but his influence on Saxon morale was considerable and he did much to stiffen the resistance of his people.

The campaign of 779 took Charles' army right across Saxon territory to their eastern boundary with the Slavs. The sudden appearance of this well-disciplined, ferocious band of Franks fighting far from their homeland was an awesome prospect and the East Saxons put up little resistance. The sheer energy of the Frankish king was a major secret of his success, as Gibbon famously observed:

> The sedentary reader is amazed by his incessant activity of mind and body; and his subjects and enemies were not less astonished at his sudden presence at the moment when they believed him at the most distant extremity of the empire.[4]

Thousands of the vanquished accepted the Christian faith, only to abandon it as soon as the crisis was over. In an attempt to give permanence to his achievements, Charles established churches and monasteries in the newly subjugated region, believing – or hoping – that the steady drip-drip of teaching, preaching and miracle-working would accomplish what necessarily brief displays of military might could not. Yet, still the Widukind problem remained, and still the spirit of the Saxons had not been broken. The Frankish chronicles, our main source of information about the wars, are triumphalist in tone and give the impression of a steady, inevitable extension of Charles' territorial control. In fact, the fighting was far from being one-sided. The Franks lost several battles and sacrificed thousands of their own warriors in the Saxon Wars.

By now Charles had been drawn into a fight to the death with his pagan neighbours. He had staked not only his own reputation but also that of the Christian Frankish people on ultimate and total victory, and this must explain why his treatment of the recalcitrant Saxons became more and more savage. There could be no going back. Fighting the common enemy had become an internal political necessity. To fail or abandon the conquest of Saxony would be to weaken the cohesion of his own people. The king was now in his thirties, the prime of life in an age when a man was reckoned old at fifty. Every year that passed, with what was now his main purpose in life unaccomplished, placed greater pressure on him. The cohesion of the Frankish state was predicated on warfare. Charles' warrior-nobles had to be kept busy against foreign enemies. They also needed to achieve success, for success meant booty, which they needed in order to pay their followers and ensure their own mounting prosperity. As long as their king could provide the means for enrichment, they would follow him. Of one of Charles' campaigns Einhard recalled: 'The memory of man cannot recall any war against the Franks by which they were so enriched and their material possessions so increased.' The haul of gold and silver, he claimed, had turned the Franks from 'paupers' into Midases.[5]

In 782 Charles held his annual gathering near Paderborn and there he resorted to a new tactic for subduing the Saxons. To military defeat and forced conversion he now added the constraint of the law. His 'First Saxon Capitulary' was a body of regulations designed to back up the Christianisation of the subject people. New laws prohibited, on pain of death, such crimes as destroying or looting churches, murdering priests, refusing baptism, reconverting to their old religion, continuing pagan practices and even eating meat in Lent. The intention was not to extract the full penalty of the law, but rather to encourage Saxon offenders to seek absolution and do penance. Charles did everything to reinforce the power and prestige of the clergy. He placed the burden of maintaining churches firmly on the shoulders of the local people, who were now obliged to provide land and slave labour for the mission communities established in their midst.

The immediate result was disaster. Months later, while Charles was busy elsewhere, some of his nobles attempted to gain prestige through an attack on a Saxon force in the mountainous region north of the Weser. They were carved to pieces with the loss of more than twenty of Francia's leading men. This led to a widespread revolt and, once again, Widukind appeared to lead it. As soon as the news reached him, the king, who was 600 kilometres away at Auxerre, immediately marched eastwards with the furious

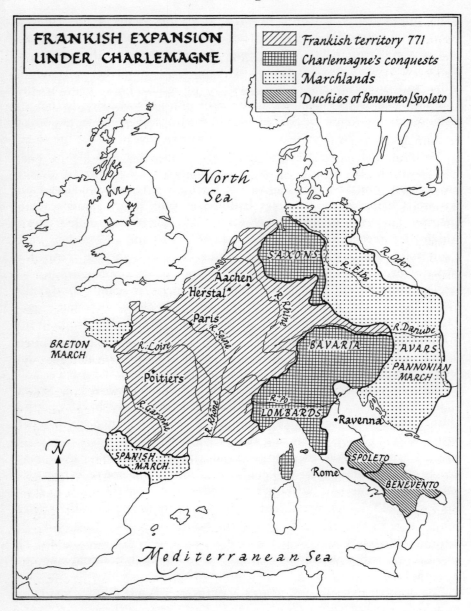

FRANKISH EXPANSION
UNDER CHARLEMAGNE

Frankish territory 771
Charlemagne's conquests
Marchlands
Duchies of Benevento/Spoleto

North Sea

SAXONS

R. Oder

R. Elbe

Aachen
Herstal

R. Rhine

Paris

R. Seine

R. Danube

BAVARIA

AVARS

BRETON MARCH

R. Loire

PANNONIAN MARCH

Poitiers

R. Rhône

R. Garonne

R. Po

LOMBARDS

Ravenna

N

SPANISH MARCH

SPOLETO

Rome

BENEVENTO

Mediterranean Sea

energy of an avenging angel. He did not have to fight a battle. Messengers sent ahead, and reports from those who had witnessed the ferocity of Charles' reaction, warned the Saxon leaders that the Frankish host was unstoppable. They hastened to disavow Widukind, who returned to Danish exile, and to make a grovelling submission. To assuage Charles' wrath they rounded up and handed over 4,500 men who had been responsible for the recent massacre. In a terrible demonstration of wrath and power, Charles had every one of the prisoners beheaded at Verden, on the banks of the Aller. The figure of 4,500 may have been an exaggeration on the part of the chronicler, who delighted in bloodthirsty detail; the mass execution was, nevertheless, a gruesome act and demonstrates Charlemagne's mounting desperation.

He doubtless hoped that it would put an end to Saxon resistance once and for all, but he was soon disappointed. There was still no lack of warrior chiefs determined not to be bullied out of their independence, and every year there were uprisings somewhere in the inadequately subdued territory. Nothing Charles tried could put an end to the Saxon problem. He rewarded any of their leading men who accepted his rule. He incorporated Saxon cohorts into his army when campaigning elsewhere. Neither bribery nor conversion achieved his objective; still he had to resort to naked force. Much of 783 and 784 was taken up with the war in Saxony, and in the latter year he stayed to continue fighting beyond the campaigning season. Throughout the winter Frankish units rampaged through the country, killing, burning and tearing down pagan shrines. This devastation and the relentless determination that inspired it finally persuaded Saxony's leaders that further resistance would be foolhardy.

Yet still all dissident voices had not been silenced and Charles knew they would not be, as long as Widukind was at liberty as a figurehead for rising generations of Saxon patriots. The king had the political acumen to realise that he could no longer gamble upon Widukind's capture or death in battle. Alive, he was a hero and a focus of the nation's hopes. Dead, he would be a martyr and an inspiration to future rebels. There would have to be talks with the elusive patriot. Charles sent a message to Widukind offering safe conduct to his villa at Attigny in the Ardennes and sending hostages as a guarantee of his good faith. It was there, in the autumn of 785, that Charles gave his arch-enemy an honourable welcome. Widukind was won over with rich gifts, a promise of pardon and, probably, appointment to official positions in the Frankish state. In return, he laid down his arms and received baptism on Christmas Day, with Charles himself standing godfather. Messengers immediately set out for Rome, carrying the good tidings and requesting that prayers of thanksgiving be offered throughout the Christian world for the end of conflict and the extension of Christ's kingdom.

The rejoicing was premature.

Notes

1 *Einhard and Notker*, pp.63–4
2 *Carolingian Chronicles*, p.48
3 Ibid., p.48
4 Gibbon, op. cit., V, p.182
5 *Einhard and Notker*, p.67

4

Enemies Within

Charlemagne was now in his forties, a good age by the standards of life expectancy in the eighth century. He would, in fact, live well into his seventies, a longer lifespan than any other male member of his family for several generations: this was not the least of his accomplishments. We can now begin to assemble a clearer picture of the great man from his actions and his early biographers.

He is described by Einhard as a benign dictator, a no-nonsense, straightforward ruler with a becoming modesty in his personal habits. He was slightly above average height and of heavy build, with a flowing moustache and wide, penetrating eyes. He dressed simply in the typical Frankish tunic over a linen shirt and long hose, over which he wore a blue cloak and, in winter, a jerkin of otter skin or ermine. Einhard tells us that the king loathed dressing up and was with difficulty persuaded to don ceremonial robes for major state or ecclesiastical occasions. A story from the highly anecdotal, ninth-century *De Carolo Magno* underlines Charles' contempt for fripperies and has a ring of truth about it. He was at Friuli when some of his courtiers arrived back from Pavia, where they had been enjoying the festival and returned flaunting fashionable clothes of silk, bedecked with feathers and ribbons. Charles insisted that they immediately accompany him on a hunting expedition. The poor men were given no time to change and for several hours were obliged to ride through forest glades and thickets, lashed by rain and briars. On their return they were not allowed to change out of their bedraggled finery. Charles kept them dancing attendance upon him till late into the night. The next morning their ordeal was not over, for Charles commanded them to present themselves in the same clothes they had worn the day before. As they stood before him, shivering in their tattered, muddy garments, the king pointed out to them the moral of their uncomfortable experience: they should not allow their manhood to be sapped by effeminate, debilitating luxury.

In 783 Charlemagne lost his wife, Hildegard, the first woman he had actually married. She was only twenty-five, but she had borne him ten children in twelve years. More remarkably, only one of them, a twin, died soon after birth. Einhard eulogised his hero as an affectionate and devoted family man who could not bear to be separated from his children and shed tears of unmanly grief over those who pre-deceased him. The biographer gives us an affecting cameo picture of Charlemagne's domestic life:

> He paid such attention to the upbringing of his sons and daughters
> that he never sat down to table without them when he was at home
> and never set out on a journey without taking them with him. His
> sons rode at his side and his daughters followed behind. Hand-picked
> guards watched over them as they closed the line of march.[1]

We can accept at face value the account of Charlemagne's love for his sons and daughters. Yet this is very far from being the whole story, nor could it be when every one of his children held political significance. They grew up in a highly pressured atmosphere, constantly aware of their importance to the dynasty and restrained by the rules imposed by a parent who totally dominated their lives. It was not only during their travels that their safety was his special care; palace security must have been very tight. It is likely that Charlemagne also well understood the need for family unity. In his own childhood he had been very close to his sister, Gisla, but subsequent events suggest that his relations with his brother had long been strained. The conflict with Carloman had come close to tearing Francia apart, and Charlemagne did not want history to repeat itself.

The boys – Charles, Carloman and Louis – were, from an early age, involved in government, nominally at least. The eldest was kept at court to learn from the king's officials. The others were sent away from home before they were many years old, to 'rule' various regions of the empire. Carloman lived in Italy and Louis was made King of Aquitania. Of course, they did not have any actual power: they were ciphers, with entourages made up of Charlemagne's most trusted officers. It was their task to maintain a high profile for the regime and to make powerful subjects aware that their overlord was no mere distant figurehead. By allocating them their own spheres of authority, Charles made clear his intentions for the future division of his realm. In 781 another strong gesture underlined the permanence of the dynasty. The second son, Carloman, had yet to be baptised. It had been agreed that the pope would perform this ceremony, but the press of affairs had hitherto prevented the king from journeying to Rome. At Easter 781 he made good the omission. But at the font he surprised the onlookers by giving his young son a different name – Pepin. It was the clearest possible statement that his firstborn was to be set aside in favour of his children by Hildegard and a warning to any who might think of using the hunchback to mount a challenge for the throne.

The boys cannot have been separated from the life of their father's court for significantly long periods of time because they received some instruction from Alcuin, the British scholar who was in charge of the 'palace school' from 782 to 796. It is from letters sent later by their teacher that we gain some impression of their characters. Charles seems to have taken his responsibilities seriously and to have been open to Alcuin's advice to be on the watch for corruption among his followers. Pepin was eager for military adventure, and Alcuin nicknamed him 'Julius'. Louis was the scholar of the family and so devout that he would later be known as 'Louis the Pious'. He was the teacher's favourite, often seeking Alcuin's guidance on religious matters. Perhaps he was too introverted, for it was said of him, 'he never showed his white teeth in a smile'. As soon as Charlemagne's boys were old enough, they accompanied him on campaign and by the time they entered their teens they were expected to lead their own forces into battle.

For their sisters, Rotruda, Bertrada and Gisla among them, life was very different. They might have expected, as soon as they reached puberty, to be married off to husbands whom Charles wished to tie to the regime by familial bonds. They could have been bestowed on foreign rulers or on Frankish magnates. However, the king kept all his daughters single and at home. Einhard tells us that this was because 'he could not live without them', but his reluctance must have been, in part, due to his nervousness about entanglement in affairs beyond his borders. At one time Rotruda was betrothed to the Eastern Emperor and there was talk of Bertrada's marriage to Offa, King of Mercia, but nothing came of these proposed alliances. Instead, the girls remained at court where they studied under Alcuin, enjoyed the luxurious indolence of pampered princesses and were closely chaperoned. But not closely enough. In the frustrating confinement of the court Rotruda fell to the blandishments of Rorgon, Count of Maine and had a son, Louis. Bertrada, the prettiest and liveliest of the sisters, had an even more passionate and long-lasting affair with one of her father's closest friends. Angilbert was a true Renaissance man – soldier, scholar, poet, courtier, statesman, diplomat and religious leader. He had been Pepin III's chief adviser and he was to be found at Charles' right hand on the battlefield and in the council chamber. To Alcuin, Angilbert was 'my Homer', 'my bosom friend' and 'the defender of my soul', although the teacher regarded his colleague as a little too much given to theatrical entertainments and counselled him, 'thy care should be for singing clerks rather than for dancing bears'. This lover of life spent his final days as lay abbot of the wealthy monastery of Saint-Riquier, his last request being to be buried beneath the threshold of the abbey church so that all who came and went to worship would tread him underfoot. Angilbert was more than thirty years Bertrada's senior, but his zest for living must have attracted the princess, for she bore him two sons. One of them, Nithard, followed in his father's footsteps as a loyal servant of the Carolingians and was to become the greatest of the early Frankish historians.

The indiscretions of Charlemagne's daughters were a source of embarrassment to his biographer, who described them as 'unfortunate experiences'. Einhard claimed that Charles 'shut his eyes to all that happened, as if no suspicion of any immoral conduct had ever reached him, or as if the rumour was without foundation'.[2] It is unlikely that the king was as shocked as the writer would like us to believe. There was a mixture of piety and earthiness about the court, as there was about Charlemagne himself. The minstrelsy that he and his family enjoyed was a rich mix of war songs, bawdry and stories of the saints. A poem written by Angilbert to Bertrada while he was away on royal business provides a charming picture of his sons and their mother uninhibitedly enjoying the relaxed life of the court, and certainly gives no hint that the king's daughter and grandsons were living under a cloud of disapproval. He pictured his little family playing in the palace garden. 'Tell the boys, poem of mine,' he writes, 'to keep safe by God's mercy within their walls from fire and thief and sickness.'[3]

The letters exchanged between Alcuin and the royal women offer us hints of the tug-of-war between Christian moral imperatives and the libertarian life of the court. He enjoyed a very close friendship with Charlemagne's spinster sister, Gisla. She became abbess of Chelles, near Paris, but paid frequent visits to her brother. Alcuin wrote often with news, gifts of 'improving' books, and spiritual counsel. For example, he exhorted her to remain steadfast in her holy vocation:

. . . always remember the husband whose bride you have become. Your bridegroom is most glorious, and seeks no other adornment in you than that of the spirit – no twisted hair-dos, but straight conduct, no empty outward show of clothes, but a noble inward splendour of purity . . .[4]

Writing again to another of the king's female relatives, Alcuin displays his concerns more specifically. He urges his correspondent to set an example of godly living to all the other maidens in the palace:

> that they may learn from your holy life to keep watch on themselves and to rise again when they fall. Let them repent before they meet their judge. Let them be noble in character as in parentage. Let them not serve carnal desires but the teaching of Christ.[5]

It requires very little reading between the lines to understand what was on Alcuin's mind. Charlemagne's illegitimate grandsons must have had many playfellows in the palace garden. Rotruda and Bertrada paid many visits to their aunt at Chelles, and Alcuin did not fail to include greetings and exhortations to these younger women in his letters to the abbess:

> I must always love the children of my Lord David (Charlemagne) . . . But the devotion of my heart tends especially to you because of the friendliness and goodness you have shown me, for which may God's mercy reward you. Good fortune and prosperity be yours for ever, dearest daughters.
>
> Tell Columba (Rotruda) to commit to memory what she has received, until he comes who may add, 'Blessed are they who hunger and thirst for righteousness, for they shall be filled.'[6]

Poems and letters give us glimpses of the king's private life that are more vivid than the eulogies of Einhard and that find no place in official annals. They show us Charles sitting with his court scholars, listening to them exchange witticisms and engage in theological argument. Like many powerful men of limited education, he held intellectuals in some awe. He consulted them on complex or disputed matters of doctrine and liturgy. Yet one gets the impression that he sometimes treated them as court entertainers – mental acrobats who existed to please and astonish the royal circle with their skills. The most important of those skills was to flatter the king by acknowledging that he was cleverer than them. 'I have sent you a discourse in handbook form on the unique and holy Trinity,' Alcuin wrote, 'not that I thought your knowledge of the catholic faith was in any way lacking, but to justify the title of "master" which some gave me, however undeservedly.' When the scholar sent Charlemagne a treatise, the semi-educated king had it read to him, then returned it to its author with his corrections. And, of course, Alcuin was profuse in his humble thanks.[7] Another cameo presents Charles in his chapel listening critically to the performance of the liturgy and suddenly pointing with his staff to one or other of his clergy-men to take up the recitation. Woe betide any man who was not ready because he had lost his place or allowed his mind to wander. One of the court poets described the great leader's homecoming: his sons falling over themselves to help him divest himself of gloves and sword, while his daughters rushed out with flowers and fruit.

Even in his most intimate moments Charlemagne had to be the centre of attention. Perhaps it would be truer to say that he had very few really intimate moments. He loved to be – and probably needed to be – surrounded by people. All the anecdotes we have about him show us the king in the company of his family or his scholars, or enjoying the camaraderie of his burly warriors on campaign or in the chase. Charlemagne loved swimming, which was one reason for his choice of Aachen, with its warm springs, as his principal residence. But he seldom, if ever, swam alone; children, friends, palace officials and even the royal guards were often invited to join him in the water.

Charles' daily routine when he was at home in one of his residences began at dawn, when he had himself woken and immediately went to matins. As soon as he returned he was ready for the business of the day. He was a workaholic and kept scribes, advisers and messengers busy with a flurry of letters, instructions and legal judgements. He received petitioners and heard some of their pleas in person. The morning ended with mass, which was followed by the main meal of the day. He followed the monastic habit of having improving texts read while he ate, his favourite book being Augustine's *City of God*. As with everything else that he did, Charles was a hearty eater. He enjoyed his meat and drink – so much so that, while observing most of the Church's rituals, he refused to fast on the prescribed days. He chose to believe that regulations about food, like those on the subject of sex, did not apply to kings. That said, he does not seem to have indulged himself excessively in either area. He was too conscious of the dignity of his person to become insensible with ale or wine. Concubines he certainly had, but there is no evidence of an 'army' of royal bastards, which would have signified a lack of sexual restraint. At table a strict ritual was observed. It was normal for the royal family to dine alone, served by high-born retainers, while the rest of the court looked on. Only when Charles rose from the meal were other palace habitués allowed to eat, in order of rank. This formality has to be set beside Einhard's portrayal of the modest, relaxed monarch who took no delight in ceremonial.

Judged by any modern standards, Charlemagne was a tyrant. His exercise of absolute power meant that wary or ambitious courtiers had to study his moods carefully. They knew that he was capable of making or breaking men on a whim, and they calculated carefully when might be the most opportune moment to approach him with their petitions. Charles knew that they knew, and his relationships with them took on the appearance almost of a game. When Notker, a monk of Saint-Gall, wrote in the 880s his account of life in Charlemagne's court, he relied on hearsay and stories passed down by others. However, when he is not being too fanciful, his anecdotes have a ring of truth about them. One is worth quoting at this point because it gives a flavour of the clamouring importunity of palace life, and Charles' preservation of his own authority by not giving way to pressure or allowing the emergence of favourites. A certain rich bishop had died and the king indicated to one of the poor scholars who served his chapel that he might be elevated to the vacant position. Scarcely able to believe his sudden good fortune, the young man threw himself at his master's feet in grovelling gratitude. Charlemagne then warned him that there would, of course, be competition for the post, as the scholar would discover if he concealed himself behind a curtain. When he was thus hidden, the king ordered his palace officials to be admitted to the presence chamber.

> . . . they all began to canvass their own claims to the bishopric through those in the close confidence of the Emperor, showing impatience at the delay and jealousy of each other. The Emperor, for his part, persisted in his plan and was not prepared to change his mind; he refused the bishopric to everyone and said he would not break his promise to the young man.

Eventually Queen Hildegard herself approached, seeking the plum job for one of her own chaplains:

> The King listened politely to her request. He said that he would not and could not refuse her anything, but he was not willing to let down his own little churchman. It is the way of all women to want their own particular plan and solution to take preference over the decisions made by their menfolk; and so the Queen concealed the anger that was rising in her heart, lowered her firm voice to a whisper and tried to sway the resolute Emperor's mind with her soft caresses. 'My Lord King,' she said, 'what can it possibly matter if this young man of yours does not receive the bishopric? I beg of you, my sweet Lord, you who are my refuge and my glory, give it instead to my own cleric, who, after all, is a faithful servant of yours, too.'

This was too much for the concealed supplicant, who saw the prize being snatched away from him. 'Hold firm, my Lord King!' he called out. Charlemagne, 'who was a great believer in frank behaviour', brought the young man out from his hiding place and confirmed his appointment before the whole court.[8]

Fond as he undoubtedly was of Hildegard, Charles did not hesitate to take another young bride within months of her death. Her name was Fastrada and she lived until 794, by which time she had provided Charles with two more daughters. This poor girl has always had a bad press. Einhard condemned her 'cruelty' and asserted, 'it was under her influence that Charlemagne seemed to have taken actions which were fundamentally opposed to his normal kindliness and good nature'. After this queen's death, the writer assures us, 'no-one ever levelled against him the slightest charge of cruelty or injustice'.[9] Such a whitewash inevitably – and rightly – rouses our suspicions. Einhard was writing for Louis the Pious and could not tell the unvarnished truth about the king's father. Charlemagne *did* on occasion give way to bad temper and acts of cruelty. He *did* make enemies among his own followers. And there were times when opposition to his rule *did* become a serious threat. The most unstable period of his reign was the decade after 785, the very year when the Saxon problem seemed to have been solved and the empire might have looked forward to a time of relative peace. It was easy for Einhard to shift the blame for the difficulties of those years onto Louis' stepmother.

Success in battle was, as we have seen, vital to the king in ensuring the continued support of his more powerful subjects. His persistence in waging war against the Saxons, and his ultimate triumph, considerably strengthened his hold on the loyalty of those warrior-barons on whom he relied. It helped to expunge from their memory an earlier campaign in which Charles had overreached himself with disastrous consequences and which we must now consider. Ironically this, his worst defeat, became the basis of those later legends that identified him as the heroic Christian knight par excellence. This was the massacre of his rearguard in the pass of Roncesvalles. The Saracen envoys who appeared at Paderborn in 777 were, no less than the representatives of papal Rome, men who were desperate to engage the help of the mighty Frankish king in their own political conflicts. The Muslim world was in a state of turmoil in the second half of the eighth century and nowhere was the situation worse than in Spain. The basic dislocation had been caused by the overthrow of the Umayyad caliphs, whose empire had ringed the Mediterranean basin for 200 years, by the Abbasids. Only in Spain were the new rulers resisted by 'Abd al-Rahman I, who established an independent Umayyad caliphate. He made his capital in Cordoba and began that transformation that would turn it into one of the most beautiful and civilised cities in Europe. However, most of his energies were devoted to making his nominal rule a reality. He was opposed, not only by Abbasid supporters, but by religious dissidents and local leaders bidding for independence. The situation was complicated, especially in the north, by the existence of sizeable Christian communities.

Sulaiman ibn Yaqdhanu'l-A'rabi, the *wali* of Barcelona, placed himself at the head of a revolt involving several of the Muslim princelings who held sway over much of the region between the Ebro and the Pyrenees. He and his allies were very vulnerable to both land and sea attack by the superior forces of the caliph. This was why Sulaiman looked across the mountains for support and betook himself to Charles' spring assembly. His was a purely hard-headed political decision and he did not hesitate to look for help to the greatest infidel in the Western world. For his part, the leader of the *populus christianus*, who was forcing baptism on his pagan neighbours, had no compunction about making common cause with Muslims. Later legends represented Charles' 778 Spanish campaign as a crusade against the unbelievers. It was nothing of the sort. His Frankish horde went to war to help one Muslim faction fight against another. And for his pains he had his nose very seriously bloodied.

The sons of the Prophet were, militarily, a very different proposition from the unsophisticated pagan levies of Saxony. They occupied strong, defensible cities, which the Franks were ill equipped to besiege. Charles was successful at Pamplona, whose defences had been seriously weakened in earlier wars, but his capture of this city proved to be a costly strategic blunder. Though under titular Muslim control, Pamplona was an ancient Basque stronghold and the local people were as hostile to demonstrations of Frankish power as they were to Ummayed suzerainty. Charles had made enemies of the people who controlled the Pyrenean passes through which he would have to travel on his return. Meanwhile, the other section of his army, advancing via a different route, made no impression on the enemy. What was worse, however, was the squabbling that broke out among Charles' allies. Either their religious allegiance was firmer than that of the Christian Franks or they were terrified of incurring 'Abd al-Rahman's wrath. Whatever their reasons, Sulaiman's co-conspirators deserted him. The Franks were not admitted to Barcelona or Zaragoza. Sulaiman was assassinated by his own erstwhile supporters. Meanwhile, the caliph's forces were marching northwards, sweeping the rebels before them. Charles had no alternative but to beat an ignominious retreat.

It was while the army was making its way through the pass of

Roncesvalles that the Basques took their revenge. They detached Charles' rearguard from the rest of the army, massacred it and then fell upon the baggage train. Before Charles could come to the aid of his countrymen, the attackers had disappeared back into the mountains. Among the slain were several of the king's leading men and friends. One was Hruodland, better known to history as Roland, the ruler of the Breton March. There is no record of the exact circumstances of his death, but Frankish bards embroidered freely upon this ignorance and, by the twelfth century, Roland was represented as the trusted friend of Charlemagne (or, in later legends, as his nephew or illegitimate son), who had been placed in command of the rearguard and who, after several remarkable feats of bravery, died while leading a heroic defence, not against the Basques, but against the Saracens. Roland became the model Christian knight and martyr.

Why did Charles embark upon an ill-advised campaign that was badly conceived and poorly executed? Sulaiman's report on the confused situation in the Ebro valley may have persuaded him that there was some political advantage to be gained from intervention. Frankish control in the south-west was of comparatively recent origin. It was Charles' grandfather and father who had pushed the Muslims back across the mountains. Their successor may have reasoned that a show of force would further secure his frontier. But it may be that family pride and ambition got the better of him. If Charles made the mistake of believing his own publicity, he may have decided to match the exploits of his forebears and take the field against the infidel. Whatever his motives, the result was disastrous, although, fortunately, only in the short term. The humiliation of defeat did not undermine his position within Francia. He and his military leaders were immediately involved in the next round of conflict with the Saxons. The royal chronicler glossed over the Spanish campaign and Charles put it behind him. The Pyrenean frontier remained secure, but not because of Charles' military reputation. Successive caliphs were too involved with internal problems to think in terms of northward expansion, and the Christian kingdoms of Asturias, Navarre, Leon, Castile, Aragon and the marchland of Barcelona formed an effective buffer. Charles never ventured again across the western mountains. Fortunately for him, he never had to.

The effective sealing off of the border with Iberia was of immense consequence not only for Charlemagne's empire, but for the development of Christian Europe. The boundaries of Frankish control and influence were largely defined and this aided the nation's self-identification. People more readily determine who they are by specifying who they are not. The Franks and their dependent tribes were not pagans. They were not Muslims. They were Christians. Since the concept of individual choice in religious matters would have seemed to them very odd, it follows that within their frontiers ethics and personal devotion, as well as law and political life, were based upon loyalty to their king.

By the age of thirty-seven, Charles had established himself as *the* ruler of the Christian West. Though there was obvious continuity with the Carolingian and Merovingian past, what had come into being was something new – a fusion of Frankish custom, Celtic spirituality and Romano-papal ecclesiastical politics. The 'new Francia' did not emerge without experiencing internal tensions. Its story was not, as the chroniclers might have us believe, the steady, triumphant extension of the nation's frontiers into previously pagan territory. The records offer reluctant glimpses of discord between the king and his subordinates, and even between the king and members of his own family.

The years 786–8 were particularly unsettled. Trouble first appeared in Thuringia, that part of the empire closest to Saxony. Pacification of the pagans on Francia's north-east frontier had not assuaged the discontents of all Charles' subjects in the region. A certain Count Hardrad gathered several of his neighbours into a conspiracy. For years they had borne the brunt of all the campaigning against the Saxons. Now that warfare was over, they may have been dissatisfied with the distribution of land and booty, feeling that their indispensable loyalty and suffering deserved more tangible recognition. Hardrad and his accomplices planned to kidnap Charles, presumably with the intention of extracting from him a more fulsome reward for their services. Unfortunately for them, the plot was betrayed and its ringleaders arrested. Einhard insists that Charlemagne only had three traitors executed and that, thanks to royal clemency, others were merely deprived of their eyes, before being shut up in monasteries to meditate on their sins. For this account to be accurate Charles must have felt extremely secure on his throne. Most rulers in his position would have grasped the opportunity for a demonstration of power *pour encourager les autres*, and it seems more than likely that the biographer, who was writing for Louis the Pious, had good reason for representing his patron's father as a model of Christian forbearance. Charles' dealings with the ruler of another border state lend some support to such suspicion.

Bavaria was a running sore. Its ruler, Tassilo III, was a member of an ancient ducal dynasty. He was a maternal cousin of Charles and was married to a daughter of Desiderius, ex-king of Lombardy. The status of the dukedom had long been a matter of dispute. Charles, like his father and grandfather before him, regarded it as a vassal territory, but Tassilo asserted his independence and in this 'arrogance' he was, according to Einhard, egged on by his wife. Since Bavaria was far removed from Charles' homeland, the duke could feel quite secure. It was largely because of the country's remoteness that matters were not pushed to a conclusion by Pepin III, nor, for several years, by his son. Tassilo took no aggressive action against the king, and he occasionally provided detachments for Charles' armies. However, the duke sometimes declined to attend the annual Frankish gathering and there were clearly other causes of friction. So fraught was the relationship that, in 781, the pope sent a message to Tassilo urging him to 'remember his former oaths and not to go back on his long-standing pledge to the Lord King Pepin, the great Lord King Charles and the Franks'.[10] Hadrian's one-sided support probably reflects a Church–state conflict in Bavaria, where the bishops resented the close scrutiny and 'interference' of Tassilo in their affairs. Months later the duke did homage at Worms and left hostages as security for his good behaviour, but, the chronicler recorded, he 'did not long keep the promises he had made'.[11]

Charles' mounting impatience with his vacillating vassal reflects his own determination to enforce his will, but it also indicates the growing importance of the eastern reaches of the empire. Now that Lombardy had been brought under Charles' direct rule, he needed unhampered access to the eastern alpine passes. Now that the extended empire abutted onto the lands of the nomadic Avars and Slavs, he wanted to control the highway of the Danube valley. Charles was also beginning to take thought for the future security of Francia. In 781 he made arrangements for the succession and, as he contemplated his young sons and the responsibilities they would inherit, he felt the need to make sure of the loyalty of his dukes and counts.

With the backing of the pope, Charles continued to put pressure on Tassilo. There is no evidence that the Bavarian ruler posed any serious threat or offered any provocation, but the king was relentless in his determination to strengthen his hold on the dukedom. He seems to have been deliberately looking for an excuse for military intervention. Tassilo was understandably worried by the hostile intentions of his overlord. In 787, when Charles was once again in Rome, Bavarian envoys arrived asking the pope to intervene as a peacemaker. Hadrian's response was to pronounce an anathema (a decree of excommunication) against the duke. If Tassilo did not submit totally to his lord, then he would be responsible for whatever consequences might ensue. This was tantamount to providing carte blanche for a royal invasion of Bavaria. Back at Worms, Charles issued an order for Tassilo to present himself and personally ratify the oath he had made 'to the Lord King Charles, his sons and the Franks'.[12] Not surprisingly, the duke was reluctant to put himself at risk. His refusal to appear was the excuse Charles had been looking for. His response was disproportionately massive.

He launched no fewer than three armies against Bavaria. From Worms he advanced in person at the head of one; a force of Saxons and East Franks was ordered to cross the Danube near Regensburg; and another was brought across the Alps from Italy under the titular leadership of his young son, Pepin.

Resistance would have been folly. There was no alternative for Tassilo but to make a humiliating submission. He yielded up the dukedom, and Charles – magnanimously, according to the annals – exacted no punishment. But that was not the end of the duke's troubles. Within months he was charged with plotting a rebellion in alliance with his Avar neighbours. How much truth there was in this accusation we cannot know. Tassilo may have found the blow to his pride too great to be endured. On the other hand, removing the hereditary ruler of Bavaria may have been Charles' objective all along – an objective frustrated by Tassilo's hasty submission. Charles' subsequent action certainly suggests his desire for a root-and-branch solution to the problem. He had Tassilo and his family, 'together with their treasure and household, extremely numerous', brought to the royal villa at Engelheim. There the duke was tried for treason and sentenced to death. Tassilo confessed to the crimes charged against him. With his wife and children at Charles' mercy, he could scarcely have done otherwise. Charles now proceeded to exterminate the ducal line – not by death, but by a punishment that was just as final. Tassilo and his sons were forcibly tonsured and sent to separate monasteries. His wife was exiled and his other dependants dispersed.

Four years later a more serious conspiracy came to light – serious because it involved Charlemagne's own kin and some of his trusted subordinates. Charles' arrangements for the succession were meant to remove any uncertainty, foster harmony and ensure a peaceful transfer of power to the next generation of his family. To further safeguard his heirs, the king had obliged all freemen to swear a solemn oath of loyalty to himself and his sons. But not everyone was happy with the declared arrangements. Charles' firstborn, Pepin the Hunchback, in particular, felt that he had been dispossessed of his rightful inheritance. The bastard was, thus, an obvious standard around whom discontented or ambitious members of the Frankish hierarchy could gather. In 791, when the king summoned all his warriors for an invasion of Avar territory (see page 71), Pepin feigned illness and stayed behind. His aim was to gather a significant band of supporters in his father's absence, have himself proclaimed king and raise a widespread rebellion. This was far from being a foolhardy plot. After the annihilation of the Bavarian ruling dynasty, several Frankish leaders became, unsurprisingly, apprehensive at the autocratic power that Charles was assuming, and Pepin would, undoubtedly, have sounded them out to calculate how much potential support he could count on. Once again conspiracy was nipped in the bud. A young monk overheard the plotters and hastened to report to the king. Pepin and his associates were rounded up and charged with violating their oath of allegiance. This they denied by claiming that the officials charged with administrating the oath had never reached them. Such arguments did not save them. Most of the plotters were hanged or beheaded, but Pepin was spared. He was sent to the distant monastery of Prüm, where a particularly severe rule was in operation. Einhard adds to his account, somewhat ingenuously, that Pepin had, in any case, professed a vocation for the religious life. After some years he was allowed to move to the more congenial atmosphere of Saint-Gall.

Notker later added a footnote to the sad story of Pepin the Hunchback. The thoroughly humbled prince was set to work in the abbey garden and there, one day, he received some visitors sent by his father. They brought a question from the king: some men had been detected in a conspiracy, and Charles demanded his son's advice about how he should deal with them. The monk paused but briefly in his labour of digging up weeds and indicated that he had no interest in politics. When the emissaries pressed him further, he advised them to tell Charlemagne what they had discovered him doing. Then he took up his trowel and continued to prod the earth, leaving his visitors to depart nonplussed. Of course, when the incident was reported to Charlemagne he immediately understood the enacted metaphor that had bemused his agents, and dealt accordingly with the offending parties. Fact or fable? It scarcely matters. What the commentaries of Einhard and Notker tell us is that one of the debates we associate with the political philosophers of the Renaissance had a long prehistory: should the epithet 'great' be accorded to a ruler who was an exemplar of Christian virtue and tempered justice with mercy, or did it more appropriately belong to a man who had the strength to be utterly ruthless when the circumstances demanded? It was certainly a moral conundrum that occupied Charlemagne's thoughts.

It seems likely that, over the long span of his reign, there were more attempted rebellions than were reluctantly recorded by the chroniclers. None of them succeeded. Was this due to the force of his personality? Was it proof of the effectiveness of his intelligence system? Probably both. Yet neither answer takes us to the heart of the matter. Why was Charlemagne able to hold together such an ethnically and linguistically diverse empire over so many years, when such an accomplishment had proved impossible to those who had preceded him and would similarly elude his successors? What was his secret? I believe it lies in the fact that he gained, and retained, the support of the power elites of Francia. The warrior-barons and the ecclesiastical leaders, most of whom came from the same families, buttressed Charles' autocratic regime because, by and large, he gave them what they wanted. He respected the traditions of what was essentially a militaristic society by involving the territorial magnates in the policy-making and administration of a more centralised state. Success in war not only enabled him to make generous distributions of booty, but also made possible the breeding of more war-horses and draught-animals and the acquisition of more weapons. This cycle of conquest and economic prosperity enhanced the wealth and prestige of Francia's aristocracy. As for the Church, Charlemagne's protection, his deliverance of the papacy from the Lombard threat, his levying of taxes for the support of clergy and religious houses, and his own personal commitment to the expansion of the Gospel community gave Francia's bishops and abbots every reason to back his regime. Malcontents resentful of the emperor's exercise of arbitrary power were never able to secure sufficient backing to present a significant threat to his authority.

Nevertheless, the disturbances and personal sadnesses of the 780s made this decade a real watershed in Charlemagne's reign. On his visit to Rome in 781 he had tried to give his extended empire harmony and security by having Pope Hadrian crown his sons and by betrothing Rotruda to the Eastern Emperor, Constantine VI, but these moves had provoked fear and jealousy, which had eventually displayed themselves in covert rebellion. The deaths of Hildegard and his mother had followed rapidly on each other in 783. He had also lost some of his closest advisers and most trusted officials. In addition to those who had fallen earlier beside Hruodland at Roncesvalles, Geilo (his constable) and Adalgisile (his chamberlain) had perished in battle in 782. His hasty marriage to Fastrada had proved unpopular. A succession of internal upheavals had violently shaken his throne. These trials had not weakened Charles' hold on power – quite the reverse. If anything, he was possessed from this time onwards by a more gritty determination. There was about his decision-making a new ambition, a new sense of destiny. He channelled his thinking into more long-lasting and grandiose objectives. They were symbolised by his decision to do something that no Frankish ruler had ever done before: found a capital city.

Notes

1 *Einhard and Notker*, p.75
2 Ibid.
3 E. S. Duckett, *Alcuin, Friend of Charlemagne*, 1951, p.94

4 S. Allott, *Alcuin of York*, 1974, p.101
5 Ibid., p.100
6 Ibid., pp.102, 104
7 Ibid., pp.86, 91
8 *Einhard and Notker*, pp.96–7
9 Ibid., p.76
10 *Royal Frankish Annals*, p.59
11 Ibid.
12 Ibid., p.65

II

Charlemagne the Emperor

The dignity of his person, the length of his reign, the prosperity
of his arms, the vigour of his government, and the reverence of
distant nations, distinguish him from the royal crowd . . .

Edward Gibbon, *The History of the Decline
and Fall of the Roman Empire*

5

Shades of Purple

There was nothing inevitable about Charles, King of the Franks, becoming Charles, Emperor in the West. If the times had not conspired to bring about a shift in the political realities of the Christian world, Charles would have been recognised by posterity as the greatest king of the Carolingian line, but nothing more. It was events in distant Constantinople and Rome that changed all that. While it is true that a man of Charlemagne's stature could not have been the mere tool of fate – a human artefact crafted and shaped by the actions of others – it is clear that those actions provided the spur to his ambitions, and the opportunities for him to define more precisely and to pursue more vigorously what he believed was his divinely ordained mission.

The Eastern Empire was in crisis. Preoccupied with problems on its own side of the Adriatic, it was losing its grip on the territories and authority it still claimed in the West. Had it only had to deal with the spreading stain of Islam, this would have been trouble enough, but Byzantium was adding to its own woes with the Iconoclastic Controversy. It may seem strange to modern minds that the collapse of the residual Roman Empire should have been due in part to an argument about whether religious pictures should be displayed in churches. Yet what appears to have been a self-indulgent and esoteric, if not downright cranky, dispute goes right to the heart of the spiritual and cultural revolution that was shaking the entire Christian world to its foundations. We tend to use the words 'Renaissance' and 'Reformation' in a very specific, fifteenth–sixteenth-century context, but the spiritual and intellectual upheaval implied by these words was experienced by Christendom in other ages and the age of Charlemagne was one of them. Thousands of devout worshippers had a deep emotional attachment to their icons of the Virgin Mary and their local saints, while monasteries had a vested interest in preserving ancient artefacts that attracted pilgrims – and their offerings. Others no less zealous espoused a purer, simpler style of piety stripped of gaudy externals. The elastic-sided Christian Church has always stretched to accommodate ascetics who shun the defilements of this world, and sensualists who reach out to the immaterial through the material. In times of fierce spiritual intensity, such as the eighth century, these approaches to the divine almost inevitably come into conflict.

In both East and West, Christianity was fighting a battle to the death with Islam and paganism. Around the Mediterranean basin from the Taurus Mountains to the Pyrenees it had spectacularly lost that battle. At the end of the eighth century the Eastern Church was still recoiling from the shock and was in defensive mode. It would be another fifty years before Byzantine Christians had the heart to take up the challenge of missions to the pagan lands to the north. As we have seen, the evangelistic thrust from the Celtic fringe and, to a lesser extent, from Rome had, by then, already made significant advances. One result was to enhance the stature of the Carolingian kings as against the rulers at Constantinople. Pepin III and Charlemagne appeared as Christian champions whose achievements contrasted markedly with those of the contemporary emperors. Another result was intense introspection on the part of the Christian community. Outstanding success and failure against other faiths both tended to highlight the same internal problems for the Church – problems of doctrine and discipline. Where God was seen to be punishing the Church, it must be for unholy living and errors of belief. Where there were new churches to be set up and thousands of converts to be instructed and nurtured, it was important that the clergy were orthodox in their teaching and holy in their living. Bishops, kings and emperors, therefore, were intensely focused on the minutiae of doctrine and ethics.

The practice of using images in devotion and worship now came to the top of the agenda at church councils, where it divided the iconoclastic sheep from the iconodulist goats. It exposed a conflict between theological fundamentals. On the one side were those who, in common with Muslims and Jews, regarded it as blasphemous to represent the divine in art. For them, God transcended human imagination and, in the Mosaic law, he had specifically forbidden the making of 'graven images'. Furthermore, they argued, filling churches with pictures of saints and members of the Trinity led inevitably to idolatry. Defenders of images counter-claimed that believers needed visual stimuli to direct their thoughts to heaven. Pictures might – indeed, should – be venerated because they conveyed something of the holiness of the person they represented. If God himself could be incarnated in Jesus, why could a painting, created by a divinely gifted artist, not also mediate grace?

The particular outbreak of violent ideological warfare known as the Iconoclastic Controversy began in 730 when the Emperor Leo III issued an edict against images. In obedience to his decree, they were removed from churches and broken up. Wall paintings were whitewashed. This provoked a backlash from Christian leaders and congregations, who had come to regard icons as an intrinsic part of their worship and devotion and who resented the intrusion of the secular power into matters of religion. There were revolts in several places, which were put down with varying degrees of ferocity. Just as the clashes of Catholics and Calvinists in sixteenth-century Europe generated numerous outrages and produced thousands of martyrs on both sides, so, 800 years earlier, rivers of Christian blood flowed in defending opposed doctrines. And, as in the later Reformation, religion and politics were inextricably bound together. In particular, the Iconoclastic Controversy heightened the tension between Constantinople and Rome. Not only did successive popes refuse to obey the imperial edicts relating to images, but they anathematised as heretics those who issued and tried to enforce them. This provided them with another reason for turning for protection to the Frankish kings. These half-civilised barbarians were far less likely to see themselves as amateur theologians and would be more amenable to being guided by their fathers in God.

In the 770s the Iconoclastic Controversy raged in the very centre of the imperial family. Leo IV was anti-images, and towards the end of his reign he renewed the persecution of iconophiles. His wife, Irene, was a fierce defender of image worship. In 780 Leo died at the age of thirty-one, leaving the empire to his ten-year-old son, Constantine VI. Irene now took over as regent and promptly reversed her late husband's religious policy. It was her dearest wish to convene an ecumenical council that would, once and for all, restore the veneration of icons as a vital part of church life. In order to secure the attendance of sympathetic delegates from the Western Church she entered into diplomatic negotiations with Charles and these culminated in the betrothal of Constantine to Rotruda in 781.

The relationship between the two rulers was a delicate one. Constantinople provided sanctuary for Adelchis, a son of Desiderius and pretender to the Lombard throne. To this cause of friction was added the intervention of Pope Hadrian, who had no desire to see a rapprochement between the two major powers that might shoulder him aside. The Rome–Ravenna conflict had not ceased with the end of Lombard rule. The Archbishop of

Ravenna still asserted his independence from the papacy and, when necessary, looked for support to Constantinople. Then there was the issue of Benevento. This Lombard duchy covered much of southern Italy and, though technically it had fallen to Charles on his triumph over Desiderius, it was far enough away from the Frankish power base to be able to enjoy independence. Its duke, Arichis, maintained good relations with the Byzantine emperors, who regarded it as a client state through which to maintain some influence in the West. To complicate matters further, the pope also had designs on Beneventan territory.

In 786–7 it was Arichis who found himself out in the diplomatic cold at a time when he needed support. His agents brought news that Charles, freed from major military obligations in the north, was about to turn his attention to Benevento. It was in vain that the duke looked to Constantinople for aid. Irene's long-desired council had been convened, only to collapse when iconoclastic members of the imperial guard sent the gathered holy men packing at swordpoint. This made the regent more determined to succeed. She went ahead with plans to have the assembly moved to Nicaea (modern Iznik), across the sea in Asia Minor. The last thing she wanted was to provoke Charles into refusing his support for the council. When, in the spring of 787, the Frankish army emerged from its winter quarters near Rome, Arichis hastened to make his submission. It was a cheap way of securing peace and, as soon as the Franks were safely back on the far side of the Alps, Arichis ignored the vows he had made, including acknowledging the pope's territorial claims. The duke died shortly afterwards, but his successor, Grimoald, continued to play off the two major powers and very successfully retained Beneventan independence. Charles did launch occasional expeditions to southern Italy, but the silence of the chronicles is eloquent commentary on their lack of success.

It was no comfort to him to know that Byzantine assaults on the duchy had also failed. The king's relationship with Irene had now soured. He refused a request for Rotruda to be sent to Constantinople to live in the imperial household with her intended. When he received the articles agreed in Nicaea, Charles rejected them, even though they had papal support. He had no sympathy with the iconoclasts but he also refused to endorse image worship. It seems that what irked him was the attitude of the emperor and his mother. Far from regarding him as a brother monarch, they patronised him as a barbarian chieftain and expected the churches in his territory to do as they were told by their 'superiors' at Nicaea. The humiliated king issued an epistle to his own bishops, denouncing 'the recent synod of the Greeks'. 'Altogether renouncing the service and veneration of images', he declared, we despise the views of the bishops gathered in Nicaea and 'without demur condemn them'. In 794 he underscored the position of the Western Church over the Eastern by summoning his own council to meet at Frankfurt.

By this time events in Constantinople had taken more dramatic twists and turns. Constantine had grown to manhood, but he was a weak-willed sybarite and it was his domineering mother who controlled the government. However, when Irene issued an order that she was to be accorded senior status in the imperial partnership, she went too far. Constantine became the focus of discontent for iconoclasts and all who opposed the power-crazed harpy. After a sequence of unseemly and increasingly vicious confrontations, Constantine managed to sever the maternal apron strings and had himself proclaimed sole ruler in 790. Irene was banished and it seemed that her son had triumphed. But the young man was too politically inept and morally bankrupt to hang on to power and to hold the respect of Constantinople's leaders. Within two years, Irene had intrigued her way back into the court. The struggle at the centre continued, with mother and son heading rival factions and using government money to buy support. Meanwhile the empire at large fell into administrative chaos and incipient rebellion. Corruption and violence in Constantinople had reached what, even by Byzantine standards, was a peak. The contrast between what we might call the old empire and the new became rapidly more apparent to all who were politically aware. And one reason for that was that Francia and Byzantium were now active in the same military theatre.

Charles may have subdued the Saxons (for a time, at least) and incorporated the Bavarians fully into his empire, but he had not secured his eastern frontier. It could not be secured because it was under constant pressure. We need to remind ourselves that the two Christian empires were small fry on the Eurasian landmass. In terms of sheer territorial occupation, they were dwarfed by the Abbasid Caliphate, by the remarkable Khazar Empire, reaching from the Caspian to the Baltic, by the Turks of Siberia and Mongolia and, beyond them, by the sprawling domain of the Tang emperors. These monoliths squeezed out their weaker neighbours and thus, from across the Asian steppes, came nomadic peoples in a never-ending migratory stream. They moved in single tribes or confederations, scrabbling with each other for precious grazing land, falling on more settled societies to plunder them for booty, slaves and grain or to demand protection money. We know little about these restless, rootless communities. Most of them were non-literate. They left no written accounts of themselves and even the archaeological record is sparse. If they have names, they are only the names that Franks or Byzantines gave them when they came into conflict with them in the territorial cockpit bounded by the Carpathians, the Danube and the Black Sea. For it was there that the migrants came up against the bastion of Christendom – irresistible force and immovable object.

The Avars were a tribe who dominated the lower Danube plain by the early seventh century. At the height of their power, in 626, this formidable people actually threatened to seize Constantinople and were denied success only by their lack of the sophisticated technology necessary for siege warfare. From that point on the Avars fell victims to another confederacy, the Bulgars, and were forced westwards until they came up against the Bavarians. To the Christians across the border they represented both a threat and a challenge so that, once again, military endeavour and missionary expansion went hand-in-hand. A familiar sequence of events now repeated itself on the frontier. When the Franks were occupied elsewhere, the Avars made incursions into Bavaria. When they were repulsed, they bought peace with hostages and offers of conversion. It was in 791 that Charles decided to intervene in person. It seems that he had a respect for the Avars out of all proportion to their actual strength, for he took a large army and, before crossing into enemy territory, ordered three days of prayer and fasting to ensure divine aid in the ordeal that lay ahead. In the event, the opposition simply crumbled, allowing the Franks to penetrate deep into Avar territory before returning home – if not triumphant, at least unmolested.

The Avars were not the force they had once been and were unable to live up to their reputation. They were weakened both by their conflict with the Bulgars and by civil war. Now it was the turn of Charles' agents to take advantage of the Avars' distraction. Duke Eric, who controlled the March of Friuli, east of the Dolomites:

> dispatched his men under the command of the Slav Wonomir into Pannonia and had them plunder the ring of the Avars, which had not been entered for ages . . . The duke sent the treasure of the ancient kings, which had been piled up over many centuries, to the Lord King Charles at the palace of Aachen. After receiving it and thanking God, the Giver of all good things, this most wise and generous man, the Lord's steward, sent Angilbert, his most beloved abbot, with a large part of it to Rome, to the threshold of the apostles. The rest he distributed among his magnates, ecclesiastical as well as lay, and his other vassals.[1]

The Avar Ring, or *Hringum*, was their main royal stronghold and holy place, a mighty fortress defended by no fewer than ten layers of circular earthworks. The apparent ease with which Wonomir was able to plunder it indicates just how debilitated the Avars had become. Their treasure was certainly prodigious, so much so that Charles despatched Pepin on a second raid to collect everything that Wonomir had missed.

This double expedition, about which we know tantalisingly little, was the biggest stroke of luck in Charles' career. It finally secured his eastern boundary. He made no attempt to incorporate Avar territory in the empire. His thoughts were already turning from expansion to consolidation and he had no intention of being drawn into the conflicts of the Balkan Slavs. It was enough that the middle Danube plain now constituted a march or buffer protecting his eastern lands from further incursions. Easy victory over the Avars dramatically enhanced Charles' reputation as God's scourge of unbelievers, particularly when it was contrasted with the inglorious military experiences of Byzantine emperors. When Constantine took the field against the Bulgars in 792, his army was routed at Marcellae and, like the Duke of Plaza-Toro, 'when his enemy ran away his place was at the fore'. But Charles' greatest stroke of good fortune was the appropriation of the vast Avar treasure. The chronicler doubtless exaggerated the king's generosity. While Charles certainly made a handsome donation to the new pope and prudently gave rewards to his most trusted counts and dukes, he devoted the bulk of his newly acquired wealth to enhancing his own prestige and particularly to providing himself with a capital 'city'.

Aachen, *Aquisgranum*, had been popular with Roman legionaries on the northern frontier for its hot sulphur springs, but, like so many other centres identified with Latin civilisation, it did not long survive the withdrawal of the conquerors. By the time of Charles' accession it was an insignificant town with a population of, probably, no more than a few hundred people. But the king loved Aachen. It was there that he chose to spend his first Christmas as an independent ruler in 768, and it was there that he died in 814. In the years between he appears to have returned there as often as his peripatetic life would permit. Einhard tells us that the baths were the main attraction for Charles, but that alone cannot explain the appeal that this small town in the far north of Austrasia held for him. Over the years the royal villa at Aachen grew into a palace. Charles erected a more substantial residence for himself and, because he made increasingly frequent visits there, the chief men of the kingdom had to build their own dwellings in close proximity to the palace. So Aachen's growth was, in some respects, a natural development. However, there was also something profoundly *un*natural about the urbanisation of the Frankish ruling class. Traditionally Charles and his nobles were the leaders of a warrior people, constantly mobile. They had to be ready to move suddenly and swiftly to ensure the loyalty of their own folk and to maintain their hegemony over conquered nations. The king had to show himself in different parts of his realm if he was to impress and inspire all his subjects and, particularly, if he was to hold his nobles in check. Frankish lifestyle had nothing in common with that of those who lived beyond the divide of the Pyrenees, the Alps and the Danube. Urban living was the basis of what passed for 'civilisation' in the twin fragments of the Roman Empire. Its denizens despised the 'barbarians' as uncouth, illiterate ruffians, who lived in tents and mud huts and were ignorant of the refinements of mosaiced atria, perfumed cubicula and temples adorned with sculptures. For their part, the Franks despised the effete inhabitants of a decadent Mediterranean world, who could not even defend themselves from invasion. In their view, Frankish towns were all very well for bishops whose cathedrals were the centres of the territories in which they exercised spiritual jurisdiction. They were not appropriate locations for men of action. What Charles did at Aachen, therefore, calls for careful explanation and interpretation.

However, it is very difficult to determine what, *precisely*, his vision was for the splendid new civil and ecclesiastical complex that his architect, Odo of Metz, was bringing into being. It cannot have been a permanent focus for the 'Western Empire' on a par with Constantinople, for Charles had already made arrangements for the division of his territory among his sons. Nor can he have entertained delusions of creating a city that could rival the ancient splendours of the eastern capital, of which he eagerly sought information, or of Rome, which he had seen for himself. These cities, and Ravenna, undoubtedly inspired his building project, but Charles knew that what he was creating could only be a pale reflection of these immense, exotic, time-hallowed *urbes*. If we can read Charles' mind at all, Aachen represented something that was essentially personal, but which also symbolised the divine nature of his mission. In obedience to God he had established a Christian empire larger and more vibrant than that ruled by the corrupt and vicious couple currently occupying the Byzantine throne. It was inconceivable that the *basileus* (the emperor) – not to mention the pope and even his own son, Pepin, in Pavia – should live in far greater splendour than himself.

As we have seen, some chroniclers suggested that Charles had begun impressive building at Paderborn in the 770s and had aimed to create there a royal 'city' that would bear his own name – 'Karlsbad'. But Paderborn was too far from the centre of Charles' realm. Once the Saxons had been subdued and once his treasury had been filled to overflowing with Avar gold, the king planned sumptuous palaces for Ingelheim and Nijmegen, but devoted most of his attention to his favourite residence of Aachen.

The royal palace at the heart of the city took its inspiration from the Lateran Palace in Rome, the ancient complex that Constantine had given to the popes as their official residence. It may be no coincidence that, from 795, Leo III undertook a massive rebuild of this very site. For the greater glory of God and Leo, he created commodious living quarters and a stunningly decorated banqueting hall. As far as we can tell from archaeology, written records and what remains of the old structures, Charles' 'new Rome' consisted of a walled enclosure dominated by two buildings. The royal hall stood at the top of a 100-metre slope, from which it looked down over the entire *palatium*. It seems to have been a simple two-storey, rectangular building with little external embellishment. The ground floor was given over to domestic offices, while above was a long room for banquets and ceremonial events. An apsidal end contained the king's throne, as was the Roman and Byzantine custom, and this may have been fitted with curtains that could be used to screen off the royal presence, thus adding to its mysterium. The private quarters of Charles and his family were adjacent to this reception hall and may have been equipped with a balcony from which the king could see, and be seen, by his subjects. The internal walls of the hall were covered with paintings. If they followed the pattern that a later poet described as adorning the corresponding room at Ingelheim, they portrayed the deeds of great martial heroes, both Frankish and Roman. We can only guess at the kind of furnishings with which this millionaire monarch surrounded himself in his home. Einhard insists that his tastes were simple, but the king understood something of the importance of display. The biographer tells us that Charles rarely gave great banquets, but when he did so his table was furnished with dishes and goblets of gold and silver. He did not commission works of art, but he did adorn his capital with objects that had been plundered from defeated peoples, removed from Italian cities with the consent of the pope or given as gifts by fellow monarchs. His will itemised such spectacular precious objects as a large square table of solid silver etched with a map of Constantinople and a similar round table portraying the main features of Rome.

Charles' real extravagance was lavished on the basilica dedicated to the Virgin Mary, which stood in the centre of the compound. A large open space stretched between the palace and the church, flanked by residences and administrative buildings. This courtyard was dominated by an equestrian statue of Theoderic the Ostrogoth, which Charles had brought from Ravenna. If Charles venerated the memory of this sixth-century conqueror, it must tell us something about how he saw himself in relation to the classical world. Theoderic was a barbarian chief who, with the blessing of the Eastern Emperor, 'liberated' Italy from its Germanic ruler, Odoacer, and governed (ostensibly as a Byzantine viceroy) for thirty-three peaceful years. By the time Charles was building Aachen, the heroic legends of Theoderic had been growing for more than two and a half centuries. He was regarded as a 'civilised' barbarian who had governed imperial territory firmly and wisely. Although he was a Byzantine official, his subjection to the emperor had been largely theoretical and most of his energies had been devoted to establishing mutual tolerance between his Roman and Gothic subjects. Charles, it would seem, regarded himself as standing in the same tradition. He, too, was a 'bridge' figure linking two cultures.

Leaving the statue of Theoderic behind him and continuing downhill, a visitor would enter a colonnaded atrium or cloister in the midst of which a fountain sparkled in the sunlight. This lay before the great, bronze west doors of St Mary's Church. It, too, represented a fusion of styles originating on either side of the Alps. This Carolingian-Romanesque building was a sixteen-sided rotunda surmounted by an octagonal drum. Advancing into the centre of this space, the visitor's eyes would be drawn upwards to the inside of the vault where, above the light-filled clerestory, stood, in glittering mosaic, the enthroned figure of Christ surrounded by worshipping denizens of heaven, offering their crowns to the King of Kings. Beyond this representation there was little in the way of votive art. Frescos filled most of the walls at lower levels, but they were didactic in intent rather than devotional. Charles rejected the worship of images and had the walls of his church painted with biblical scenes. His no-nonsense concept of Christianity demanded that people should understand their faith and not be slaves to empty, superstitious icon-worship. That is not to say that he espoused a stark, puritanical approach to worship. Quite the contrary; he provided his church with a rich array of ornaments and precious vessels and kitted out his clergy in sumptuous vestments. These were the acts of a wealthy and devout layman intent on beautifying the worship of God without falling over into idolatry. And, as God's representative, he placed himself centrally in this sacred building, for, beneath the glowing figure of Christ Pantocrator, stood the royal throne.

The new capital, then, expressed a fusion of Charles' Christian commitment and his imperial ambition – but what, exactly, did 'imperial' mean? What kind of imperium did Charles and his setting project? The most obvious fact is the one of size. Charles ruled a personal fiefdom such as had not been seen since the days of Constantine, a fiefdom called 'Europe', which claimed continuity with the old Roman Empire while being distinguished from the area ruled by the eastern *basileus*. His writ ran throughout a territory corresponding to the modern nations of France (excluding Celtic Brittany), Germany, Belgium, Holland, Luxembourg, Switzerland, Austria, Poland, Slovenia, the Czech Republic, Hungary and the greater part of Italy. Charles could justifiably claim that he had re-established the major portion of the Roman Empire in the West. He saw himself as the steward of a great inheritance and not as a barbarian conqueror. Unlike Theoderic, Charles was no Byzantine appointee. He owed nothing to the gracious generosity of the emperor in distant Constantinople. The territory he ruled had been inherited from his ancestors and added to by his own endeavours.

Since those endeavours had been singularly successful, who could doubt that they had been blessed by God? The key to Charles' developing understanding of his divine mission lies in his belief in a Providence deeply involved in the affairs of men. Taking that as his starting point, everything else followed with a simple logic. It was not just that God had spectacularly blessed almost all his works; as Charles surveyed the political scene elsewhere, he observed nothing but chaos and corruption.

In Constantinople, where it might have been supposed that things could not possibly get worse, they had done just that. It is not for nothing that the adjective 'Byzantine' has come to signify a mixture of the complex and the sinister. The ineffectual Constantine and his insufferable mother were king cobras in a squirming snakepit of factions. Palace officials, captains of the guard and monastic leaders were scheming against each other, constantly wielding both metaphorical and actual knives. Constantine had already been pronounced heretic by one religious grouping for his moral failings and, when he returned in disgrace from the disastrous Bulgar campaign, he lost the respect of the military clique. His reaction was to try to buy the support of the iconoclasts. This infuriated Irene, who had been waiting for an opportunity to get rid of her son ever since he had humiliated her by temporarily excluding her from power. One day in the summer of 797 she had him ambushed. He was confined to the palace where, shortly afterwards, his eyes were gouged out in such a vicious fashion that he died of his wounds. Irene now became sole emperor (not empress) and the first woman in the long history of the Roman Empire ever to hold that office. But, in achieving her ambition, she had fatally weakened her position. Too many men whose support she needed were appalled by her filicide and when, as a result of cutting taxes as a popularity gesture, she plunged the empire into bankruptcy, it became clear that her days were numbered. In Rome, indeed, her days were considered to be over. The pope was horrified at the thought of a woman presuming to the semi-divine office of emperor. The official view in the western half of the empire was that the throne was empty.

But if Rome affected to be shocked by events in the sister city, it was very much a case of the pot calling the kettle black. Hadrian I died in

795 and Charles wept sad tears at his passing. Well might he do so. Hadrian had occupied St Peter's chair almost from the moment of Charles' emergence as sole king, and the two men had established a working relationship based on mutual respect and affection. It had never been an easy relationship because the basic interests of the two men were diametrically opposed. Throughout his dominions Charles took an increasing interest in ecclesiastical discipline. He sent directives to his bishops about clerical morals. He summoned theologians to discuss points of doctrine. He carved out new dioceses in conquered territory, and chose the men who were to preside over all the dioceses in Francia. In these matters Charles corresponded with the pope and seriously considered his advice, but he was quite clear in his own mind about the limitations of papal power. The epitaph he caused to be engraved on Hadrian's tomb included the words, 'I unite the names with shining titles: Hadrian and Charles, I a king, you a father.' There could be no clearer distinction between temporal and spiritual authority. But in Italy, Hadrian was a temporal ruler. He was reliant on the Frankish king for the protection of his patrimony, but he had no intention of yielding up his sovereignty to Charles. This he made symbolically clear when Charles came to Rome. He received the visitor with all the pomp due to a *patricius Romanorum*, a Roman aristocrat, but insisted that Charles should not spend any night within the city precincts. In other words, Hadrian wanted this powerful monarch as a friend and protector, but not as an overlord. Charles' political thinking, however, was based entirely on the fact that he *was* an overlord to all the leading men throughout his dominions, both lay and ecclesiastical. He refused to be used as a stick with which to beat Hadrian's enemies, and he declined to augment papal authority and temporal possessions whenever he was asked to do so. However, despite the many unresolved issues between the two men, they enjoyed a close friendship. The same was not true of the relationship between Charles and Hadrian's successor.

The election of Leo III divided Rome into warring factions. This may have been because the new pope did not belong to any of the city's elite families or because, as his enemies insisted, Leo was guilty of fornication and perjury. Whatever the truth of the matter, the early months of Leo's pontificate were marred by serious disturbances. In April 799 these culminated in a murderous assault led by members of the papal staff. During a saints' day procession Leo was dragged from his place and attacked with knives. The objective was the time-honoured custom of skewering out the victim's eyes and, for good measure, severing his tongue. However, the attackers bungled their job and the pope survived the ordeal. Within days his supporters were spreading the story that his destroyed organs had been miraculously restored. This encouraged Charles' man, Duke Winigis of Spoleto, to take the wounded pontiff under his roof. From there, Leo was escorted to the royal court at Paderborn to seek his protector's aid to regain the city and to be restored to his position.

Charles was at a loss to know what action to take (see also page 79). He did not want to appear to be at the beck and call of the pontiff, but neither could he turn his back on Leo's plight. At Paderborn he listened to both sides of the story and, meanwhile, sent to his wisest advisers for their comments. Alcuin, who had never met the pope and could know nothing of the rights and wrongs of the case, was outraged that anyone should have lifted up violent hands against him. For Alcuin it was enough that Leo had been delivered from his enemies. 'God has restrained the hands of the wicked from carrying out their evil will,' he insisted. Later, when he had more details of events, he wrote:

> Has not the worst impiety been committed in Rome, where the greatest piety was once to be seen? Blind in their hearts, they have blinded their own head. There is no fear of God there or wisdom or love. If they feared God they would not have dared; if they had wisdom they would not have willed it; if they had love they would never have done it.

For Alcuin, this was proof that the Church was in deep crisis. 'Deep bogs of evil spread their mists where the springs of righteousness should send forth streams of holiness,' he complained. He speculated that this might be an indication that the world was in its last days. And he drew a conclusion that must have given Charles much food for thought:

> There have hitherto been three persons of great eminence in the world, namely the Pope, who rules the see of Peter, the chief of apostles, as his successor – and you have kindly informed me what has happened to him. The second is the Emperor who holds sway over the second Rome – and common report has now made known how wickedly the governor of such an empire has been deposed, not by strangers but by his own people in his own city. The third is the throne on which our Lord Jesus Christ has placed you to rule over our Christian people, with greater power, clearer insight and more exalted royalty than the aforementioned dignitaries. On you alone the whole safety of the churches of Christ depends. You punish wrongdoers, guide the straying, console the sorrowful and advance the good.[2]

Even when we strip away the obligatory flattery, there is no denying that Alcuin's assessment of the current dire situation was pretty accurate. The decadence and violence in both the Mediterranean Christian capitals, particularly when contrasted with the widely renowned splendour and sophistication of the Muslim court of Harun al-Raschid in Baghdad, might well have suggested that the fiery judgement of God was at hand. The question for Charles was what role was he divinely ordained to play in the restoration of peace and dignity to the Church. He may have known that the great Theoderic the Ostrogoth had, 300 years before, acted as judge in papal affairs during the so-called Laurentian Schism. Then, the temporal ruler of Rome had decided which of two rival popes should be acknowledged. On that occasion, also, accusations of criminal and immoral conduct were levelled against Symmachus, who eventually gained Theoderic's support. The strategy employed by this Symmachus had included issuing the notorious Symmachan Forgeries, which purported to be ancient documents asserting, among other things, that the pope was above all human judgement. It was this licence to sin that Leo now claimed in his dispute with his enemies. It seemed to work.

Charles responded decisively to the crisis, but his action had negative as well as positive aspects. He had Leo escorted back to Rome and arranged to follow later, in order to deal with the pope's accusers. But this was not because he had weighed all the evidence and decided in the pope's favour. It was because he had accepted the judgement of the theologians that St Peter's successor was above human law. Yet there is likely to have been another, deeper motivation – either conscious or unconscious. If the state of the Christian world was as bad as Alcuin and others suggested, Charles must have seen it as his responsibility to restore unity and order. A protracted trial of the pope would certainly not have served that end. When the pursuit of truth and justice was weighed in the balance against political stability, it was the latter that proved the heavier. Now the Symmachan Forgeries came to Charles' aid. He accepted the casuistry of the ecclesiastical establishment, which insisted that he had no right to stand in judgement on St Peter's successor. It was on this dubious moral basis that the Rome–Aachen axis was renewed at Paderborn. The return of the pope with an escort of Frankish troops was not likely to satisfy the feuding parties in Rome, but at least phase one of the restoration of peace and order had been achieved. Phase two would have to wait until Charles could travel south to overawe the city with his own presence.

For centuries historians have speculated, and speculated in vain, about what passed between the two leaders at Paderborn. In view of what followed the next year, the understanding reached between king and pope was of crucial importance, but since no record remains of their discussions we are obliged to speculate as well. It is, however, informative to examine some of Charles' other activities in the years 797–800, and particularly the way he spent the months between Leo's departure and his own appearance in the papal capital. The handling of Frankish diplomacy changed at this time. As soon as the Byzantine throne became, in his opinion, vacant, Charles opened up strengthened diplomatic ties with the other great Levantine ruler, Sultan Harun al-Raschid. The Muslim emperor had always conducted business with Constantinople, but he was no less scandalised than the leader of Latin Christendom by a woman's usurpation of the Byzantine throne and now regarded Charles as the only spokesperson for Christian Europe. Charles also received delegations from the Patriarch of Jerusalem. The leader of the Church in the Holy City had always looked to the emperor as the 'protector' of the sacred sites, though such a position was symbolic rather than practical. Now he, too, declined to do business with a woman and acknowledged that a Frankish warrior-chief had become the *de facto* successor to the caesars.

Gratifying though his enhanced status in the wider world was to Charles, his principal concern was the allegiance of everyone within his borders. If he aspired to be recognised as something more than King of the Franks, this would have to be sold to all his nobles, bishops and abbots. He spent much of 800 on tour, imposing his personality and taking advice from his political and spiritual deputies. In March he was on the Channel coast overseeing a new project – the construction of a fleet of ships to meet the mounting challenge of raids from Denmark. He spent Easter at Saint-Riquier, where Angilbert was abbot of the large and impressively embellished monastery. His itinerary then took him via Rouen to Tours, where he held a family conference with his three sons, as well as with the wise Alcuin. A circular route brought him to Orléans, Paris and Aachen. In August he summoned his chief men to a gathering at Mainz and from there made his way southwards into Italy. He spent time with Pepin in Ravenna before continuing his leisurely (or was it contemplative?) way to Rome. What momentous matters were discussed at all these meetings we cannot know. All that is clear is that whatever Charles intended to do on this, his last, visit to Rome was well thought out.

Leo came forth in person to meet the king at the twelfth milestone. The symbolism was significant. As an honoured *patricius Romanorum*, Charles might have expected to be greeted by a delegation on behalf of the pope two kilometres beyond the city wall. The elaborate welcome he now received betokened a marked change of status. The next day (24 November), in an even more elaborate ceremony before a crowd of citizens, Leo received

Charles on the steps of St Peter's. After the public celebrations the two men and their retinues retired to the Lateran Palace for private talks. There Charles discovered that Leo, too, had been busy since their last meeting. He had re-mosaiced the walls of the main audience chamber. The theme of the decoration was the divine commissioning of apostles and other leaders of the Church and, in a prominent position, Charles himself was portrayed as one of three figures. In the centre St Peter was represented. He was handing a stole of office to Pope Leo on his right and a battle standard to Charles on his left. This may have implied no more than the traditional role of the Frankish king as protector of the Church. That was what most interested Leo. But the recent welcome and subsequent events made it clear that a new relationship was in the process of being forged.

The most urgent matter to be attended to was defusing the situation in Rome. Leo might have been reinstated, but that had not silenced his critics. The citizens had to be induced to accept the decision Charles had already made about the pope's innocence. He summoned a synod, ostensibly to examine Leo's conduct. In reality it was there to validate a whitewash. With king and pope so publicly hand in glove, it is scarcely surprising that witnesses were not tumbling over themselves to support the initial accusations. Charles made no attempt to sit in judgement on the head of the Church. Instead, by a prior agreement, Leo swore an oath on the Gospel that he was not guilty of any wrongdoing. And that was that. Or, rather, that was that for everyone except the pope's enemies. Charles condemned them to death, a sentence later commuted to exile. Fortuitously, the same day that Leo slipped deftly from the hook, Charles' envoy arrived back from Jerusalem. He bore a magnificent gift – the keys to the sacred sites. Of course there was no question of Charles being in a position to protect his co-religionists in the Holy Land, but the presentation was a propaganda coup and a snub to the Emperor Irene. Yet worse was still to come for the regime in Constantinople whose members believed that, whatever the moral standing of the holder of the imperial office, the empire remained one and indivisible. Messengers were soon scurrying to the Byzantine capital with the shocking news that the barbarian Charles had dared to wrap himself in the imperial purple.

Christmas Day 800 has been hailed as one of the major turning points in European history, yet historians have argued for generations about exactly what happened on that day, who was responsible for it and what it signified. About the simple facts there is no dispute. Charles attended the Nativity mass in St Peter's. At the head of the congregation he prostrated himself for the petitionary prayers. At their conclusion he rose, and it was as he did so that the pope stepped forward and placed a circlet of gold upon his head. At this, the assembled throng acclaimed Charles as emperor: *Carolo piisimo augusto, a Deo coronato magno et pacifico imperatore, vita et victoria!* 'Long life and victory to Charles, the most pious Augustus, the great, peace-loving emperor, crowned by God!' Then everyone from the pope down made obeisance. So much for the central event.

It is when we seek to discover who organised it, and what they intended by it, that we run into difficulties. The only available written analysis dates from years and, in some cases, decades later and the memories of the writers were inevitably coloured by subsequent events and personal prejudice. It was around 803 when the scribe of the Lorsch Annals (so called from the Rhineland abbey where they were thought to originate) set down what may be considered the official Frankish apologia:

> When, in the land of the Greeks, there was no longer an emperor and when the imperial power was being exercised by a woman, it seemed to Pope Leo himself and to all the holy fathers who were then assembled in the council, and thus to the whole Christian people, that it would be fitting to give the title of emperor to the king of the Franks, Charles, who had the city of Rome, the normal residence of the Caesars, in his power, as well as the other cities of Italy, Gaul and Germany. The Almighty God having consented to place them all under his suzerainty, it seemed to them fitting that, according to the desire of the Christian people, he should also bear the imperial title. This request Charles in no way wished to refuse but, submitting himself humbly to God at the same time as to the desire expressed by the priests and the Christian people, he received the title of emperor and the consecration from Pope Leo.[3]

The suggestion is that Charles' elevation was a well-planned event, the details of which were hammered out at the synod that he had convened in November. Charles' biographer, Einhard, tells a different story:

> Charlemagne really came to Rome to restore the Church, which was in a very bad state indeed, but in the end he spent the whole winter there. It was on this occasion that he received the title of Emperor and Augustus. At first he was far from wanting this. He made it clear that he would not have entered the cathedral that day, although it was the greatest of all the festivals of the Church, if he had known in advance what the Pope was planning to do. Once he had accepted the title, he endured with great patience the jealousy of the so-called Roman Emperors, who were most indignant at what had happened.[4]

It may be that Einhard wanted to ascribe to his hero a becoming modesty or, perhaps, there was a diplomatic point to his words; the desire to show that the challenge to Constantinople had originated not in Charles' ambition, but in the universal desire of the people of God, to which the pope gave expression. However, we should be cautious about writing off Einhard's reservations. He may have been present in the basilica as a member of the royal entourage. If he was not, he would certainly have received detailed accounts of what happened from eye-witnesses when they returned to Aachen.

The conflicting versions cannot be completely reconciled. The ultimate responsibility for Charles' elevation lies either with himself or with the pope. Yet perhaps the very divergence of the evidence betokens an ambiguity that is essential to our understanding of the event. Rome's Christmas gift to the world was, at one and the same time, epoch-making and evanescent. Edward Gibbon, looking down the long corridor of history, insisted, 'Europe dates a new era from his restoration of the Western empire.'[5] But contemporaries did not see the coronation as a world-changing event. There were no spectacular celebrations, and Charles was far from clear about how he should carry his new dignity. If we want to understand what the coronation meant to the new emperor and his empire we must set aside, for the time being, any thoughts about its historical significance.

Notes

1 *Carolingian Chronicles*, p.74
2 Allott, op. cit., pp. 87, 110, 111
3 *Annales Laureshamenses*, ed. G. H. Pertz, 1826, p.28; cf. L. Halphen (trs. G. de Nie, 1977), *Charlemagne and the Carolingian Empire*, p.93
4 *Einhard and Notker*, p.81
5 Gibbon, op. cit., VI, p.184

6

David and Josiah

Brief is our life, now in the midst of years,
And death with silent footfall draweth near.
His dreaded fingers are upon the gates,
And entering in, takes all thou hast.
Look forward to that day, and to that unloved hour
That when Christ comes from heaven
He finds the father of the house still watching,
And then thou shalt be blessed.
Happy the day when thou shalt hear the voice
Of thy gentle Judge, and for thy toil rejoicing:
'Come, my most faithful servant, enter in
The kingdom of the Father everlasting.'
That day, remember me and say:
'O Christ most gentle.
Have mercy on a poor man, Alcuin.'[1]

We are fortunate in having many poems and letters by the English scholar Alcuin or Albinus. Not only do they reveal a most attractive character, but they admit us to the world of the Carolingian intelligentsia and provide insights to the thinking of Charlemagne that we would otherwise lack. The king was much more than a semi-literate barbarian. He was more than an efficient warrior and formidable commander of men. He was even more than a pious or superstitious religious enthusiast. Charles, like many semi-educated politicians, held scholars in genuine awe. As his territory grew, he certainly had need of them as administrators, emissaries and diplomats. But, as his correspondence with Alcuin and other churchmen indicates, his relationship with the intellectual *haut monde* went well beyond the merely practical. He had an inquisitive and energetic mind and loved to engage his experts in doctrinal, liturgical, ethical and even political debate.

Alcuin was the last of the prominent scholars of the first great phase of English learning. He was born in about 735, the year that Bede died, and he stood squarely in the Northumbrian tradition of scholarly devotion that had its roots in the Celtic revival. Alcuin spent most of his life in York, where he was ordained deacon and where he eventually became director of the archiepiscopal school. He immersed himself in the Bible and the Church fathers, but was also intoxicated by the great Latin authors. When he adopted the academic conceit of a classical nickname, he elected to be known as 'Flaccus', after the poet Horace (Quintus Horatius Flaccus). Teaching, study and worship in the abbey occupied most of his time, but he also kept up a lively correspondence and swapped verses with his counterparts throughout Britain and abroad. The interconnectedness of monastic communities and the conducting of Church business, which involved travel along the roads that led to Rome, created and sustained an international brotherhood of men who shared a passion for learning. By 778 Alcuin had already made a couple of trips to the continent to consult books in the libraries of Frankish monasteries.

By this time the life of contemplatives in Northumbria was becoming difficult. Internal dissension was followed by the devastating raids of the Vikings. 'I cry from my heart before Christ's altar,' Alcuin wrote when he heard of the sack of Lindisfarne in 793, 'O Lord, spare thy people and do not give the Gentiles thine inheritance, lest the heathen say, "Where is the God of the Christians?"'[2] Charlemagne was equally appalled by events across the North Sea. His coastline was also threatened by the Scandinavian raiders, but that was not the only kind of outrage that troubled him. He was incensed to hear of the murder of the Northumbrian king by a band of his own nobles and he gave sanctuary to the exiled heir. Like every crowned head, Charles had a vested interest in opposing regicide and anarchy wherever they appeared.

The man who kept him closely informed of affairs in Britain was Alcuin. Charles had met the scholar at Parma in 781 when Alcuin was returning from a mission to Rome on behalf of his archbishop. What he encountered was no diffident, retiring scholar, but an ebullient enthusiast. Alcuin was a large man who approached life with gusto, held strong opinions and was not afraid to air them. One of the reasons the two men developed a close friendship was that, although Alcuin well understood the subservient attitude expected of courtiers, he was no mere sycophant. The emperor could rely on him for straight advice. The chemistry between them must have established itself very quickly, because Charlemagne invited the Briton to accompany him to Aachen to take over the running of the 'palace school'. Alcuin spent the next fifteen years at the royal court and, after his retirement to the monastery of Tours in 796, he continued to correspond with the emperor. Just as he was to Charlemagne 'your Flaccus', so Charlemagne was to him 'my Lord David', named after the victorious Old Testament king, and Alcuin performed what might almost be considered the role of a prophet, advising, warning and expounding the word of God to his sovereign. Thus, for example, Alcuin pointed out the danger of sword-point conversions:

> Careful thought must be given to the right method of preaching and baptising, that the washing of the body in baptism be not made useless by lack in the soul of an understanding of the faith . . . the Lord told his disciples in the gospel, 'Go, teach all nations, baptising them in the name of Father, Son and Holy Spirit' (Matthew 28.19). The blessed Jerome in his commentary on St Matthew's gospel explains the order of this commandment as follows: 'First they teach all nations, and then dip them in water. The body cannot receive the sacrament of baptism if the soul has not first received the truth of the faith.'

On another occasion he urged his royal master to spare the rebellious people of Benevento, and rely on diplomacy rather than force. And in 'preachy' letters he did not hesitate to tell Charles how to govern:

> Forasmuch as imperial rank is ordained by God, its purpose must be to lead and serve people; hence power and wisdom is given by God to his chosen, power to crush the arrogant and defend the lowly against the wicked, and wisdom to rule and teach his subjects with virtuous care . . . What then is your religious duty in time of peace, when the soldier's belt is undone and the whole people turns to you in peace for government . . . if it be not to decide what is right for every rank, to proclaim your enactments and to give holy counsel that each may go home happy with the teachings of eternal salvation? . . .
>
> Spare your Christian people and defend the churches of Christ, that the blessing of the heavenly king may strengthen you against the pagans. We read that one of the old poets, writing in praise of the ideal rulers of the Roman Empire, said, if I remember rightly, 'To

spare his subjects and defeat the proud' (Virgil, *Aeneid*, IV, 854), a line which St Augustine expounded with much praise in his *City of God* (1, 6). Yet we should heed the teaching of the gospel more than the poetry of Virgil. Our Lord said, 'Blessed are the merciful, for they shall obtain mercy' (Matthew 5.7), and elsewhere, 'Be merciful as your heavenly father is merciful' (Luke 6.36).[3]

Alcuin knew very well that he was dealing with a man of hearty and varied appetites and variable temper. He was, therefore, less forthright in advising the emperor on more personal aspects of his conduct, such as keeping concubines, but he did not hesitate to admonish Charlemagne's son, 'Have joy with the wife of your youth, and keep free from other women, that the blessing God has given you may lead to a long line of descendants (Proverbs 5.17–18).'[4] The letters of Charles' teacher, prophet and friend possess an affectionate frankness, not overly tinged with flattery, which reveal to us an emperor who valued the advice of scholars and holy men. Charles read (though he never mastered the skill of writing) and was well versed in the Bible, St Augustine, St Ambrose and other books recommended by Alcuin. He eagerly collected examples of liturgy for use in his chapel and he had 'Flaccus' draw up for him tables of daily devotion for his private use. If he followed rigorously the spiritual exercises recommended to him, Charles must have spent long hours every day on his knees or before church altars. How much time competing inclinations and the demands of a busy life actually allowed him to spend with his God we cannot know, but there can be no doubt about the sincerity and depth of his religious convictions. As Professor Barraclough has remarked, 'Few things about him are more astounding than the way this man, who was incessantly engaged in campaigns and fighting, who forewent none of the pleasures of life, spent his time on abstruse questions, deeply engaged, for example, in the intricacies of Easter tables and the Christian calendar.'[5]

In congratulating Leo III on his election, Charles defined the responsibilities of temporal and spiritual leadership in a Christian state:

My duty is by divine aid to defend everywhere with armed might the Church of Christ from inroads of pagans and from ravaging of infidels without; from within to fortify it by the learning of the Catholic faith. It is your part, holy father, to support our fighting by hands raised to God as those of Moses, so that, through your intercession and the guidance and gift of God, Christian people may ever have victory over his enemies, and the name of our Lord Jesus Christ be glorified throughout the world.[6]

There is an element of realpolitik in all this. Napoleon laid down the dictum that government is impossible without law, and law is unthinkable without religion. Charlemagne, like his later imitator, had a diverse empire to hold together and this required the cement that only Christianity could provide. However, the fact that the problems faced by the two dictators were similar does not mean that their motivations can be aligned. There was no trace of sophisticated cynicism in Charlemagne. He was a genuine visionary in a way that the little Corsican never was.

He derived his image of the perfect society from Augustine's *City of God* and *De Ordine*. The thinker of antiquity had insisted that a true Christian state should model itself on the heavenly city where perfect order and harmony reigned. The achievement of a semi-divine *ordo* in the kingdoms of men involved establishing peace and justice for all. It was the ruler's responsibility to pay close attention to the minutiae of all regulations pertaining to the relationship between man and man, man and state and, above all, man and God. It is Charlemagne's commitment to the Augustinian ideal that explains his constant obsession with regulating the religious and secular life of his people. Though Alcuin saw him as a David, the Old Testament parallel that the emperor preferred was Josiah, the seventh-century BC reforming King of Judah, who rediscovered the Deuteronomic law and purified the religion of his people. Education and law had to go together because the heterogeneous traditions represented throughout his empire had to be brought into submission to the perfect law of God, and the people had to understand what was required of them. For the moment, we must defer our examination of Charlemagne's educational reforms and concentrate here on his attempts to get to grips with the problem of laying down a juridical foundation.

As we have suggested, establishing a legal framework was both a practical necessity and a religious duty. As such, Charlemagne needed no urging from Alcuin to make it a priority. His mindset was that of a systematiser rather than an innovator. Whether in the secular or religious sphere, what mattered was discovering what was sanctified by custom or divine mandate and setting it out for his subjects to obey. He armed himself with a copy of the Rule of St Benedict in order to eradicate abuses that had crept into monastic life in some centres. He set Alcuin to work on a revision of the Vulgate, in order to provide his priests with one, authoritative, version of the Bible in place of the confusion of texts hitherto in use. In the same way he ordered from Rome a standard sacramentary so that the mass would be everywhere celebrated 'properly'. Intent on regulating the life of the clergy, he obtained from Pope Hadrian a set of ecclesiastical laws, the *Dionysio Hadriana*.

The expansion of Frankish territory during the first three decades of Charles' rule necessitated frequent revision of the laws. Each region and tribe had its own set of ordinances. They were based on custom, few were written and all were jealously cherished as part of the culture that determined the identity of the people who lived by them. Charlemagne's task was to have these disparate codes set down for the benefit of local judges and administrators while ensuring that they were not at variance with Frankish law. Einhard suggests that it was only after he was crowned emperor that Charles realised the importance of standardising the laws, but in reality this was an ongoing process that began early in his reign. From time to time the king called his leading men together to discuss and promulgate capitularies, collections of ordinances and regulations for the better governance of his peoples. It may be no accident that the first in this series of legislative gatherings was convened in 778.

In the previous months Charles had suffered serious setbacks and reverses – Saxon revolt, the fiasco of Roncesvalles and unrest in Aquitania. This could not have failed to have a profound effect upon a man steeped in the Old Testament, particularly in the chronicles of the kings of Israel and Judah. Charles believed implicitly in an almighty warrior God, the Lord of Hosts, whose terrible power was ranged alongside righteous rulers and turned against those who forsook the Lord their God. Up to this point he had attributed all his victories to divine aid. How could it be otherwise when thousands of pagans were brought to their knees before the Cross of Christ? Now he had tasted defeat, humiliation and the loss of some of his dearest companions in arms. Logic as well as piety obliged him to face up to the withdrawal of divine favour. What had he done, or failed to do, to forfeit the support of the God of Battles? Nor would Charles have been the only one to be asking the question. His warrior chiefs followed him cheerfully as long as he led them to victory and was obviously the favourite of heaven. But if the tide of war turned against him, they too might have their doubts. In 788 Charles chose to hold his assembly in the Meuse valley, the area where his dynasty had originated, at the ancient palace of Herstal where he may well have been born. There, like Josiah, he gave his people a new set of laws. It was the beginning of a long-term reforming programme that he hoped would please God and help to create a holy nation.

The result was the *Admonitio Generalis*, a comprehensive set of laws governing Church and state and intended as a blueprint for reform. The kernel of the legislative code was the *Dionysio Hadriana* that Charles had obtained from the pope, but regulations governing the moral conduct of monks and the proper performance of the canonical offices shaded into the religious and ethical behaviour of the laity. Thus, for example, god-parents were required *by law* to teach the Lord's Prayer and the creeds to their charges. In a preface to this utopian schema, Charlemagne made a clear statement of his own belief in his divine mission. His prime responsibilities, he stated, were the extension of the kingdom of God, the care of the Church in his dominions and the correct teaching of the faith. There followed a list of regulations for the clergy. Charles had had them from Hadrian, but did not hesitate to make his own amendments and additions. The first and most important task of bishops and priests, he asserted, was preaching. They were engaged in a battle for the hearts and minds of the peoples of the empire, who had to be weaned away from their old practices and beliefs, not just nominally but in very truth.

From this it was a straightforward move to issues of ethics and law:

The people were to be taught an essentially redemptive philosophy, and told that their lives were fundamentally dedicated to God. All this adds up to a way of life which permitted few compromises and was both designed and destined to become the very bones and spirit of the medieval way of thinking about society.[7]

In a Christian society anyone who offended against the king or the common good was sinning against God, and reprisals under the secular law were expressions of divine retribution. In a sense we should not really talk of 'secular law' at all in Carolingian Europe. All the regulations that Charles made about living in the material world on a variety of subjects – from coinage to care of the sick, and from tithe collection to the maintenance of bridges – were made with one eye on the spiritual realm.

The *Admonitio Generalis*, though the most comprehensive legal document of the reign, was only the first of a series promulgated by this passionately reformist monarch. As the years advanced, an ever-increasing deluge of written instructions, laws, regulations, letters and admonitions poured from the royal chancellery. These capitularies were usually issued by the king after consultation with his advisers. Where Charlemagne led, his bishops followed. They wrote and circulated their own exhortations concerning the observance of canon law, as well as tracts explaining the holy mysteries and the importance of correct performance of the liturgy. From very early in his reign Charles had attended to an overhaul of ecclesiastical structure. Where bishoprics were vacant, held 'temporarily' by heads of religious houses or simply held by unworthy occupants, he installed men he could trust to carry out his policies. But there was no question of Charles making the rules and then leaving his senior clergy to get on

with the business of enforcing them. His commitment to reform and ortho-
doxy was too strong for that. He frequently summoned his bishops and
abbots to church councils where he could discuss with them issues of
doctrine, liturgical observance and spiritual discipline. Thus, in 794, he
summoned bishops from within and without his domains to meet him at
Frankfurt to discuss, among other things, the refutation of the Adoptionist
heresy being taught by Bishop Felix in his Pyrenean diocese (see pages
111–112). This had about it all the elements of one of the great ecumenical
councils of the Church, and Charles had no doubt that it stood in that
ancient tradition.

One of Charlemagne's priorities after the imperial coronation of 800
was the planning of another major assembly. This eventually took place at
Aachen in October 802. It was comprehensive in the subjects it covered.
According to the *Lorsch Annals*, Charles

> asked the bishops along with the priests and deans to read all of
> the canons which had been adopted by the synod, as well as the
> decretals of the popes. He ordered that these decrees be translated
> before all the bishops, priests and deans. In a similar manner he
> assembled all the monks and abbots who were present at the synod
> and asked them to read the rule of the holy father Benedict which
> was translated for all the abbots and monks . . . Then the emperor
> himself assembled all dukes, counts and other Christians along with
> the legal scholars and had all the laws of the empire read out and
> translated so that each man heard his own law. He ordered that
> improvements be made wherever necessary, and that the improved
> law be written down to enable the judges to make their decisions
> on the basis of written law and not accept any gifts. So, all the people,
> rich and poor alike, were to have justice.[8]

Significantly, Charlemagne also had everyone swear an oath to him as
emperor, for it was one thing to enact sweeping, comprehensive legisla-
tion and another to have it universally accepted.

It was in the 780s that Charles began to make his court a centre of
religious scholarship. He had always had an inclination to intellectual
enquiry. Now it became a passion. He was determined to control the intellectual life of his empire; in effect to tell his people what to believe and
think. He sent to monastic libraries at home and abroad for books that
might be kept at court or copied to be sent on to other schools and centres
of learning throughout the empire. In this way Charles ensured that future
generations of churchmen and literate lay leaders were well versed in Holy

Scripture, commentaries, patristic works and most of the great classical authors. At the same time the king kept on the lookout for men of learning. Such were the blandishments that he and his agents offered that teachers of real stature were lured to the peripatetic Frankish court or took up positions in Frankish abbeys. From Italy came Peter, later Bishop of Pisa; the historian Paul the Deacon; Paulinus, whose clear theological exposition and lucid style drew from Alcuin the comment, 'Happy is the Church and the Christian people as long as it has even one such defender of the faith.'[9] Alcuin was not the only scholar poached from Britain. Notker tells a story about the arrival of two Celtic monks on the Frankish coast. It is a parable rather than historical narrative. According to the chronicler, the new arrivals puzzled the townsmen they encountered by calling out in the market places, 'Wisdom for sale!' News of this odd behaviour reached the king and he sent for the monks. 'What is this wisdom you offer,' he demanded, 'and what do you charge for it?' They replied that they came to instruct people in the ways of God, seeking no remuneration, but only 'a place suitable for us to teach in and talented minds to train'. The delighted Charles immediately employed them at his court and later put them in charge of educating boys drawn from the noble houses of the realm.[10]

Like the best of legends, the tale expounds essential truths. The Christian message in all its complexity intrigued and bewildered Charles' subjects, reared as they were to believe in a world of spirits who communicated with the living via priests and holy men. For his part, Charles was committed to enlightening his people in the higher knowledge of the Christian revelation. He recognised this to be a formidable undertaking, which would require the talents of every teacher he could find who was well versed in the Bible and the ancient writings. As for the men of learning who now resourced the educational crusade, they recognised in Charles' zeal a force that would empower the Christian mission throughout his wide dominions and beyond. While evangelists ventured into pagan lands and monks interceded for them, teachers could ensure that the future leaders of the empire were trained to provide and sustain a secular government that would support the Church in all its endeavours.

But what *was* this empire? How did this ruler who aimed to control the very thoughts and beliefs of all his people understand his own *imperium*? In order to attempt an answer to this question the first point we need to grasp is that Charles was not thinking in territorial terms. In 806 he nominated his three sons by Hildegard as his heirs and divided his territory between them. The reality is that he had no choice. To have ignored Louis and Pepin in favour of their brother, Charles, would have been to invite fraternal strife and aristocratic rebellion. The regional dukes and counts would not have tolerated such a flouting of Frankish tradition. But what emerges from a closer study of this formidable military leader in that Charles had no interest in creating a 'thousand-year reich'. His conquests had not been for the glory of the Carolingian dynasty; they had been for the glory of God. What he created in the West was an *imperium Christianum,* a civilisation based on divine law. The Franks were the new Israel, just as Charles himself was the new Josiah. These Old Testament parallels were powerful and were repeatedly stressed in the capitularies and ordinances that poured from the imperial chancellery. Within Charlemagne's domin-ions there were numerous lands and tribes and he did not attempt the impossible task of merging their identities within a greater Francia. He simply ensured, as far as he was able, that pagan practices were abolished, that local laws did not conflict with those of the central authority and that Christian preaching and teaching had the powerful backing of the government.

The second point we should note is that Charles' attitude to his task did not fundamentally change after Christmas Day 800. There was a continuum about the building of a Christian society that had its origins early in his reign. The imperial coronation may appear to be a momen-tous event and, in terms of its perceived challenge to the Byzantine emperor and to Frankish traditions, it was so. Yet it was also just another step in a process that had about it an air of inevitability. Charlemagne was aware of the progressive revelation of God's will for him. He could not be disobedi-ent to the heavenly vision – whatever political complications it might involve. He could not but see the dramatic events of 798–9 in Constantinople and Rome as divine signposts to his own future. Nor did the process end in 800. Charlemagne spent the next twelve years seeking a *modus vivendi* with an outraged Byzantine court, which refused to recog-nise that the Roman Empire had been split into eastern and western segments. After the coronation, his *imperium* still needed to be defined. Charles' first attempt at definition took some months to evolve. Not until May 801 do we find him using the following formula: 'Charles, the most serene Augustus, crowned by God as great and pacific Emperor, governing the Roman Empire, King of the Franks and Lombards by the grace of God'. He accepted the mantle of the ancient caesars because the imperial throne was, in the view of most Western observers, empty; but even so he refrained from calling himself 'Roman Emperor'. In later years, as we shall see, he omitted all reference to 'Roman' in his title. It never entered his thinking to march an army to the Golden Horn to assert his authority. All this indicates that his *imperium* was something personal, rather than institutional, and that it was an evolving concept.

The question, then, re-emerges: was Charles ready and willing to receive the crown, whatever it might imply, on that unforgettable Christmas Day, or was he the object of a papal coup? Leo III was a subtle schemer who maintained himself in power for nineteen years despite his very questionable moral standing and his array of enemies. He had every reason to stage a dramatic event that would strengthen his personal position and make permanent the papacy's switch of allegiance from Constantinople to Aachen. Byzantine claims cramped the pope's style and limited his authority without offering any effective protection to the Church in the West. Leo's predecessors had sheltered behind the Carolingian shield because they needed a military champion to safeguard the territorial integrity of the papal state, and because they resented the emperor's claim to authority in matters doctrinal and liturgical. As far as the latter point is concerned, Hadrian and, now, Leo had exchanged a distant lion for a closer tiger, for Charles maintained tight control of all aspects of Church life. On balance, however, Leo adjudged that the future lay with an energetic and devout West rather than a decadent East.

So much for the longer term. Leo's immediate need, in the late autumn of 800, was to bind the Frankish leader to him with iron bands of obligation. His thought patterns were quite different from Charles'. As a member of the Roman curia, his mind was set in an institutional mould and he was no stranger to intrigue. Whatever the Gospel might teach, Leo was convinced that ends justified means. He would, therefore, do anything to enhance the power of the papacy. That involved careful planning, when possible, coupled within an intuitive readiness to grab opportunities and take risks when necessary. His talks with Charles at Paderborn had shown him that the king was disgusted with the scandalous goings-on in Constantinople and that he was open to guidance about his own destiny. Charles needed no flattering courtiers to convince him that he was *de facto* leader of the Christian West and, arguably, leader of the Christian world. All he lacked was the purple. But this was not in the pope's gift. Emperors were traditionally created by the people. They were acclaimed, quite often by factions of the army. What Leo needed to do was choreograph a demonstration of popular support, and this is precisely what he did in the days leading up to the Christmas celebrations.

It seems to me quite consistent with what we know of Charlemagne's character that he might have been genuinely taken aback by the seemingly impromptu crowning ceremony while, at the same time, accepting – even welcoming – its implications. It did little more than confirm an existing reality, but it was, or could be seen as, one more divine signpost. As such, Charles could not ignore it.

As for its long-term significance, we cannot accept the assumption that Gibbon and most later historians held to be axiomatic. J. Bryce expressed the traditional view when he wrote, 'The coronation of Charles is not only the central event of the Middle Ages; it is also one of those very few events of which, taking them singly, it may be said that if they had not happened, the history of the world would have been different.'[11] Of itself, Christmas Day 800 changed nothing. Charlemagne's empire was an ephemeral entity. What the ceremony in St Peter's symbolised, however, *was* of timeless significance. It acknowledged the consolidation of the Latin Christian West as something distinct from the Greek Christian East. World history would certainly have been profoundly different if Charles, his clergy and his scholars had not imposed a cultural unity on the disparate peoples of Europe. Those peoples would have gone their own ways with their own customs, languages, religions and laws. No other unifying factor could have emerged, to inspire in rulers and ruled a desire for cohesion round a core of common beliefs and values. Several nations *did* arise, as we know, frequently warring with each other and jockeying for supremacy, but always their rivalries were expressed within the framework of a common culture. It is this tension − this sense of belonging to a *family*, however quarrelsome and, at times, dysfunctional − that has given Europe a unique and powerful position in the world. That is what human history owes to Charlemagne. As for Charlemagne's coronation, that might reasonably be characterised as one of the most momentous non-events in history.

Notes

1 H. Waddell (ed.), *More Latin Lyrics from Virgil to Milton*, 1976, p.203
2 Allott, op. cit., p.36
3 Ibid., pp.73, 78, 86
4 Ibid., p.77
5 Barraclough, op. cit., p.23
6 See Duckett, op. cit., p.87
7 R. McKitterick, *The Frankish Church and the Carolingian Reforms, 789–895*, 1977, p.9
8 Cf. M. Becher, *Charlemagne*, New Haven, 2003, pp.104–5
9 Allott, op. cit., p.119
10 *Einhard and Notker*, pp.93–4
11 J. Bryce, *The Holy Roman Empire*, 1919, p.50

7

Friends and Neighbours

The Byzantines had a saying that the Franks were good friends and bad neighbours. They, of course, angrily rejected the claims of the 'upstart barbarian' who had presumed to challenge the right of the divine *basileus* to rule over the undivided empire. To them this was just another rebellion by one of the uncouth subject peoples. But behind the bluster there was real fear. From Constantinople the steady encroachment of the war-like Franks had been watched with mounting apprehension. Lombardy and Bavaria had been brought under Charles' rule. From Friuli his agents had made the thrust that had crushed the once-mighty Avars, a success that stood in stark contrast to Constantine VI's failure against the Bulgars. Venice, the commercially important Byzantine enclave at the head of the Adriatic, was split between pro- and anti-Frankish factions and, in 805, the reigning doge did homage to Charles at Aachen and returned home with a Frankish bride. Between the eastern edge of Charlemagne's territory and the northernmost outposts of effective Byzantine rule lay a region contested by various Slavic tribes and alliances. Should the Frankish king be drawn into this area, where might he stop? He had been proclaimed emperor. It seemed reasonable to expect that he would try to make good his claim to rule the indivisible Roman Empire.

For both Charlemagne and Irene held the conviction that the empire *was* indivisible. There was no question of allowing the Frankish king to rule some entity called the 'Western Empire'. It was a matter of theological conviction that, just as God was one, his people were also one and there could be only one deputy to exercise his authority on earth. Thus what was essentially at stake was the legitimacy of Irene's grasping of power, for, if the Byzantine court looked upon Charles as a usurper, Charles' supporters regarded their mistress in the same light. Both sides were, of course, in the grip of a legal fiction. It is obvious to us that the Greco-Slavic East and the Romano-Germanic West were on divergent paths long before the end of the eighth century. Whether anyone could see this at the time is doubtful. What is certain is that no one wanted to acknowledge it.

Yet, having said that, it seems that for the man who now saw himself as *imperium Romanum gubernans* the practicalities of reconciling fact and fiction were fraught with difficulty. Charles had no intention of mounting a military campaign against Constantinople. The effort required would have strained the resources of his realm beyond endurance – and probably the loyalty of his generals also. If he hesitated about accepting the coronation as the only logical outcome of the political situation after 797, as I believe he did, the main reason was his concern about the reaction it would provoke in the East. One of his first acts as *augustus* was to send a new diplomatic mission to Constantinople. According to a solitary Byzantine source, the envoys were empowered to offer their master's hand in marriage to Irene. Most scholars tend to dismiss this overture as very unlikely, but it does have a certain logical appeal. One might say that, from Charles' point of view, it offered the only peaceful way out of the impasse in which the leadership of the Christian world found itself. His fourth wife had recently died. Irene was a widow. Perhaps God's hand was to be seen in all this. The idea of uniting the two great dynasties was not a new one; twenty years before, Charles and Irene had engaged in serious negotiations about a marriage between their children. The only alternative to some such union would be to demand the submission of the lady emperor, and that could only have unfortunate diplomatic consequences. The suggestion may not have been without appeal to Irene. Charles could offer her two highly attractive things that she lacked – a full-to-bursting treasury and the support of an awesomely effective military force. To keep herself in power she had had to tax her people to the hilt, and the threat from her faction-ridden court and army was mounting steadily.

In the event, Charles' proposal (if it was offered) very soon became irrelevant. Irene was so unpopular among her own officials that a palace coup was virtually inevitable. Rumours of her marriage to the despised barbarian may well have been the final straw. Sophisticated Byzantine officials would have been horrified at the prospect of having to submit to rule by a hairy, uncouth, uneducated, axe-wielding savage whose ancestors had only recently emerged from the northern forests. The plot that unseated Irene in 802 (while Charles' representatives were still in Constantinople) was headed by her own chancellor, Nicephorus. Irene's fate was, perhaps, better than she deserved. She was allowed to retire to the island of Lesbos, where she died in 803.

Subsequent events in the eastern part of the empire might well have reinforced the belief in the West that God had forsaken those who claimed to rule from Constantinople. Charlemagne lived to see four more occupants of the Byzantine throne. One was killed in military action, his skull being thereafter used as a drinking vessel by a Bulgar warlord. One died of battle wounds within months of being elected. A third abdicated and retired to a monastery after a miserably ineffective period in office. The emperor who was in place at the time of Charles' death was hacked to pieces in his own chapel six years later.

Throughout most of this period a state of cold war existed between the two imperial regimes. Envoys passed back and forth making claims and counter-claims and there were minor clashes of arms, but neither side would commit to a course of action designed to settle once and for all the question of who ruled the empire. The reasons were simple. No cause would have been served and no problem solved by all-out conflict. On the contrary, war between the two Christian empires would have played into the hands of their numerous enemies. The territories ruled by Charlemagne and by Nicephorus I and his successors were under pressure from various directions. It was all they could do to maintain the integrity of their boundaries. Nicephorus was obliged to campaign in what are now Greece and Bulgaria. Charles' last years were ones of containment during which, as well as the ever-present insecurity of the eastern lands, he had to cope with seaborne predators on the North Sea, Channel and Mediterranean coasts. Neither emperor could muster the military might that would have been necessary to overthrow the other. To have stretched their resources in an attempt to establish overall mastery would only have torn their domains apart and placed intolerable strains on the allegiance of their subordinates. Confrontations could only be small-scale.

They were confined to Italy and the lands bordering the Adriatic and it fell to Pepin, as King of the Lombards, to act as his father's military and political representative. He did not make a very good job of it. In southern Italy the Byzantines encouraged Grimoald III, Duke of Benevento, to resume his bid for independence from Charlemagne's overlordship. Pepin launched campaigns in 800 and 801. The Frankish chronicles are ominously silent on the outcome of these raids, beyond claiming victories at Ortona on the Adriatic and Lucera in Puglia. The following year things went seriously wrong for the Frankish interest. Grimoald made short work of overwhelming the recently installed garrison in Lucera and captured Winigis, one of Charles' most able and trusted lieutenants.

Worse was to follow when Pepin took the field in person to secure Venice's continuing loyalty. He became embroiled in three years of intermittent warfare, which achieved nothing. Until recently this semi-independent trading centre had been under Byzantine protection. Doge Obelario, believing that he was simply acknowledging political reality, had transferred his allegiance to Charlemagne and taken a Frankish bride, but his action only split the community into rival factions. The traditionalists turned to Constantinople for aid, and Nicephorus sent ships and men to reinforce the garrison. Obelario called on Pepin for help and initially the pro-Frankish faction was successful. However, Obelario and his party were subsequently overthrown and sent into exile. Pepin was obliged to restore his authority and advanced on Venice with a land army. Although he easily took possession of the mainland, he found his path across the lagoon blocked by rows of viciously pointed stakes, from behind which the populace assailed his troops with missiles. Angry and frustrated, Pepin settled down to invest the city and starve out its inhabitants. But Venice commanded the sea and was kept supplied by a fleet from Constantinople. The defenders pointed out the futility of Pepin's tactics by lobbing loaves of bread over their barricades. After some inconsequential naval engagements along the Dalmatian coast, Pepin – now in his forties and past his prime – reluctantly agreed to a parley. He accepted ransom money and withdrew his forces. Not long afterwards, in the summer of 810, he died.

This was a serious blow to Charlemagne. Pepin had been the repository of all his father's hopes for controlling Italy, protecting papal interests and balking Byzantine hopes of reasserting influence in the West. Charles was now eager to establish a lasting peace with the Greeks and received envoys from Nicephorus. Negotiations came to fruition in 812 during the brief reign of Michael I Rhangabe. The Eastern Empire was then at the nadir of its fortunes. Battle after battle against the Bulgars had been lost and before Michael's miserable reign came to an end, the enemy would be at the gates of Constantinople. Small wonder that the Byzantine emissaries were prepared to concede whatever Charlemagne demanded to put an end to the distraction of hostility between the two Christian empires. And what *did* Charlemagne demand? Simply the recognition of his equal status with the eastern ruler. Michael agreed that, in future, he and his successors would address Charles as 'brother' and allow him to use the title 'Emperor'. But emperor of what? The word had been emptied of all but honorary significance because Charles agreed to drop the words 'governing the Roman Empire' from his extended title and to abandon his claims to southern Italy and Venice. Was this, then, all that the years of wrangling had been about? Was the Western Empire, as Louis Halphen insisted, nothing but a 'personal apotheosis of Charlemagne'?[1]

The removal of Irene had disposed of the basis on which Charles and Leo had justified their action in 800. Once Nicephorus had been acclaimed, the Eastern Empire had a ruler whose legitimacy was on a par with Charles' own. Theoretically, the Roman Empire now had two rival emperors, but, as we have seen, Charles made no effort to unseat the incumbent at Constantinople. As for the flashpoints that did flare up, only the squabble over Venice was new. The struggle for control of southern Italy had been going on for several decades. Nor is there any evidence that Venice held any long-term strategic importance for Charles. We have to look, not to his external relationships, but to the workings of his own government machine to see why the imperial title, once assumed, had to be vested with as much substance as possible and why it mattered that his eastern counterpart should acknowledge it.

The empire that Charles had devoted the best thirty years of his life to building was a heterogeneous bundle of territories whose peoples spoke different languages, revered different customs, had frequently been at war with each other and whose rulers were only tied to him by a variety of personal obligations. By no means did his writ run large throughout the territory we might designate on a map as 'Francia in 814'. Despite the overall success of his military and diplomatic activities, there were still regions where little or no attention was paid to instructions from Aachen; and in all regions the people looked to their local warrior-lords for leadership rather than to a distant emperor whom they had seldom, if ever, seen.

On the fringes of empire were fiercely independent proto-nations so culturally distinct from the Carolingians that it was in their very nature to resist incorporation. Out in the west lay Celtic Brittany, where Charles had totally failed to impose his will. The Romans had not fared much better in the land they called Armorica and, after their withdrawal, British immigrants fleeing from Anglo-Saxon conquerors settled in the peninsula, bringing with them Celtic missionaries who were still as suspicious of Rome as their neighbours were of Aachen. Charles undertook two extensive campaigns in Brittany in 786 and 799, but all he could extract from the local rulers were vague and unreliable pledges of loyalty.

Matters were more complicated, but no more satisfactory, in the region bordering the Umayyad caliphate. The mountainous Pyrenean corridor stretching from the Mediterranean to the Atlantic was the home of the fiercely independent Gascons and Basques, both descended from the Vascones whom the Romans had encountered there. Gascony, to the north of the mountains, had, theoretically, been brought under Frankish rule, but the debacle at Roncesvalles in 778 indicated just how loosely the people of the region sat to their allegiance. Moreover, that celebrated massacre was only one of several bloody confrontations between the Franks and their unruly subjects. The guardians of the passes never hesitated to fall upon Frankish contingents passing through their territory. Charlemagne knew that there was no effective way of enforcing his will on the people of this rugged, intractable terrain and he gave them as wide a berth as possible. He allowed the traditionally hot-headed Gascons to be governed by their hereditary ducal family and interfered as little as possible with the hornet's nest of tribal pride. As for their cousins, the Basques, all he could do was rely on them to police the marchland that extended southwards to the valley of the Ebro and the Umayyad border.

Aquitania, to the north of Gascony, was a land no less aware and proud of its heritage. During the centuries of Roman occupation this had been the most Latinised part of Europa and its people still looked down on the 'uncivilised' Franks. Merovingian rulers treated Aquitania with kid gloves, but their Carolingian successors found it impossible to reach an accommodation. At the outset of his reign Charles had been faced with a revolt led by the old ducal house and, as we have seen, had been obliged to impose his suzerainty on the land in 769. He was, however, wise enough to realise that force needed to be tempered with respect for Aquitania's own traditions and the dignity of its people. In 781 he raised the duchy to the distinction of a sub-kingdom under the nominal rule of his infant son, Louis. Although the political status of Aquitania had not changed, it now had its own royal court and a government that issued its own decrees and laws (albeit its activities being merely rubber-stamped decisions made in Aachen).

Charles' long struggle with Bavaria had resulted in the deposition of Tassilo and the end of his ducal dynasty. Again, the Frankish overlord did not change the political status of the country. He simply replaced the ruler with a duke of his own choosing – his brother-in-law, Gerold. When Gerold died in 799, Charles seems to have had some difficulty in finding a trustworthy individual to succeed him. He installed a pair of 'prefects' to govern the territory, which retained its territorial integrity and its ancient institutions.

Saxony and Frisia in the north-east could not be treated with the same generosity. These were conquered lands whose subjection had been bought at the cost of much Frankish blood. Moreover, they were restless under the hand of their overlord and required close supervision from the imperial centre. An additional complication was their political structure. They had no single king or duke with whom Charles and his agents could negotiate. The land was dominated by regional warlords. Widukind was far from being the only charismatic leader capable of gathering a following and making himself a nuisance to the Frankish 'master race'. The peace Charles had imposed in 785 lasted for ten years. Then, between 795 and 802 a series of risings flared up, like sudden conflagrations in a fire-blackened landscape. Charles' mounting irritation showed itself in increasingly draconian measures. He occupied a divide-and-rule policy, rewarding faithful Saxons and sending them into battle against their recalcitrant kinsmen. He drove rebels from their lands and settled Franks in the occupied areas. When the East Saxons across the Elbe continued to defy him, he resorted to 'clearance': he rounded up the inhabitants of the infected areas, marched them south and relocated them in other parts of the empire. That done, he awarded the purged region to his Slav allies, the Abodrites.

In southern Italy, as we have seen, Charlemagne had to admit defeat. There he was dealing with more sophisticated local rulers, and their connection with Constantinople added political complications. From their hilltop strongholds the dukes of Benevento and Spoleto had little difficulty in asserting effective independence. Charles, as King of Lombardy, continued to claim suzerainty over them and backed his claim by occasional military sorties, but neither he nor his son, Pepin, could maintain the sort of presence that would enable them to make Frankish rule a permanent reality. When Pepin died, in 810, Lombardy and its appurtenances remained part of the imperial domain, for Charles had Pepin's young son, Bernard, crowned as his father's successor.

The empire that Charlemagne ruled was bounded almost entirely by sea and neutralised marches. Yet within those frontiers the variety of political relationships could hardly have been wider. From the Austrasian and Neustrian heartland of the Franks to the suppressed colonies of Saxony, local peoples were connected to the central government through a diversity of political agencies. Charles did not try to meld them into an organisational sameness. There remained a tension between the centre and the regions that was never – and perhaps could never be – resolved. This suggests a significant failure on Charlemagne's part. He took his divinely appointed role completely seriously and, as we shall see, devoted enormous energy to the administration of his extensive possessions: corresponding with religious and secular officials, drawing up regulations, sending out messengers and travelling in person long distances every year. Yet, despite all the capitularies that were despatched, despite the system of imperial counts and envoys, despite even the zealous Christianising missions, Charlemagne did not bring his people under a single legislative system.

Common law is an essential ingredient in the cement that binds peoples together. It governs all relationships between individuals, and between individuals and the state. It gives society its structure, at once liberating and confining those who live within it. The *Lex Romana* had been one of the glories of the later Roman Empire, whose citizens could know that wherever they were within its far-flung borders they were protected by the same laws and enjoyed the same rights. That disappeared with the legions, and no attempt was made to replace it until another emperor introduced the *Code Napoléon*.

An empire without a unifying code of laws is a contradiction in terms, but conquered states with their own revered customs always pose a problem to the conqueror. Machiavelli succinctly stated that such a conqueror had only three options with such states: 'the first is to ruin them, the next is to reside there in person, the third is to permit them to live under their own laws, drawing a tribute, and establishing within it an oligarchy which will keep it friendly to you'.[2] Ninth-century Francia was not fifteenth-century Italy, but it was subject to the same political realism. Charlemagne preferred to avoid the most drastic solution of crushing conquered peoples, but, as we have seen, was quite prepared to do so when all else failed. Elsewhere in his empire he tended to adopt the Florentine's third option of allowing subject peoples to live under their own laws, although he also paid regard to Machiavelli's second suggestion. He could not live permanently in the potentially troublesome parts of his realm, but he took great pains to make his presence felt there through an army of agents and through occasional visits.

If he made no effort to bring all regions under one legal code it was not because he discounted the importance of law. Quite the contrary. He scarcely needed the admonition of Alcuin who, on hearing of his master's coronation, wrote, 'My dear son, show justice and mercy among your Christian people, for Solomon tells us that this is what exalts a throne and makes a king's power praiseworthy and acceptable to God.'[3] Charles would be remembered in after-years as a great law-giver – and not without cause. He was a stickler for law and justice. He had the customary codes of all the regions of the empire collected and committed to writing. He was equally fastidious in causing the Church's canon laws to be documented and circulated. As we have seen, he issued numerous capitularies to supplement the regional law books. Yet he refused to trespass on the rights of each section of the empire to live by its own revered ancient customs. This meant that issues such as the right of inheritance, the age of majority, the trial of suspected offenders and the types of punishment meted out to criminals varied from region to region. Thus most of Charlemagne's subjects lived under their own tribal leaders and their own laws.

This degree of flexibility means that, although we use the word 'empire' as a useful convention, the vast area under Carolingian control cannot be called an empire in any meaningful sense of the word. It was a personal condominium, driven by Charlemagne's religious zeal, his personality, his energy and his organising genius, and it worked only as long as there was a strong man at the helm. One aspect of Charles' genius was his pragmatic flexibility. He understood well what he could enforce and what he could not. It follows that he relied to a large extent on his status. Like most leaders isolated by power, he experienced an element of insecurity. He had about him many who flattered him to his face, but were those officials equally in awe of him when they returned to their own localities? The Monk of Saint-Gall told the story of some envoys from Harun al-Raschid. One day when they had partaken rather too freely of the emperor's hospitality, they blurted out to him that he was more honoured in their country than in his own. When Charlemagne pressed them for an explanation, they replied:

We Persians ... and the Medes, Arminians, Indians, Parthians, Elamites and all the people of the East fear you much more than we do our own ruler, Harun. As for the Macedonians and all the Greeks, what can we say of them? They dread your overwhelming greatness more than they fear the waves of the Ionian Sea. The inhabitants of all the islands through which we passed on our journey were as ready and keen to obey you as if they had been brought up in your palace and loaded by you with immense favours. On the other hand, or so it seems to us, the nobles of your own territories have little respect for you except when they are in your presence. When we came to them as strangers and asked that for love of you they should show us some human kindness, and when we explained that we were trying to find our way to you, they gave us no help at all but sent us empty away.[4]

The story concludes with the emperor sending for the offending officials and dismissing them forthwith. Whether or not the incident was literally true, as recorded two generations after Charles' death, it does highlight a very real problem that Charlemagne faced. He was a living legend and, just as wondrous tales about him grew with the passage of the years, so they increased with distance during his own lifetime. Foreign visitors were attracted to Aachen by exaggerated accounts of the glowing accomplishments of the Frankish super-king.

Those more intimately acquainted with the man himself were much less likely to be dazzled, especially as Charles avoided the gaudy trappings that other monarchs used to impress their subjects. He knew that the princelings of his empire followed him for a variety of motives – devotion, greed, self-interest, fear – and that, in many localities, potential rebellion bubbled not far below the surface. Alcuin understood the situation well and described it simply to a friend:

> I am certain of the good intention of our lord and emperor and that he seeks to order everything in the realm granted to him by God according to what is just. However, I am also certain that he has more followers who seek to undermine justice than who seek to support it, that is more *praedatores*, robbers, of justice than its *praedicatores,* preachers, that there are more who seek their own advantage than those who look after God's advantage.[5]

In feudal society (and we may think of the Frankish polity as proto-feudal) the wealth of the aristocrat class was derived primarily from land and the profits of local administration. Some had licence to mint their own coins. Warrior-magnates were dependent on participation in successful royal campaigns for booty, but otherwise they could exist independently of their kings and exploit their situation for personal advantage, with scant regard for any higher principles that their distant rulers might urge on them. Charlemagne was well aware that his laws were often flouted by the very men who should have been indifferently administering them, but he could not afford to be too heavy-handed in his treatment of these semi-autonomous lords, many of whom enjoyed jealously guarded hereditary rights extending back over several generations. The frequent capitularies issuing from the court, and the complex system of local governors and imperial inspectors (see below), are not so much proof of Charlemagne's administrative ability as indications of how difficult it was to maintain control of his more powerful subjects.

That difficulty explains why the imperial title was so important to him. It raised his standing *within* the empire. It demonstrated to his people that he was no longer just a Frankish king. He had *international* status. He was an equal partner with the Eastern Emperor as co-leader of the Christian world. His determination to have his new official status recognised (and, by implication, the anxiety that he felt on the subject) became clear in the annual assembly convened in 802. Charles decreed that all subjects over the age of twelve were to swear an oath of allegiance to him as 'Caesar', whether or not they had already pledged themselves to him as king. The agents charged with administering the oath were to stress its solemnity. They were to point out that the offences covered by their vow went far beyond mere disobedience to the emperor, including crimes 'against the holy churches of God or against widows, orphans and travellers, because our master, the Emperor, had set himself up to be . . . their protector and patron'. Non-payment of government dues or church tithes would constitute a breach of the subject's oath, as would any attempt to evade military service. Once the subject understood that there was hardly any area of his life that was not covered by the oath, and had been warned of the dire consequences that would follow any breach, he was to swear over a holy relic brought along for the purpose.

At the same assembly Charles also promulgated an extensive set of decrees that his secretariat had been working on for months. Known as the Programmatic Capitulary, the ordinances were at pains to point out that the new title would not affect his peoples' traditional rights and freedoms. All their laws would remain in force, except any that might be considered inequitable. These would be referred to the emperor for his consideration. Charlemagne's own involvement in the dispensing of justice seems to have increased after his imperial coronation. The Frankish court had long been the final resort for subjects seeking the redress of perceived wrongs, but its judicial work now increased hugely. It was headed up by the count of the palace, a lay official who was provided with a large staff to reach and circulate verdicts.

Charlemagne's main regular point of contact with his magnates was the *campus maii*. Once a year, usually in May (hence the name), he summoned them all to meet him. This was an ancient tradition with a military basis. In this assembly plans were made for the forthcoming campaign season. But it was also an acknowledgement that power derived from the people and, as the reign wore on, Charles used it to discuss an increasing range of subjects with the temporal and spiritual leaders of the empire. The results of these discussions, as we have seen, often resulted in detailed capitularies for dissemination throughout Charles' domains.

The men responsible for carrying out these instructions were the counts, officials trained at the imperial court in Frankish administrative methods. They were handpicked by Charles for their personal loyalty and came, for the most part, from good Frankish stock in Neustria or Austrasia. They were provided with land for their support in the area under their jurisdiction and, since they tended to pass their office on to their eldest sons, they became, in effect, another order of landed aristocracy. The counts were provided with a staff to enable them to carry out their duties efficiently and they were responsible for all aspects of local administration.

Their primary task, however, was to oversee the operation of the law courts. Judicial sessions were held in each county three times a year, and the count was aided in his task by a body of legal experts (*scabini*). These sessions were expected to deal with all sorts of cases, except those that directly concerned the emperor or his *fisc* (domain). The counts were ordered to mete out justice impartially – that is, they were not to be bribed or bullied into favouring the rich and powerful at the expense of the poor.

It might be thought that this system provided enough checks and balances to make local government work with a reasonable degree of fairness and efficiency. However, in the hierarchy of officialdom not even the counts were completely free from close imperial supervision. Every year they were subject to scrutiny by a band of Charlemagne's personal envoys, the *missi dominici*. These men were chosen from among the counts and bishops, travelled in pairs and had the authority to inspect every aspect of local administration. They had freedom to summon witnesses, demand sight of records and hear complaints. The authorities upon whom they were sent to snoop were warned against trying to conceal anything from the emperor's representatives:

> Above all, take care that you are not overheard, you or your subordinates, saying to people with the intention of thwarting or delaying the execution of justice, 'Say nothing until the *missi* have departed; thereafter we will settle the matter between us.'[6]

This almost throwaway line in the middle of a long set of instructions is very revealing. It shows us Charlemagne in a different light from the one provided by the annalists. This is not the bluff, good-humoured, self-confident super-king, whose martial prowess is matched only by his wisdom and piety. Here is a ruler who has learned to be canny and suspicious almost to the point of paranoia. The incessant travelling, the constant flow of instructions, the repeated insistence on having everything – even minor details – reported back to him are the marks of a man obsessed with the anxiety of things getting out of control.

There was one element in the political life of the empire that Charlemagne did not feel threatened by, because he exercised a greater degree of control over it and because he looked on it as a partner in the pursuit of his divine mission. The Church not only provided him with bishops, abbots, monks and priests to do the work of evangelism and teach the fundamentals of the Christian religion; they constituted his secretariat, his intelligentsia, his senior administrators, and were the guardians of the faith/philosophy/ethical code that alone could unite the disparate parts of his empire.

Charles' relationship with his senior clergy was complex. On the one hand, they were prominent landowners in their own right. Most of them belonged to the empire's great aristocratic families and some of them rivalled their kinsfolk in conspicuous consumption. The Monk of Saint-Gall describes an entertainment offered by one bishop to the emperor's envoys:

> The banquet which followed was served so lavishly, on plate of gold and silver, and in vessels studded with jewels, that it was capable of tickling the palate of even the most dainty eaters . . . The bishop sat on the softest of cushions. He was dressed in the most precious of silken stuffs and wore the imperial purple. Indeed, he was a king in all but name and sceptre . . . in order to demonstrate to them even more his own magnificence and glory the bishop ordered skilled choristers to advance: they were accompanied by every musical instrument one could think of, and by the sound of their singing they could have softened the hardest hearts . . . Every imaginable variety of drink, mixed with all kinds of flavouring and colouring matter, garlanded with herbs and flowers, which set off the gleam of the jewels and the gold and at the same time imparted a new sheen to them, grew lukewarm in their hands, for their stomachs could take no more. At the same time pastry cooks, roasters of meat, bakers of fine bread and stuffers of chicken were striving to stimulate their appetite with the viands which they had prepared with such artistry; but, alas, their bellies were full.[7]

We might fancy ourselves in the fabled world of Harun al-Raschid and the *Thousand and One Nights*, but there is no reason to think the writer guilty of exaggeration on a vast scale.

Favoured imperial servants, as well as men and women whose relatives were in a position to whisper in the imperial ear, accumulated enormous ecclesiastical estates. Alcuin, for example, was abbot of no fewer than seven monasteries. Charlemagne, then, was complicit in the aggrandisement of wealthy churchmen. Grants of ecclesiastical titles and land were an easy way of demonstrating favour and, hopefully, of binding the recipients more firmly to the Crown. Charlemagne also extended his personal control by the system of 'immunities'. Rulers of ecclesiastical estates were exempted from 'interference' by all imperial agents and were responsible directly to the emperor. Another advantage that holders of church lands enjoyed was the tithe. All Charlemagne's subjects were liable to pay annually one-tenth of the value of all landed wealth for the upkeep of the Frankish Church. This indicates just how firm and valuable Charlemagne's commitment was to the leaders of the spiritualty. His determination to encourage the Christianisation of his empire put senior clerics in a strong position and inevitably increased that very temptation he was concerned to eradicate: the temptation for prelates and abbots to divert the profits of office to worldly ends.

All he could do was apply a carrot-and-stick policy. He kept his church leaders under close scrutiny. Whereas it was difficult for Charlemagne to rid himself of lay lords, he could – and did – hire and fire bishops and abbots at will. The Monk of Saint-Gall tells us that Charles once sacked a bishop for being too drunk to attend the night office. The top church jobs remained in Charles' gift and, as long as the Frankish ruler was a strong man, closely involved in ecclesiastical affairs, there was no question of controlling influence being exerted by powerful aristocrats – and certainly not by the pope. However, all the elements were in place that would enable the Church in later ages to challenge the power of the state.

When he came to power Charles discovered a Church that had, by and large, descended into a state of lethargy after the heady days of Boniface and his zealous colleagues. Scores of new monasteries and nunneries had been founded, and hundreds of men had taken up vocations to the secular priesthood, but then complaisant institutionalism had set in. Instead of using prayer and study as springboards to evangelism and the moral renewal of society, clergy and religious adherents were content to enjoy the security and status of their privileged position. Bishops no longer summoned regular synods to keep their clergy up to scratch. Many of those clergy were educationally sub-standard, with the result that preaching was inadequate both in quantity and quality. Within the religious houses a variety of rules of life were practised and, as the result of generous benefactions by pious donors, abbatial officers had to devote much of their time to administering large estates. The monastery of Fulda, for example, had 15,000 separate properties to supervise, and Saint-Gall was at the heart of a city of several thousand souls, all of whom served the brothers in one capacity or another.

Charles, the new Josiah, struggled throughout his long reign with the problems of ecclesiastical discipline. Control, proscription, supervision – these seemed to him the appropriate means for fulfilling his divine mandate as God's deputy. Through the rituals of worship and the veneration of holy relics, the religious impulses of his people could all be focused on a common set of beliefs, and this would lead to a truly Christian society in which people lived together in peace, moral values were honoured, widows and orphans were cared for and subjects were as loyal to their emperor as he was assiduous in caring for their well-being. This, at least, was Charlemagne's vision. The realisation of that vision was as beset with difficulties as was the achievement of the emperor's political goals. Not only were Christian dogmas variously understood (or misunderstood), and Christian rites variously observed from locality to locality, but theological and liturgical differences ran like fissures through the churches under his command.

Charles' 'control freakery' in matters religious was driven in part by his desire to tie his peoples together with the bonds of faith, but there was also in it a streak of superstition. He believed that there was one proper canon of the mass, one right way of chanting the psalms, one faultless text of Scripture, and that erring from the correct forms was 'unlucky' because displeasing to God. There was for Charles and most of his contemporaries a certain incantatory magic about religious formulae. In 790 he demanded from the pope an authorised sacramental liturgy, which he then had copied and distributed with strict instructions that no variations from the set form were permitted. It was in the same spirit that he commissioned from Alcuin a clean copy of the Vulgate text. He went further in his obsession to get things 'right'. Since some wrong usage stemmed from scribal errors that were almost inevitable during the long and laborious process of manuscript copying, Charles set in hand a reform of calligraphy. The result was Carolingian minuscule, a clear, standardised script which was so precise and attractive that, though it did not catch on in the ninth century, it was resurrected 600 years later and forms the origin of all modern European printed alphabets. Another of Charles' reform measures was similarly destined not to come to fruition until after his death. He obtained a copy of St Benedict's order, as practised at Monte Cassino, and tried to have it adopted throughout his dominions. Faced with the ingrained habits of the existing institutions, this met with little success until the reign of Charles' son, Louis the Pious.

Again we turn to the capitularies to discover those issues that were causing Charles particular concern. He first set out his programme for church reform in the *Admonitio Generalis* of 789. In it he earnestly reminded the bishops that their prime responsibilities were 'to lead the people of God to the pastures of eternal life' and 'to carry erring sheep back inside the walls of the ecclesiastical fortress on the shoulders of good example and exhortation'. To this end he ordered bishops not to absent themselves from their dioceses, to summon regular synods, to visit all their parishes, to ensure that mass was properly celebrated and that the lives of the clergy were above reproach. He blamed the ecclesiastical hierarchy for the secularisation of church affairs, while urging that religious principles should govern every aspect of what might be considered secular life – the operation of the law courts, the upkeep of buildings and even the issue of coin. Charles was deeply interested in every aspect of the application of Christianity to the life of the individual and society. The numerous issues he discussed with advisers such as Alcuin ranged from the correction of the church calendar to the mystery of the Trinity. No subject was too arcane for this semi-educated warrior-king of barbarian stock, who profoundly respected learning and yearned to be the leader of a civilised Christian state. Alcuin assured his master that:

> many follow your well-known interest that a new Athens is being created in France, indeed a far finer one. For that which is ennobled by the teaching of our Lord Christ surpasses all academic education; that which had only Plato's teaching owed its reputation to the seven arts, while ours is enriched by the seven-fold Spirit and so excels all earthly wisdom.[8]

As well as summoning his leading clerics to the annual *campus maii*, Charlemagne frequently called church synods and presided in person to discuss with his bishops and abbots matters of discipline, liturgy and theology. Sometimes there were issues of real urgency and import to consider. The attack on Leo III and the charges made against him in 799 caused Charles much heart-searching. A blow against the pope was a blow against the unity of the Christian West, but if Leo really was guilty of serious immorality, how could Charles demand that his own churchmen should live as examples to the flock? Furthermore, if Leo was not worthy of his office, did Charles have the authority to remove him? His advisers answered the last question in the negative and it was this, apparently confirmed by Leo's 'miraculous' recovery, that decided Charles to put his authority behind the pope – with such momentous consequences.

Heresy was another matter on which this theological amateur issued instructions. At the great Frankfurt Council of 794 Charles and his scholar-councillors dealt with two currently important doctrinal disputes. We have already considered their intervention in Byzantium's Iconoclastic Controversy (see pages 69-70). The other problem issued from within his own dominions. Down in the far south-west, in the small Pyrenean diocese of Urgel, the bishop, Felix, had become infected with some unorthodox christological notions currently circulating in the Spanish churches. The novel explanation of the relationship between Christ's human and divine natures was called 'Adoptionism'. As soon as news of this heresy reached Charles, he summoned Felix before him and demanded a recantation. That was in 792. Two years later, at Frankfurt, Charles launched a detailed examination and denunciation of Adoptionism, and the findings of the council were circulated in a special encyclical. Though this particular heresy was never a widespread problem, controversy rumbled on for many years, providing an opportunity for Alcuin, Paulinus of Aquileia and other scholars to air their erudition in a series of profound tomes. It is more than likely that the finer points of this debate went well over Charles' head. What was important for him was fulfilling what he regarded as his solemn responsibility for the purity of the faith throughout his dominions.

After the imperial coronation his concern for the spiritual well-being of all his people deepened. So, it would seem, did his frustration with his lack of progress. A council at Aachen in 802 repeated earlier exhortations to secular clergy to obey canon law, and to monks to follow the rule of St Benedict. The language of his capitularies became more and more insistent and Charles' ecclesiastical law-giving culminated in 813, when he summoned no fewer than five councils to meet simultaneously and provided them with an agenda that deprecated the sins of all the religious 'professionals', called for national repentance and fasts, urged the importance of works of charity and ordered more regular administration of the sacraments.

There was an air of disillusionment about Charlemagne's last decade. It was not just that, by the standards of the age, he was now an old man and the vigour and optimism of youth had left him. The unpalatable truth was that the horizon was darkening. The glory days were past. The once-invincible empire was on the defensive, under pressure from many directions. Goals that had once seemed attainable now looked as far away as ever. There was no obvious improvement in the moral and spiritual tone of Frankish society, and he was still having to pursue the reform agenda that he had drawn up at the beginning of his reign.

Charles also felt the lack of intellectual stimulus. The scholarly camaraderie of the 880s and early 890s was no more. The spark had gone out of the 'palace academy' because most of its members had dispersed. Paulinus, Paul the Deacon, Peter of Pisa, Angilbert – these and others had departed to spend their remaining days in distant monasteries or had been promoted to bishoprics. In 796 Alcuin left for the abbey of St Martin in Tours, one of the rich religious houses bestowed upon him by a grateful monarch. Charles found other, younger men to serve his chapel and classroom in the splendid surroundings of Aachen, but the excitement and cheerful banter of an earlier era had gone. Reading the letters exchanged by Alcuin and his royal master in the years immediately following the Christmas coronation, it is difficult to avoid the feeling that the aged scholar was glad to have made his escape. There are traces of weariness and disillusionment to be discerned amidst the dutiful flattery and the exhortations to piety of Alcuin's elegant lines. Charles often invited his old friend to visit the court, but Alcuin always managed to find some excuse (usually poor health) for declining. In one reply the ex-teacher was more frank; he indicated that he no longer enjoyed the rough atmosphere of the royal palace where the king and his ministers were constantly on the watch for treason, where war was the only topic of conversation at table and the favourite subject of minstrelsy:

> So I humbly beg that your Flaccus may be allowed to come to . . . happiness in a land of peace and joy and not of division and war. What can a weakling like Flaccus do among arms, a leveret among boars, a lamb among lions, a child of peace, unversed in war? While you have the teachings of the Lord God, let the coward stay at home so as not to make others afraid. So Virgil wrote to Augustus: 'You chase the boars; I watch the nets.'[9]

Alcuin would not have been the first or the last Christian to discover that state religion, with its inevitable compromises, no longer answered his own spiritual needs.

Death also continued to deprive Charlemagne of his closest companions. In 800 his latest wife, Liudgard, died. On hearing the news, Alcuin wrote his master a long letter of condolence:

> Do not mourn for another's happiness. She has finished her toil among the thorns and flown to Him who made her. Such is the condition of our frailty after our first condemnation; we are born to die and die to live. Is there any happier way to life than death? . . . May she live happily to all eternity, and dear to God, I pray, as she is dear to me.[10]

Unfortunately, the relationship between Charlemagne and his scholar friend was not destined to end on a note of mutual support and affection. Towards the end of Alcuin's life (he died in 804) he fell out with the emperor. The altercation was over a cleric from the diocese of Orléans who had been condemned for some misdemeanour, had escaped justice and taken refuge in St Martin's abbey. Here he claimed that he had been unfairly treated by Theodulf, his bishop, and asked to be conveyed to Aachen to present his case before the emperor. Theodulf sent armed servants to arrest him. The monks of Tours resisted. They were aided by the townsfolk and the result was bloody confrontation. Theodulf complained to Charlemagne, and Alcuin also made representations to the emperor. There had been a time when Charlemagne would have carefully weighed what his old tutor wrote, even when he was being most critical of royal policy, but now – ever on the lookout for clerical misdemeanours – he chose to accept the bishop's version of events. 'We are exceedingly surprised', he wrote angrily to the Abbot of Tours:

> that it has seemed good to you . . . to oppose our authority and ordering. It is perfectly evident that such decrees as ours have their origin in ancient usage and in constitutional law and that no one has the right to hold them in contempt. We are the more exceedingly astonished that you preferred to yield to this criminal's prayers rather than to obey our will.[11]

There is no evidence of a reconciliation between the two men.

The king who loved company was to find himself more and more alone during the darkening days that marked the remainder of his reign. With his new capital, his new title, his new position as the acknowledged equal of the Eastern Emperor, and three sons to inherit his extensive lands, he might have considered his life's work to be nearing successful completion. But daunting problems such as he had never yet had to face lay ahead and he would bury two of his legitimate sons before the time came for him to lay down his own earthly burden. Alcuin had once written to console him on the deaths of two of his most trusted lieutenants:

> This life is a road to our country. If it be rough and narrow, we must walk on it manfully; if it is level and easy, we must run carefully, for many lie in wait to trap us. God's providence knows who needs a long journey on this road, and for whom it is best to end the labour of the journey quickly.[12]

As he strode the last miles of his own lonely journey, impatient for results that seemed to elude him, Charlemagne may sometimes have had cause to remember his erstwhile friend's advice.

Notes
1 Halphen, op. cit., p.98
2 N. Machiavelli, *The Prince* (trs. W. K. Marriott), 1908, p.21
3 Allott, op. cit., p.98
4 *Einhard and Notker*, p.146
5 cf. Becher, op. cit., p.119

6 cf. Halphen, op. cit., p.107
7 *Einhard and Notker*, pp.112–13
8 Allott, op. cit., p.93
9 Ibid., p.94
10 Ibid., pp.106–7
11 cf. Duckett, op. cit., pp.291–2
12 Ibid., p.107

8

Renaissance and Requiem

It may seem strange to have deferred until this point a consideration of what it has become customary to call the 'Carolingian Renaissance'. The reason for so doing is simple: the revival of classical studies and the educational reforms that Charles set in hand were not ends in themselves, but must be seen in the light of his desire to establish a Christian empire. The copying and dissemination of books, the establishing of schools and the encouraging of a better understanding of Latin were all elements of a crusade to produce a corpus of clergy who could preach, properly administer the sacraments and staff the imperial administration.

Yet it would be wrong to envisage Charles as a boorish warrior-king with no appreciation of culture, or as a cynical pragmatist interested only in using scholars and scholarship for his own ends. Charles had a deep and genuine love of learning for its own sake and an almost adulatory appreciation of those who had mastered the mysteries of ancient wisdom. From his earliest days at his father's court he had been in contact with the Christian intelligentsia, that sophisticated brotherhood of scholars who shared arcane wisdom through the magic of the written word and who even had their own language. We get a flavour of that international fellowship from a poem written by Alcuin in 781, shortly before he took up residence at the Frankish court. In eighty-one lines of affectionate banter, which include quotations from Virgil and Ovid, he imagines his verses making a tour of his erudite friends on the continent (most of them bishops or abbots, and some of them referred to by their academic nicknames):

Ask for the house of Samuel the priest,
And be sure to knock on the door with the Muses' fiddle,
And say in modest poetical voice to the lad that opens the door,
'Alcuin sent me from England's side of the world
To bring kind greetings to a well-loved father'.
And if you have the chance to speak to him in person,
Kneel on the ground and kiss his blessed feet . . .
If as may be
He should think it fit to take you to the palace,
Hurry round all the great ones, fathers, brethren,
Salute them fair, but at the King's own feet
Sing every song you have.
Say to him over and over, 'Best of all Kings, all hail!
Be my protector and guardian and thou my defender
From all the envious tongues that will carp at me,
Paulinus and Peter and Alberic and Samuel and Jonas,
Or whoever is minded to set a tooth in my vitals:
For terror of thee they will flee and go harmless away'.
Say in hushed whisper, 'Greetings, Schoolmaster Peter'.
(He strikes with Hercules' club when he's angry, beware!)
But put your arms round master Paulinus' neck,
And kiss him ten times over, honey sweet.
Riculfus, Raegfot, Rado duly greet
And sing in their ears, but with caution, a little song,
'O happy band of brothers, fare ye well'.[1]

Several members of this band came, like Alcuin, from across the North Sea. They had settled in the monastic centres founded by the Celtic pioneers of the previous couple of centuries – Luxeuil, Saint-Gall, Corbie – and in the multitude of houses that had sprung up since thanks to the patronage of the royal family and their aristocratic imitators – Saint-Denis, Saint-Riquier, Saint-Benoît-sur-Loire. They represented that asceticism of mind and body that revealed itself in simple piety and rigid mental discipline. Pepin the Short had trawled such centres of learning for the best brains to staff the educational and administrative offices of his court.

These, therefore, were the kind of men Charles had known since infancy. He had not, in his early days, been a forthcoming scholar – or, perhaps, his father had not allowed him much time in the classroom – and he tried to make up the deficiency in later years. Einhard informs us that Charles received tuition from Alcuin in rhetoric, dialectic, astrology and mathematics, but he left it too late to acquire the intellectual discipline necessary to master any of these subjects. Study always had to be fitted in with his other multifarious activities and responsibilities. Charlemagne had one of those minds that abhors idleness and always has to be active. Every day he had to make decisions and inaugurate plans. He discussed or corresponded with his advisers on a range of subjects from military strategy to liturgical niceties. He was an executive head, reliant on his experts for information and guidance, while remaining in command and not allowing himself to become dependent on any of his subordinates. He was debarred by temperament and pressure of affairs from organising his time in such a way as to acquire new skills or delve below the surface of complex subjects. Thus, for example, although he gained some facility in reading Latin, thanks to the patient tutelage of Peter the Deacon, he could not form his own letters. Einhard gives us a picture of the earnest monarch keeping tablets and notebooks beneath his pillow in order to grab a few moments' practice before going to sleep – but all to no avail. What he did have a flair for was languages. He spoke Latin, understood Greek and could converse in several of the tongues spoken in various parts of the empire. However, this was the result of having a good ear and being obliged to practise.

Peter the Deacon was a representative of the second stream of scholar-ship that merged with the Celtic in Charles' Francia. He originated, as did several of his colleagues, south of the Alps. When Charles added Lombardy to his domains, he came into contact with the sophisticated court at Pavia where several eminent scholars were already engaged. The culture-hungry Frank eagerly recruited them to his staff. Some of those friends mentioned by Alcuin in his poem were among their number. Paul the Deacon was one of the great historians of the Middle Ages. Originally from Friuli, he was the author of a suitably Christianised Roman history, as well as commentaries on Latin authors and the Order of St Benedict. Through such scholars Charles reached back into the classical past and found, or thought he found, links with the greats of antiquity. Paulinus, also from Friuli, was well grounded in the Roman authors as well as Scripture and the Church fathers. His most enduring work was a *florilegium*, a collection of precepts draw from both pagan and Christian authors on the subject of the virtuous life. Such manuals, as well as serving the needs of private devotion, were a vital part of the curriculum in Charles' palace school and other such establishments that he founded or caused to be founded.

We have already met another member of the court's scholarly elite, the biographer Einhard. But writing was only one of his gifts. He was educated in the monastery of Fulda, north-east of Frankfurt, and was later employed in the abbey scriptorium. Charles poached him from there in around 791. What may have attracted the king's attention was Einhard's many practical talents. He was certainly a scholar, and Alcuin regarded him as an expert on the works of Virgil, but he was primarily an artist skilled in crafts as diverse as book illustration and sculpture. Charles was at that time heavily involved in the construction of the palace complex at Aachen and he made Einhard his master of works, with special responsibility for the decorative schema. This busy, bustling little man, as he was described by contemporaries, obviously satisfied his master, who later entrusted him with important diplomatic missions. The craftsman of Aachen was much in demand by bishops and abbots elsewhere, who wanted their churches and secular buildings adorned by the man who had beautified the capital. These were just some of the men who enjoyed Charlemagne's patronage and with whom he delighted to surround himself.

The politician-historian François Guizot represented the proprietorial French view of Charlemagne when he deduced from the emperor's choice of companions that 'his predominating idea was the design of civilising his people'.[2] When Guizot, who had already translated Gibbon's *Decline and Fall*, wrote in the early nineteenth century, 'civilisation' was a word carrying a great deal of baggage that our own less self-assured age has discarded. Culturally and emotionally we have moved a long way in the last 176 years. In fact, the assumptions underlying Guizot's world view were much closer to those of Charlemagne's day than they are to ours. Alcuin and Guizot would both have agreed that the twin tap-roots of ultimate human attainment were classical learning and Christianity – the highest achievements of the human spirit and the revelation of divine truth. They would have shared a revulsion for 'barbarism'; Alcuin because he saw the devil in paganism, and Guizot because he had witnessed the satanic revolutionary mobs that had borne his father to the guillotine. They would have seen the world as a battleground of darkness and light, chaos and harmony, ignorance and enlightenment. These writers, separated by a millennium, both hailed Charlemagne as a unique hero in this ongoing conflict, a philosopher-king striving to raise his subjects to a higher level of being:

> Happy is the people ruled by a good and wise prince, as we read in Plato's dictum that kingdoms are happy if philosophers, that is lovers of wisdom, are their kings or if kings devote themselves to philosophy. For nothing in the world can be compared to wisdom . . . I know it was your chief concern, my Lord David, to love and preach it. You were eager to encourage all to learn and stimulated them by

rewards and honours, and you invited lovers of wisdom from different parts of the world to help in your plans.[3]

Does this come close to uncovering the true motivation of Charles, son of Pepin, or does he need rescuing from the flattery of contemporary courtiers and later historians?

Much has been made of the palace school presided over by Alcuin for fourteen years. Early writers described in awestruck terms this institution, to which the sons of royal and aristocratic fathers came to be instructed in the *trivium* and the *quadrivium*, which together made up the seven liberal arts of grammar, logic, rhetoric, arithmetic, geometry, music and astronomy. However, the impression of a static 'school' with regular hours and a rigid curriculum must be discarded. The imperial court was too peripatetic to allow for a regular scholarly regime. The only 'place of learning' is likely to have been at Herstal, where future administrators were trained by Alcuin and members of the royal chapel staff. Yet it was remarkable that young members of the Frankish warrior caste did receive some book learning under royal patronage. It was certainly a new experience for them. The problems they had to bend their minds to were altogether different from those related to the traditional training, and there was a mutual lack of sympathy between the two kinds of upbringing. If the intelligentsia considered themselves superior to their boorish neighbours, those neighbours regarded themselves as 'real men' in sharp contrast to the effete lovers of book learning. The youngsters, as in any age, divided themselves between a scholarly minority who were genuinely enthralled by poetry, philosophical speculation and mind-stretching mathematical problems and their companions who found riding, hunting and swordplay much more congenial. And, as in any age, there were those who emerged from school as a credit to their teacher, and those who lived to be a disappointment to him. Few young men can ever have received the kind of lashing that Alcuin gave to one former pupil who had gone to the bad:

Look at your fellow pupil who has always wholeheartedly kept close to God and now holds an eminent bishopric, loved, praised and sought after by all. But you, wretched creature, wander through the undergrowth of sin, honoured by none and criticised by all. Remember how far more brilliantly gifted you were, more accomplished in learning, keener of thought and outstanding in all the teaching of the church, but now, like a hut in a vineyard, abandoned to be the lair of foxes and wild beasts who devour the vineyard of Christ. He, once your equal and fellow scholar, a temple of the living God, a dwelling of the Holy Spirit, loved by God and men, is daily preparing his eternal home in heaven, while you go after earthly filth and rush on the miserable road to ruin over the precipices of vice.[4]

Alcuin must often have been frustrated in his attempts to civilise his young charges, for it will have been difficult for them to hold the two cultures in equilibrium. Nevertheless, this was the goal that the schoolmaster shared with his royal patron. While Charles certainly wanted to train men for the top positions of a Church that was increasingly in need of educated leadership as the bounds of the Christian empire widened, he also wished to raise up a generation of lay rulers who did not despise learning and piety. The unity of the empire depended to a great extent on aristocrats, churchmen and imperial officials being able to work together. Thus, when Charles ordered every monastic and cathedral establishment to provide a school, his motives were mixed.

Charles was able to appreciate both the traditions of his fathers and the legacy of the ancient Mediterranean world and saw no reason not to expect others to do the same. At palace feasts he delighted to hear bards reciting the songs and poems of the heroes of old, but on other mealtime occasions he had Augustine's *City of God* read to him. He joined raucously with his nobles in songs of war, love and the hunting field, but daily listened attentively to the plainsong chant of his chapel staff. The highly decorated walls of palaces and churches similarly displayed a mixture of styles and subject matter. The villa frescos at Ingleheim represented armed Frankish warriors in combat alongside scenes from classical mythology. In the chapel at Aachen architectural proportion and chaste symmetry combined (or perhaps competed) with a polychromatic riot of wall painting and mosaic decoration, reflecting the Germanic love of colour and geometric patterns. Aachen inspired a spate of new church building and extensions, such as the first cathedrals at Cologne and Rheims and the abbey church at Saint-Riquier, executed in what has been called the Carolingian style. While basilicas were laid out according to Romanesque convention, slender towers and pinnacles reached above them, expressing that yearning for heaven that would eventually reach its climax in the soaring Gothic. This was not a 'rebirth' of classical forms; it was a refashioning of Roman and Byzantine forms in a Frankish idiom.

The one area of cultural activity that comes closest to being designated as 'renaissance' was book production. It followed from Charles' passion for learning that scholars needed texts to study. It was to meet the urgent and extensive needs of the palace school, and the other schools around the empire, that he had his agents scour libraries in order to borrow almost any manuscripts of interest that they could find, and his scriptorium was kept busy copying them. They were then distributed to various monasteries, especially those of royal foundation. In this way the works of Virgil and Horace, Pliny, Livy and Seneca, Martial, Juvenal and Terence were among those preserved for posterity. The greatest cultural debt that later ages owe to Charlemagne is the rescuing of many classical texts that would otherwise have been lost to us. The extent of that indebtedness can be numerically expressed. From AD 0 to AD 800 some 1,800 manuscripts and fragments survive. From the following 100 years we have more than 7,000.

Few of Charlemagne's scholars had any real understanding of the antique world. For all their reading of the poets, philosophers and dramatists, they were unable to see them in a chronological context that would illuminate the development of ideas. Even if they could have assembled the literary bricks from which to construct an edifice of the past, this would have been of little interest to them. Objectivity was not their goal. They studied the writings of pagan and Christian authors in order to 'assert eternal Providence and justify the ways of God to men'. Unlike the humanists of seven centuries later, they were not seeking to reinstate the values of the Greek and Latin masters. They were interested in fitting the classical writers into a biblical world view; making their wisdom support the higher wisdom of divine revelation. As Alcuin observed, 'we should heed the teaching of the Gospel more than the poetry of Virgil'.

We must not allow the survival of the writings of a scholarly minority to give us a distorted view of Carolingian life. To the vast majority of Charlemagne's subjects the issues that preoccupied the Alcuin circle seemed esoteric in the extreme. Their concerns were with administering their estates, tending their crops and livestock, feeding their families, and trade. The primary advantages they drew from the empire were homeland peace; and the freedom from fear of marauding hordes raiding across insecure borders to ransack their homes, burn their crops, drive off their cattle and carry their sons and daughters into slavery. Where the emperor's writ ran, people enjoyed the benefits of law and order. This meant, among other things, that despite the ever-present scourge of brigandage, wayfarers could travel the great king's territory in comparative security. Pilgrims could make their way to distant shrines and merchants trundle their wagons from market to market.

Trade was vital to the Carolingian economy. The vast territory that lay under one crown produced numerous marketable commodities for both internal and external consumption: grain, wine, iron, lead, military hardware, salt, wool, to mention but a few. Traders moved from fair to fair across the land, buying and selling. Out of their profits came taxes and dues, some to the local aristocrats or abbots who organised the fairs, some to the Crown in the form of levies on carts and pack animals and tolls on roads and bridges. In the heyday of the empire the leading markets were cosmopolitan meeting places. Tall, flaxen-haired Norwegians came bearing the skins of beaver, marten and bear. Sleek Venetians travelled up from the south bringing silks and spices. Jews came from the Abbasid Levant with musk, sandalwood and camphor. Caravans from beyond the Pyrenees carried the unrivalled leatherwork of Cordoba.

Not all commerce had the blessing of the emperor. The word 'slave' ('*sclavus*', '*esclave*') derives from the name of peoples beyond the eastern frontier – Slavs. Lines of manacled war prisoners from the eastern campaigns were a frequent sight on the roads of Francia. They were en route for Mediterranean ports and the Islamic lands beyond. Charlemagne and his pious advisers were very uncomfortable with this human traffic. They opposed it in principle, especially if the 'merchandise' had accepted Christian baptism; and there was also the practical consideration that it was not a good idea to allow brawny Slav warriors to swell the military ranks of the empire's enemies. Much the same argument was used about the export of weapons. The blacksmiths of the Rhineland were masters of their craft. From their workshops came sword blades and axe heads of superior quality that were highly prized by international merchants. Charlemagne was incensed at the thought of his warriors being hacked down in battle by weapons that had been manufactured by their own countrymen. He issued capitularies prohibiting the sale of such items in designated markets where they might fall into the hands of traders from Spain or the Baltic lands. Any found guilty of such commerce were to suffer the confiscation of all their goods. Such regulations, doubtless, worked up to a point, but they also encouraged smuggling.

The traffic in slaves was even more difficult to police. Charlemagne attempted a degree of regulation by ordering that transactions were to be closely monitored by the local count or bishop. He condemned the practice of having slaves castrated in order to be sold to Muslim customers as harem guards. He urged the redemption of slaves who accepted Christianity. But he also had to accept economic reality. The Bishop of Lyon protested vigorously when he discovered that his master had forbidden slaves to accept baptism without the permission of their owners. Human rights, it seems, had to bow before social stability and the profit motive.

The picture we gain of the commercial life of Francia in the early ninth century is of an empire prospering from the industry of its people and its geographical position. Controlling most of the landmass between the Baltic, the North Sea and the Mediterranean, Charlemagne was able to offer reasonably secure conditions for long-distance trade. The beginnings of urban self-consciousness can be discerned, as towns became the regular venues for fairs and markets and established their own regulations for the conduct of business. Commercial highways extended from Dorestad at the mouth of the Rhine to Marseille, from Bordeaux to Corvey in Saxony. Success breeds success, and more and more foreigners were attracted to Francia's rich trading centres. Despite Charlemagne's attempts to exercise a monopoly in the minting of money, more than thirty towns issued their own coins in order to facilitate business. Quentovic, the main port for traffic to and from Britain situated near modern Calais, Rouen, Paris, Narbonne and Maastricht, as well as the imperial mint, were among the places where coins were struck. And the fact that the number of mints was steadily increasing is a good indication that the moneyers were having to keep pace with rising demand.

But wealth was a magnet for other visitors as well as honest traders:

> Woe on the day that brought to all men sorrow,
> When the heathen host from the far verge of the world
> Came rowing swiftly sudden on our coasts,
> Dishonouring our father's reverend graves,
> Fouling the churches consecrate to God.[5]

That was Alcuin's response to the Viking sack of Lindisfarne in 793. This seaborne threat might, at first, have seemed sufficiently distant and small-scale not to cause Charlemagne any sleepless nights. He was not disposed to deal with the wasps' nest just because his neighbour had been stung. His court poet saw things from a different perspective:

> Broad Asia groans, shackled in heathen chains,
> Oppressed and spoiled by a God-hating race.
> And Africa, third part of the great world,
> Is slave to pestilential masters.
> The Spanish folk, a race once proud in war,
> Bow to a hated sceptre.
> Whatever men held fair, whatever beauty
> Was in their churches, this the pagan shattered
> Or ravished for himself.
> No time, there is no time for private sorrow:

So vast the evil,
So universal through the whole wide world,
A man's own grief seems lighter.[6]

The security of the great empire seemed fragile to Alcuin, when looked at in the context of a wider world. He was well aware not only of the external threats to its integrity, but also of the internal tensions that might weaken it, and he saw with something of a prophet's eye what might befall the Frankish realm. He did not live to see the disintegration, nor did Charlemagne, but in the closing years of the emperor's reign various storm clouds – each no bigger than a man's hand – began to converge, threatening the deluge that would sweep away most of what Charles had built. For the time being he dealt with each problem as it arose.

The first he had to confront was the expanding Danish kingdom. The renewal of conflict with the Saxons between 795 and 805 provided opportunities for the Danes to intervene in the affairs of the empire. Their king, Godfred, may well have been concerned that Francia's borders were advancing too close to his own territory, especially when bishoprics were founded at Hamburg and Bremen as advance bases for Christian mission. The religious and political life of his realm seemed under threat, so he moved a large force of ships and cavalry to Schleswig. At the same time, bands of Danish marauders worried the North Sea and Channel coasts, though these may well have been free-enterprise piratical raids rather than centrally planned military operations. Charlemagne's enemies were not slow to take advantage of the friction between the two kings, and Saxon fugitives placed themselves under Godfred's protection. Franco-Danish relations worsened, but neither side was prepared to start overt hostilities and, in 804, moves were made to open negotiations. However, nothing came of them, and Charles and Godfred continued to eye each other warily.

One reason for Charles' caution and concern was that he found himself facing a different kind of enemy. Contemporaries knew little about the Vikings, and modern historians have discovered little more of the origins of these non-literate societies. To this day scholars disagree about the precise origins of the various bands of seaborne invaders who descended on the Atlantic coasts of their neighbours. They set out from the inlets and fjords of Denmark, Sweden and Norway, but were they traders-turned-brigands, or outlaws from their own societies, or landless men forced to seek loot and eventually *Lebensraum* in other lands? Even the word 'Viking' is inaccurate because it suggests a common identity for these highly individualistic warriors. There are several theories about the derivation and meaning of the word and, in any case, the name was not widely used in

Europe. Significantly, the Scandinavians were usually referred to merely as 'Northerners', 'Strangers' or 'Oarsmen'. Many were the stories told about these mysterious men who came out of the inhospitable North. Early travellers to the Baltic were impressed by the hardiness of the Scandinavians. They had a reputation for being formidable fighting men, toughened by the sparseness of their environment. They were bold adventurers who travelled in small groups far from their homelands, either as traders or brigands. They were coarse and ruthless and they struck terror into the hearts of those who suffered from their depredations. Above all, they were feared because they were 'different', a race untouched by the civilising influences of the classical world or Christianity. But they were also men on the wave of a technological revolution, who had brought to perfection a prodigious fighting machine. Anyone who has seen the Oseberg ship and the Gokstad ship in Oslo's Ship Museum can easily imagine the awe that coastal dwellers felt when they first caught sight of the Northmen's beautiful vessels. 'Never before has such a terror appeared in Britain as we have suffered from a pagan race, nor was it thought that such an inroad from the sea could be made.' Alcuin's description of the historic Lindisfarne raid was based on the horrified reports of several of his friends. Watchers from the shore looked on amazed as the sleek warships with their high, carved prows, shield-edged sides and dyed sails came racing towards them through the waves. The Vikings' vessels, whether used for trade or war, were the peak of the shipwright's art. These streamlined, clinker-built craft had very little draught and were built for speed, but deep keels also gave them stability. So impressed were the Franks with these ships that some of their chroniclers called the warriors who manned them '*Ascomanni*', 'Ashmen', after the wood used in their construction.

Though the Viking impact was shattering for those who suffered at their hands, their raids were sporadic in the early years of the ninth century, and the Northmen seem to have been very wary of attacking the land of the mighty Charlemagne. The Monk of Saint-Gall tells a story that has more than an element of hindsight about it. According to him, the emperor was present in a coastal town when the cry went up that raiders were approaching. Defenders immediately put to sea and drove off the attackers. Charlemagne stood at a window watching the action with tears streaming down his face. Eventually he explained his mood in these words: 'I am not afraid that these ruffians will be able to do me any harm; but I am sick at heart to think that even in my lifetime they have dared to attack this coast, and I am horror-stricken when I foresee what evil they will do to my descendants and their subjects.'[7] Charles' immediate response to the new threat was to erect watchtowers and to build up his own fleet.

He was more concerned about the problems posed by Godfred. In 808 the Danish king marched into the north-eastern borderland of the empire and launched an assault against Charlemagne's Slav allies. In a series of furiously fought engagements he killed many of the defenders and – more importantly for Charlemagne – captured several of their forts, destroyed a Baltic trading centre, carried the merchants away as slaves and then:

> decided to fortify the border of his kingdom against Saxony with a rampart, so that a protective bulwark would stretch from the eastern bay, called Ostarsalt as far as the western sea, along the entire north bank of the River Eider and broken by a single gate through which wagons and horsemen would be able to leave and enter.[8]

The emperor sent his son, Charles, to deal with this latest incursion, but the latter avoided a major engagement with the Danes. He contented himself with punitive sallies against former allies who had changed sides, before returning across the Elbe, 'with his army unimpaired'. Charlemagne at the height of his powers would not have hesitated to attempt a final reckoning with Godfred, but his son was not man enough for the task. Thus, Franks and Danes returned to a restless peace, each suspicious of the expansionist ambitions of the other.

Charlemagne knew that a showdown could not long be avoided, but he may well have been in two minds about whether to plan for it and to ensure that it took place on his terms. The emperor was now in his sixties and concerned more with the affairs of the next world than this one. The chronicler informs us that, while critical negotiations were in progress with Godfred the following year, Charlemagne was at Aachen presiding over a council 'about the procession of the Holy Spirit'. Nevertheless, he recognised his responsibility to hand on his realm in a secure state to his heirs. He calculated that his northern neighbour could not be conquered and that, even if he were, his sons would be unlikely to hold on to Danish territory. He was more than willing to reach an accommodation with Godfred, but this was made difficult by the provocative actions of the tribes in the marchland on either side of the Elbe. Their rivalries constantly threatened to drag their more powerful allies into conflict. In 809 further efforts at negotiation were once again frustrated by Slav groups in the border region and led to Charlemagne setting up forts in positions east of the Elbe.

The end of the conflict, when it came, had nothing to do with military victory or defeat. Dynastic strife broke out in Denmark and, in the summer of 810, Godfred was murdered by a rival for his throne. The successful faction sued for peace, and the chaos in their homeland prevented them from further disturbing Charlemagne's last years. Having disposed of the Danish threat, Charlemagne sent two armies into Slav lands beyond the Elbe to reassert his authority there. Godfred's death had not removed the risk of independent maritime marauders, and the emperor applied himself vigorously to the potential problem. He immediately set in hand a fresh ship-building programme and the following year he personally toured the Channel coast to oversee the work. He also restored an old lighthouse that the Romans had built at Boulogne.

It was not only the Atlantic seaboard that was vulnerable to attack. Pepin, as we have seen, was busy guarding his interests in the Adriatic, but he was too far away to deal effectively with a more pressing threat. Islamic expansionism was directed at Christian islands in the Mediterranean. From the mid-790s Arabs launched repeated attacks from bases in Africa and Spain. Charlemagne responded by placing the Balearic Islands under his protection in 798 and by increasing the size of his own fleet in southern waters. From 806 to 813 his commanders were involved in naval campaigns almost annually. They were by no means always successful. Corsica and Sardinia were badly mauled by the Arabs in 809–10. Then, in 812, alarming news reached Aachen: a combined African and Spanish fleet was reported to be on its way to invade Italy. The aged emperor sent his grandson, Bernard, to organise the defence of his territory and waited anxiously for news. He also ordered his cousin, Wala (grandson of an illegitimate son of Charles Martel), to keep an eye on the young man 'until the outcome of the matter would assure the safety of our people'.

That somewhat enigmatic comment by the chronicler hints at an atmosphere of genuine alarm in the Frankish capital. The southern crisis came as the last in a succession of tragedies for the empire and the dynasty. In 810 a bovine epidemic had swept Charlemagne's domain from end to end, carrying off virtually all the cattle and bringing to a halt the season's campaigning. In the same year Pepin, King of Italy, had died, to be followed to the grave within months by his brother, Charles. This left Charlemagne's least favourite son, Louis (who had recently been responsible for a humiliatingly unsuccessful campaign in the Ebro valley) as his only heir. The emperor, well aware that his own vitality was fading, now had to make urgent plans for the succession. The division of Francia which he had set out in 806 obviously no longer applied, but what arrangement could replace it that would command sufficient support from the powerful clan leaders of the land? The question was by no means an easy one to answer. This was one of the reasons for sending his trusted kinsman, Wala, to Italy with Bernard. Charlemagne may well have been concerned for the young man's safety, but he was equally anxious to avoid Bernard becoming the focus of factions aiming at the throne. Wala and his brother, Adalhard, were lifelong companions of Charles and were foremost among his trusted lieutenants. They would be vital in ensuring that his wishes for the succession were carried out.

There was still more bad news to come. Hard on the heels of the report about the Arab invasion fleet came information that the Emperor Nicephorus had been killed in battle. It was only recently that, after a decade of argument and negotiation, Charlemagne had brought his 'brother' monarch to the point of signing a treaty of perpetual peace. Now everything depended on the attitude of the new ruler who had seized power in Constantinople, Michael I Rhangabe. Charlemagne waited anxiously for the return of his envoys. Fortunately, they brought good tidings. Michael wanted to be rid of the complication of the long-running feud over the imperial title and, in return for the abandonment of Frankish claims to Venice, was prepared to accord Charlemagne the ill-defined honorific of 'Emperor'.

That matter settled at long last, Charles was able to deal with the succession issue. He called a major assembly at Aachen. There, in the presence of all the leaders of Church and state, he crowned Louis as joint-emperor and installed Bernard as King of Italy in his father's place, with Wala and Adelhard to assist him. There was no question of the pope presiding at this solemn ceremony; Charlemagne clearly did not regard the imperial title as being in the gift of the papacy. What is more interesting is that he now saw it as a hereditary title. He had sought it as a personal honour, but now that it was securely in his grasp he staked a dynastic claim to it. From this point of view the 813 ceremony is more significant than the 800 one. All Charlemagne's efforts now were directed towards securing peace. He had established cordial relations with the Danes and the Byzantines and, the chronicles report, despatched three armies to the imperial marchlands in order to settle minor disputes and create stability on the borders. Now he also sent representatives to Duke Grimoald of Benevento to receive tribute and ensure his loyalty to young Bernard.

Only in the south were his efforts to leave his heir an empire enjoying peace and security frustrated. His commanders failed to repulse the Arab attacks of 812. The invaders stormed Corsica and the Italian mainland, looting at will. When Count Irmingar successfully waylaid the returning fleet near Majorca, he regained a large amount of booty and liberated more than 500 prisoners. This, however, did not deter the Muslims. They were soon back in action, carrying out raids on Sardinia and on coastal settlements north of Rome and around Nice.

Consideration of the governmental activities of the years 810–13 might lead us to picture a clear-sighted ruler with a vision for the future. We could be seduced into imagining Charlemagne consolidating the gains of his reign in order to bequeath to Louis a Christian reich united within its borders and poised for possible further expansion into pagan and Muslim lands. Such may well have accorded, at least in part, with the emperor's devout ambition for the spread of the Gospel, but he was by no means obsessed with the idea of sustaining and extending a territorial empire and, even if he had been, the realities of the Frankish state would have frustrated any such grand scheme. When we consider Charlemagne's legacy, and the rapid collapse of the greater Francia that he created, we are confronted by an apparent ambiguity. He bequeathed to Louis an inheritance whole and entire, but without the material means adequately to sustain it, and without a political framework capable of withstanding the pressures that he must have foreseen.

Charles was not oblivious to the insurmountable problems attendant upon maintaining a territorial empire. There were three factors that prevented him successfully inaugurating a lasting *European* state. For most of his core supporters, Charles was still a *Frankish* king, bound by the customs and expectations of his warrior-aristocrats. For the clergy and the intelligentsia, he was a *Christian* ruler whose prime responsibility was to God and the Church. These two concepts could never be made to dovetail neatly together. Both were hampered by the third factor: the governmental mechanism that operated the imperial administration was, at best, rudimentary.

Nothing better illustrates the competing ideologies to which Charles was prey than the will that he drew up in 811, while two of his legitimate sons were still living. He had accumulated vast wealth from plunder, tribute and taxation and, if his principal concern had been the continuance of the empire, he might have left a full treasury to his elder son. However, Frankish custom and religious scruples intervened. Charlemagne was concerned above all else with the repose of his soul. Accordingly, he immediately gave two-thirds of his portable wealth to the Church. The remainder he kept for his own use until he either died or retreated into a monastery (a possibility he was obviously contemplating). When he had no further need for earthly goods, this final portion was to be divided between his surviving children and grandchildren, his household servants, the poor and, once again, the Church.

One key – probably the most important one – to Charlemagne's political thought is Augustine's *City of God*, which, next to the Bible, was his favourite book. In reflecting on the temporal and heavenly realms, the patriarch took issue with ascetics who urged withdrawal from fallen human society in pursuit of an attainable holiness. He pointed out that perfection is impossible in this world, where divine and satanic forces are locked in constant conflict. The only sinless society will be that which gathers round the throne of God at the end of time. The moral for the leaders of both Church and state was not withdrawal, or even the establishment of monasteries as gateways to perfection, but earnest engagement in the battle against the forces of evil. It followed from this that territorial boundaries were of little spiritual consequence. No ruler could create a truly 'Christian' empire, within whose bounds truth and purity would prevail, and beyond which would lie unredeemed humanity and the chaos of unbelief. Moreover, his thoughts and aspirations should be focused on the New Jerusalem and on assuring himself of a place among its citizenry. To achieve that desired objective he had to shoulder the solemn responsibility of drawing his people ever closer to the ideal of the heavenly city. That involved scrupulous attention to divine 'order' in the life of Church and state.

We can readily understand why Augustine's analysis should have appealed to Charlemagne. It accorded the earthly ruler a well-defined place in the divine order of things. It gave meaning to the burdens of office. The annual campaigning, the frequent councils, the ceaseless travelling – Charles could convince himself that all this was not merely the pursuit of a transitory earthly glory. More specifically, Augustine's schema did not involve the subordination of state to Church and assert the power of spiritual over temporal rulers. Emperor, no less than pope, had his priesthood. This was a divine calling to which Charles applied himself ever more zealously as the years passed and as the day drew nearer when he would have to render his account to God. It was no mere over-gilded flattery when the Council of Mainz, in 813, addressed Charles as:

a ruler who exerted himself by untiring labour to increase the Christian flock; who joyfully honoured the churches of Christ and occupied himself in extracting as many souls as possible from the mouth of the hideous dragon, to lead them into the bosom of our holy mother the Church and to direct them all together towards the joys of Paradise and the Kingdom of Heaven; a ruler, finally, who surpassed all other kings of the earth in his holy wisdom and pious zeal.[9]

Right up to the end Charlemagne was applying his mind to the moral and spiritual improvement of his subjects. The five church councils that met in 813 all reported back to him. Their deliberations ranged over a wide variety of subjects, but the underlying concern of Charles and his leading ecclesiastics was moral renewal. The resulting decrees endorsed by the emperor denounced the besetting sins of clergy and laity. They called all men to make confession and to be regular in their attendance at mass. They proposed national fasts and exhorted the wealthy to be more generous in their charitable giving. Above all, they enjoined Charles' people to remain constant in prayer for their leader, his health in this world and his repose in the next.

Those intercessions were earnestly and sorrowfully offered up the following winter when the news spread rapidly round the empire that Charles was dead. In mid-January 814 he took to his bed with a fever. Within days his lungs were inflamed. The mighty constitution that had survived injuries in battle and the hunting field, as well as diseases encountered during his long, peripatetic, reign, succumbed at last to pleurisy on 28 January. He was buried the same day in his chapel at Aachen.

Contemporaries were conscious of the passing of a phenomenon. The greatest figure they had ever known was no more. They were aware that he had changed their world, but it would only be as they adjusted themselves to life without him that they would be able to evaluate just what he had achieved. As the ensuing years and decades passed, it may well have seemed that the impact of this colossus had been overestimated. Charlemagne had created a personal empire, a temporary federation of war-like nations held together by its leader's personality and by a common ideology – that Christianity which, thanks to its unique mixture of uncompromising certainty and practical flexibility, had made itself available to all the pagan tribes north of the Alps. There was never any likelihood of the survival of this political unit. There was no constitutional provision for it. Tribal loyalties and rivalries were too strong for it. Tensions within the Carolingian family were too disruptive. Charles had not imprinted on Germanic society some culture derived from the classical past. The emperor's model was not a long-faded memory of Roman hegemony, even though one aspect of his motivating conviction was that beyond the frontiers of Francia and Byzantium lay nothing but barbarism. His inspiration for territorial expansion and his justification for it were religious. He believed himself to be God's viceroy, charged with the solemn duties of extending the boundaries of Christendom and ensuring that divine law was respected within it. Like the faithful kings of the Old Testament, he attributed his successes to the Lord of Hosts' endorsement of his mission. In human terms, the reasons for his military achievements were his own determination, his organising ability and the size of his armies. Thanks to the economic stability he inherited and improved upon, he was able to put into the field every year large bodies of well-equipped warriors, sustained by provisions and equipment carried in huge baggage trains. The Frankish war machine was so massive that it wore down opposition by besieging enemy strongholds; Charlemagne fought very few pitched battles in open country. Success in war meant booty, and booty bought the continuing loyalty of his military elite. Charlemagne knew what every statesman knows – that the best way to deflect attention from any failings of government is to keep the attention of the political nation focused on external enemies. It was the expansionist policies he pursued for the greater part of his reign that enhanced his own authority and that of his subordinate warlords. However, in his latter days he was forced onto the defensive and then the authority of his regime begin to waver. It would need another Charlemagne to rise to the new generation of challenges. Such a heroic figure did not emerge.

In hindsight, the reign of Charles, son of Pepin, could have been seen as a 'flash in the pan', a brilliant interlude in the long history of tribal warfare that inevitably resulted from the withdrawal of the Roman legions and the continuing westward incursion of barbarian hordes into a finite geographical region bounded by the limitless ocean. In reality, during the ensuing centuries the common memory persisted that once there had been a united, expansionist western Christendom that had taken the offensive against paganism and Islam. What Charlemagne had achieved (and what a growing mythology added to his achievements) acted as a vision of what might once again become possible. It informed the internationalism of the crusades and the chivalric code that became the philosophy of the warrior caste of Christian nations. It became a standard to be taken up by both autocrats and democrats of later ages who believed that they, too, had a mission to improve the lot of humankind. Nor was all this founded on a myth. Charlemagne *was* an internationalist. He *did* believe in respect for customary law within the framework of Christian cultural hegemony. He read and spoke Latin with ease; he even mastered diplomatic Greek. His interest in the common pursuits of scholars from several lands was genuine and enthusiastic. Like them, he was passionate about recovering earlier – and supposedly purer – forms of religion and culture. On 28 January 814 this Great Adventurer in the realms of practical statesmanship and intellectual speculation died. The Great Adventure had scarcely begun.

Notes

1 Waddell, op. cit., p.153
2 F. Guizot, *The History of Civilization in Europe* (trs. K. W. Hazlitt), 1997, p.60

3 Allott, op. cit., pp.83–4
4 Ibid., p.134
5 Waddell, op. cit., p.173
6 Ibid., p.165
7 *Einhard and Notker*, p.159
8 *Carolingian Chronicles*, p.89
9 Halphen, op. cit., p.150

III

Charlemagne the Myth

He is a myth evolved by the popular imagination, a communal poetic creation, a Protean figure: we can all shape him to our likeness, for the myth is endlessly adaptable.

Edwin Muir (on Robert Burns)

9

Sic transit gloria mundi

From the rising of the sun to the shore of the sea where it sets all hearts are full of sorrow. Alas! The Franks, the Romans and all the Christian peoples weep, bowed in sorrows . . . The kingdom of the Franks has suffered many disasters but never has it suffered such great grief as in the moment when the awe-inspiring and eloquent Charlemagne was laid to rest at Aachen. O Christ, welcome the pious Charlemagne into your blessed home among the apostles.[1]

T
he lament of an anonymous monk was echoed by thousands throughout the empire, for the passing of Charlemagne was one of those rare events that leaves a gap in the lives of all contemporaries. Put very simply, Charles *was* the empire. He had been its ruler longer than most men could remember. He had extended its boundaries farther than most men would have thought possible. He had given it strong centralised government and internal stability. He had kept the warrior-nobles happy with war booty, and the church leaders content with pious reform. He was that combination of charisma and pragmatism that appears rarely in the annals of human governance. Only after his death did it become apparent just how much had depended on the force of Charles' personality. His empire and, indeed, Carolingian rule itself were soon shown to be very fragile. Small wonder that his subjects mourned for him – and for themselves as they faced an uncertain future.

Grief might have been widespread, but it was neither universal nor unmixed. Though most men respected the late emperor, many of them saw his passing as the opportunity to settle what they considered unfinished business. Territorial claims, dynastic feuds and party factions came to the surface as soon as Charles' firm hand was removed. Administrative problems that he had not solved, or had only partially solved, remained to be tackled. The question uppermost in many minds was whether the new regime would be able to hold in balance the political forces within the empire as effectively as Charles had done. Regional loyalties as well as aristocratic rivalries and ambitions were ever-constant threats to the stability of Francia, and to these were added tensions within the imperial family. Charles was scarcely buried before his relatives were squabbling over the will, and Louis, who was thirty-six in 814, would have to show himself decisive and ruthless if he was to ward off the claims made by his half-brothers, his sons and by aristocratic supporters whom they might win to their various causes, and if he was to prevent his imperial inheritance being fragmented.

The fundamental flaw in imperial policy was that the meaning of 'empire' had never been resolved. As long as Charles was in control, and asserting by word and deed '*l'état c'est moi*', there could be little debate on the subject. Now that he was gone, rival concepts were quick to assert themselves. Louis and his chosen advisers regarded the empire as a Christian political entity under hereditary rule. A strong aristocratic caucus insisted that it consisted simply of the patrimony of the Frankish king. Louis's sons were caught up in the conflict and, throughout the half-century following Charles' death, his empire was torn apart by the wars and intrigues of the contending parties. Louis himself was twice deposed and subsequently restored; he shut up all his sisters and half-brothers in religious houses; he murdered his nephew, Bernard; and he was forced to make a series of territorial accommodations with other family members, which left the political situation in chaos at the time of his death. It is against this turbulent background that we have to see the beginnings of the creation of the Charlemagne legend.

Myths are like flowers; some grow naturally in the wild and others are carefully cultivated. Most are developed by hybridisation, free-growing species being crossed with others to produce more exotic blooms. The Charlemagne myth began life as a piece of deliberate political horticulture. We have frequently referred to Einhard's *Vita Karoli*, the first biography of the emperor, and we must now consider the circumstances under which it was written. As well as being a friend of Charlemagne, Einhard was very close to Louis, and his book was almost certainly composed during the first years of the latter's reign. What he offered the new emperor was a panegyric of his father – and that for a specific political reason. The book's concluding words give a broad hint at the reason for its composition.

Having described the provisions of Charles' will in great detail, Einhard observes, 'Charlemagne's son Louis, who succeeded him by divine right, read this statement and acted upon it with complete scrupulousness as soon as he possibly could after his father's death.'² Through the copies that were rapidly circulated, the official version of events was disseminated: Louis had arranged for the disposition of his father's goods and had exercised supreme power fully in accordance with Charles' own wishes and the wishes of the people. Einhard sets this out more explicitly in his description of Louis's coronation of 813: 'This decision of Charlemagne's [to nominate Louis as joint-emperor] was accepted with great enthusiasm by all who were there, for it seemed to have come to him by a divine inspiration for the welfare of the state.'³ But it was precisely the constitutional arrangements for the new reign that were being hotly disputed. The *Vita* was nothing more or less than a piece of court propaganda designed to silence critics of the new regime. It bolstered the reputation of Charlemagne, associated Louis intimately with the late, great emperor and claimed that the arrangements for the succession had been endorsed by all the Frankish leaders. Einhard emphasised that the crowning of 813 was a *Frankish* ceremony. And here, surely, lies the reason for Einhard's treatment of that other coronation in 800. The writer wanted to make clear Charles' reluctance to receive the imperial crown from the hands of the pope. Einhard had in the forefront of his mind an audience many of whose members resented the 'interference' of Rome.

We cannot accuse Einhard of producing a version of the reign of Charlemagne that was a wanton distortion of the truth, because neither he nor any of his contemporaries would have understood the modern insistence on scientific accuracy in such matters. It is simply unfortunate that our best source for the life of Charlemagne is a one-sided interpretation of the emperor's character and a highly selective account of the major events in which he was involved. Any inconvenient facts were simply omitted from Einhard's description of 'this most distinguished and deservedly most famous king'. We have already seen that the author was reticent, even silent, about military campaigns that had gone badly for the Franks. He drew an equally discreet veil over relationships in which his subject behaved less than honourably. He tells us nothing pertinent about Charles' dealings with his brother Carloman, or of his treatment of his first, discarded, actual wife, the nameless daughter of Desiderius, or of the seizure of Bavaria and the displacing of Tassilo III. He is less than informative about the revolt of Pepin the Hunchback. As for Charles' domestic life, Einhard gives only the merest hint of the scandalous behaviour of the princesses (whom their brother despatched to nunneries as soon as he

Charles the Bald (823–877), Charlemagne's grandson, revived some of his ancestor's cultural glories and forged a close alliance with the Church. Here he is shown receiving a Bible from Count Vivian and the monks of Saint-Martin de Tours, c. 843. However, militarily, his reign was a disaster, being spent largely in power struggles with Charlemagne's other descendants.

Charlemagne had his son Louis crowned as joint emperor and successor in 813. Illustration from *Les Grandes Chroniques de France*.

Portrait of Emperor Lothair I (795–855), Charlemagne's grandson. He attempted to rule the whole empire in defiance of his brothers. Though he was allowed to retain the imperial title he had to be content with possession of only a third of the Frankish empire.

Jongleurs, the court entertainers who composed and performed the Roland epic and other *chansons de geste*. Picture from a 10th century manuscript.

According to Church propaganda going on crusade was part of a Christian knight's holy calling. In this 13th century manuscript Christ is depicted leading the crusaders into battle.

The elaborate, martial sport of the tournament was conducted according to a strict chivalric code.

The investiture of knights was accompanied by high and solemn ceremony but the sanctifying of the pursuit of arms rarely led to the kind of virtuous, chivalric behaviour of which medieval literature spoke and which this 13th century French manuscript suggests.

Scenes from the Chanson de Roland
made such an impact that they were
represented in the ambulatory
windows of Chartres Cathedral.

The Emperor Charles V (1500–1558) on Horseback in Muhlberg, 1548 by Titian.
Not until 1519 did another monarch appear who ruled an empire comparable in size to
that of Charlemagne. Charles V was Holy Roman Emperor until his abdication in 1556.

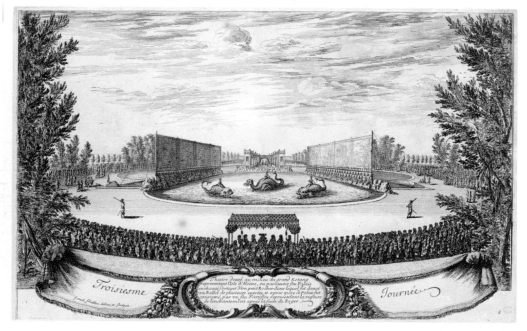

Stage on the Large Pond representing the Isle of Alcine, third day of 'Les Plaisirs de l'Ile Enchantée', 9th May 1664. In this spectacular allegorical presentation based in part on Charlemagne's legends the young Louis XIV took part.

Henri Paul Motte created this highly suggestive image of Napoleon's 'pilgrimage' to the throne of Charlemagne in 1804, shortly before his own coronation. The artist captured the dictator's ambition very clearly.

Francois Guizot (1787–1874) after a painting by Paul Delaroche (1797–1856) *c*.1878.
Guizot, an historian and politician, regarded Charlemagne as one of the great
standard-bearers of European civilisation.

came to power), being content to present Charles as a dotingly affectionate and over-indulgent father.

The *Life of Charlemagne* has made an impact down the centuries, and doubtless made an impact on the more scholarly of Einhard's contemporaries because it was the first political biography written since the classical age. Indeed, Einhard based his work on ancient Roman models, particularly Suetonius' *De vita Caesarum*. He deliberately set out to draw a parallel between the Frankish emperor and the leading rulers of antiquity. Thus, for example, he lists certain portents that had preceded Charlemagne's death, just as strange events gave warning of the assassination of Julius Caesar. The moral was obvious: the heavens cannot prevent themselves signalling the departure of great men. It is clear from the sheer number of copies of the *Vita Karoli* that have survived that numerous scribes were set to work on Einhard's manuscript in order to ensure the greatest possible dissemination. As for the author, it is probably no coincidence that in 816 Louis bestowed upon him the lay abbacies of two monasteries in Ghent.

Unfortunately for the new regime, Einhard's book seems to have had little effect in uniting Charlemagne's people in obedience to Charlemagne's heir. Louis is known to posterity as 'Louis the Pious' and there seems little doubt that he would have made a better monk than an emperor. He was given to violent rages during which he would authorise draconian measures, only to follow them with emotional excesses of remorse and acts of penance (sometimes public). It is not surprising that his government lurched from one crisis to another, nor that his own sons decided that he was incapable of ruling. At the beginning of his reign he associated his two elder sons with his rule by making Lothar and Pepin nominal kings of Bavaria and Aquitania respectively. In 817 Bernard, in Italy, was the first to challenge the constitutional settlement. He allowed himself to become the leader of a rebellious aristocratic faction. The revolt failed and the enraged Louis had the boy's eyes put out (which proved fatal). The removal of Bernard necessitated the first of many readjustments. However, the emperor's squabbling sons were never content, and things were made worse when Louis remarried and sired a fourth son, Charles, who also had to be provided with territory and titles. In 829 Lothar, who had been crowned and acclaimed as emperor-elect in 817, was supported in a challenge to his father by his brothers and by magnates who resented Louis's autocratic behaviour. The emperor was briefly deposed, but was then restored on condition that in future he would only act in concert with the Frankish assembly. The truce lasted less than two years. It was not until 835 that Louis was allowed to enjoy his throne in relative security, but even then the squabbles and manoeuvrings continued. When he died, in 840, he left a land that had descended into chaos.

When the three remaining sons reached an accord at Verdun in 843 it marked the formal death of Charlemagne's empire. Francia was parcelled up into three wedges of territory; two of them would, in the fullness of time, become France and Germany, and the land between – Lorraine and the Rhineland – would be their frequent battleground. With Lothar's death in 855 his central portion of the empire was further subdivided between his three sons. The eldest retained the title of 'Emperor', but it was devoid of all meaning. Whatever it was that Charles had bequeathed to posterity was fragmented by the ambitions and jealousies of Francia's leaders. Eventually the forces of localism, regionalism and dynasticism proved too strong for any grander vision to be sustained. This was not solely the fault of the emperor's heirs, but Gibbon's ringing condemnation of them is not entirely unjustified:

> The dregs of the Carolingian race no longer exhibited any symptoms of virtue or power, and the ridiculous epithets of the *bald*, the *stammerer*, the *fat*, and the *simple*, distinguished the tame and uniform features of a crowd of kings alike deserving of oblivion.[4]

By the tenth century the Carolingian blood coursing through the veins of the rulers of West and East Francia and Lotharingia had become very diluted. Italy was ruled by a local aristocratic dynasty. Independent states had been established in Provence and Burgundy. Yet the *idea* of a political empire never entirely went away. It lay, like some radiantly illuminated book, revered but unread and gathering dust, until a ruler of real stature – such as Otto I or Otto III – should take it up and become inspired by the achievements of Charles the Great.

Meanwhile what had happened to the land whose rulers had been indulging in their power games? The basic answer is economic decline, exacerbated by social disruption and foreign invasion. When the military resources of the warrior-lords were turned upon each other, rather than being employed in foreign wars, and when the flow of booty from such wars dried up, the consequences on commercial and agricultural life could not but be disastrous. Internal disruption provided opportunities that the empire's enemies were not slow to grasp. Saracen raids on Mediterranean islands and coastal settlements increased and were seldom effectively rebuffed. They reached the summit of their power with the sack of Rome in 846. Salvation came at last from the dislocation of the Muslim states, a revitalised Byzantium and the vigour of the counts of Provence, whose

North Sea

SAXONY

Meersen•

Aachen•

THURINGIA

LOTHARINGIA

Laon• FRANCONIA

BRITTANY Paris•

•Verdun

NEUSTRIA Regensburg•

②

Bourges• SWABIA BAVARIA

•Basle OSTMARK

① ③

BURGUNDY

AQUITAINE CARINTHIA

LOMBARDY

Milan•

Pavia•

PROVENCE

PATRIMONIUM
PETRI

SPOLETO

Rome•

Mediterranean Sea

THE DIVISION OF
CHARLEMAGNE'S EMPIRE

| 0 | 100 | 200 | 300 miles |
| 0 | 100 200 300 | 400 | 500 km |

The Empire at Charlemagne's death in 814,
and under Louis the Pious (Emperor, 813–40)

① The Kingdom of West Francia under
Charles the Bald (reigned 843–77,
Emperor 875–7)

② The Middle Kingdom of Lothar I (reigned 843–55),
divided between his three sons—Lewis II of Italy
(reigned 855–75), Lothar II (reigned 855–69)
and Charles of Provence (reigned 855–63)

③ The Kingdom of East Francia under
Lewis the German (reigned 840–76)

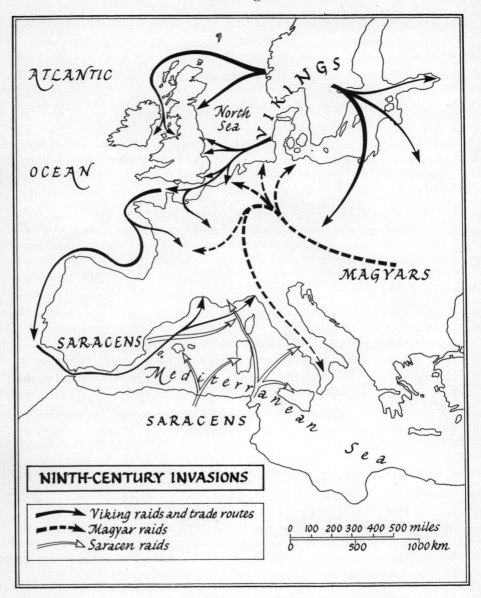

ATLANTIC

OCEAN

North
Sea

VIKINGS

MAGYARS

SARACENS

Mediterranean

SARACENS

Sea

NINTH-CENTURY INVASIONS

Viking raids and trade routes
Magyar raids
Saracen raids

0 100 200 300 400 500 *miles*
0   500   1000 *km*

reputation and power grew in direct proportion to their ability to defend
the soft underbelly of the empire.

The Magyars were a bigger problem. The latest invaders from the steppes
reached the Hungarian plain in the second half of the ninth century.
Charlemagne's eastern march was ill equipped to deal with this new menace.

The Magyars were in some respects a land version of the Vikings: fierce horseback warriors, they were masters of unfamiliar military techniques. They struck in fast-moving bands and moved on before a response could be mounted. Francia's rulers could not bring the invaders to face the kind of pitched battle in which their own armies excelled. Ironically it was the conquest of the troublesome Saxons and Avars that had left the frontier vulnerable to the magnificent Magyar horsemen. The Saxon and Avar forts had been dismantled, their war leaders removed and their command structures broken down. With little difficulty the new invaders swept through their territory and onwards into the heartlands of Francia, burning, looting and creating terrified panic wherever they went. For half a century they attacked at will, reaching Paris and Tours in the west, the lower Rhône valley and, in the south, the very tip of Italy. Thereafter they gradually withdrew to live a settled life in what is now Hungary, but not before they had decimated large areas of the Carolingian lands.

But it was the Vikings who posed the biggest and most continuous threat. The Northerners became bolder year on year, appearing in larger numbers and, increasingly, wintering in the regions they had conquered. They penetrated far inland along the Rhine, Scheldt, Seine, Loire and – having by the end of the ninth century ventured into the Mediterranean – the Rhône. Successive kings confronted the Vikings with little success, and the chroniclers were left to contemplate their burned towns and wasted farmland and record their lament: 'There did not exist a road which was not littered with dead – priests and laymen, women, children and babies. Despair spread through the land and it seemed that all Christian people would perish.'[5] The heirs of Charlemagne were driven to the humiliation of paying protection money to the invaders, or hiring Viking leaders as mercenaries to drive out rival bands of their own countrymen. In the tenth and eleventh centuries the Franks progressively abandoned to the newcomers that territory which became the Duchy of Normandy.

All empires disappear. They may fall prey to stronger neighbours. They may fragment, becoming victims of local, tribal and regional ambitions. Usually their disintegration is the result of both external and internal pressures. Charlemagne's empire was no exception. Yet two factors mark it out as different – indeed, unique. The first is its brevity. If we generously reckon its duration as covering the years from Charles' assumption of sole rule in 771 to the division of Lothar I's portion between his three sons in 855, we are left with just eighty-four years. They were followed by two centuries of anarchy as local rulers broke the shackles of centralised monarchy and became preoccupied in fighting each other and protecting their lands from foreign invasion. The second factor is that, despite political and social disintegration, the *idea* of a European empire survived. The body of Charlemagne's legacy may have perished, but its soul lived on. The Carolingians and later dynasties that replaced them continued to use the imperial title and, from time to time, there were efforts to reunite the patrimony of Charlemagne. Europe was a land of many races and languages, but by 1254, when the title was first officially adopted, it was accepted that the 'Holy Roman Empire' was a political reality. That appellation was an attempt to provide physical expression for something that gave 'Europe' a meaningful identity. What marked out the old Carolingian lands as distinct from their neighbours (except Britain) was religion. Europe would for the next millennium be defined as Latin Christendom, and it would be the Roman Church and its satellites that had a vested interest in bringing spiritual aspiration and territorial reality into alignment. Part of their propaganda armoury was the creation and encouragement of Charlemagne legends.

Notes

1 See Becher, op. cit., p.135
2 *Einhard and Notker*, p.90
3 Ibid., p.83
4 Gibbon, op. cit., VI, p.109
5 See J. Bronsted, *The Vikings*, 1973, pp.50–1

10

A Hero for All Seasons

S ome time in the second half of the twelfth century an anonymous monk wrote *The Pilgrimage of Charlemagne to Constantinople and Jerusalem*. In it he described how the emperor made a devout journey to the Holy City and, on arrival, immediately went, with twelve companions, to a church to attend mass. They noticed twelve chairs with a thirteenth set in the midst of them, and sat down to rest. A Jew who happened to be passing was so overwhelmed by the radiant visage of the royal visitor that he rushed straight to the Patriarch of Jerusalem, threw himself at the startled man's feet and begged to receive Christian baptism. The patriarch hurried to discover what had given rise to this display and was equally stunned by what he saw: Charlemagne and his attendants had taken their places in the very seats that Christ and his apostles had occupied. This man must, indeed, be a king among kings. The Franks were not allowed to leave before the keeper of the holy places had pressed upon them a large number of precious relics, including the shroud of Christ and the crown of thorns. So embellished had the Charlemagne myth become in three and a half centuries that the person of the warrior-king had assumed almost divine qualities. The pilgrimage story even came to be depicted in stained glass at Chartres Cathedral.

Yet this was only one of the attributes attached to the reputation of Charlemagne during the Middle Ages. No other figure in the whole of western history has been more transformed in the popular imagination. More than a thousand partially or wholly spurious stories were added to the canon of his exploits. The Charlemagne legend became a veritable portmanteau into which chroniclers, troubadours, churchmen and kings stuffed whatever ideological baggage they needed for their own purposes. Pilgrim, crusader, Christian warrior, chivalrous knight, pattern of perfect monarchy, moral exemplar, scholar-prince, ancestor claimed by rival dynasts, protector of the Church, saint – in hindsight, Charles, son of Pepin, became all these things. Every age invents its own heroes by mixing truth and fiction. Britain has, among others, King Arthur, Robin Hood and Francis Drake, champions around whom a multitude of legends have gathered and been celebrated in prose, verse, song and film. But no other national hero in any European country approaches the stature achieved by Charlemagne in popular imagination. He became for later ages an all-purpose charismatic figure, an amalgam of everything a Christian king should be, an example of whatever, from time to time, was esteemed by the prevailing political correctness. The myth was built up, layer upon layer, and we learn from the process more about the passing scene than we do about the increasingly obscured original.

In the decades immediately following Charles' death it was the church hierarchy that had the biggest vested interest in idolising the late emperor. The papacy was still in need of a powerful protector and this inevitably involved successive popes in the Carolingian family squabbles. But that was only one corner of a much bigger picture – the integrity of Latin Christendom. It is part of the genius of Christianity that it is amazingly adaptable. Over the centuries it has established lodgement in all major cultures. A twenty-first-century visitor from another planet who experienced Tridentine high mass amidst the baroque splendours of the Gesù church in Rome, the stark simplicity of a word-based service in the John Knox chapel in Geneva, a charismatic rave-up in the Crystal Cathedral of California's Orange County, the elaborately re-created mystery of the liturgy in St Basil's, Moscow, and the unique combination of informality, zeal and spontaneity of worship in a South African shanty town might take some convincing that he or she was witnessing different expressions of the same religion, although that would, in fact, be the case. Peel back the cultural wrappings and the enclosed theological package is essentially the same in all cases. The ancient faith not only survives, but breathes through regional, linguistic and aesthetic impositions. As we have seen, local variants of belief and practice had appeared in the churches of post-Roman Europe. This did not suit the heirs of St Peter, who were concerned about the purity of the faith, the continuance of the Church's mission to the pagan world, and their own position as leaders in the western part of the empire. Successive popes had laboured to enforce unity and uniformity as well as obedience to the Bishop of Rome. Charlemagne had been their greatest ally in this process. In the anarchy that followed his departure they exerted their authority through the ecclesiastical network to achieve political power and to ensure that, while territorial boundaries changed, the Church in the West remained whole and entire.

Politically their greatest coup was the coronation of Lother in 823. Louis the Pious had firmly resisted papal pretensions by crowning his eldest son with his own hands, but the young man was later persuaded, in the interests of enhancing his position, to travel to Rome for a second ceremony. The full implications of this would not be manifested for many years, but it was a significant coup. Where Rome led, other churchmen followed over the next couple of centuries. In order to strengthen their own positions, abbots ordered the forging of 'ancient' charters, the majority of which were attributed to Charlemagne. Of the 262 such documents bearing his seal that survive, ninety-eight are fakes. It was relatively easy to produce a parchment purporting to carry the unassailable authority of the great emperor, and the perpetrators of such deceptions presumably operated on the basis of ends justifying means. In their conflicts with grasping magnates, monasteries provided themselves with legal proof of their ancient rights, thus ensuring their own survival and that of the prayer life that undergirded the security of the realm.

'Forgery' is not quite the right word to apply to late Carolingian historical writings, but they certainly continued the tradition of political manipulation of the recording of events and, in the process, added their own garish colours to the portrait of Charlemagne. The first text to appear to add anything to Einhard's *Vita Karoli* was the *Gesta Karoli*, *The Deeds of Charles*, by the Monk of Saint-Gall, to which we have already referred. The writer was probably a man called Notker Balbulus, Notker the Stammerer, who spent most of his life in the Benedictine house situated in the hills above Lake Constance. He seems to have devoted himself to work in the scriptorium as a copyist and author, and his *Deeds of Charles* was written between 883 and 886, during the reign of Charles the Fat, who united the empire under his rule in 884 and was deposed three years later. Just as Einhard wrote to legitimate the rule of Louis the Pious, so Notker set out to perform the same service for his grandson. His unfinished book lauded the characters and achievements of Pepin III and his successors, purporting to set down information gathered from eyewitnesses. But, while the *Gesta Karoli* does add some probably accurate details about the life and habits of Charlemagne at home and on campaign, it is largely a collection of wonder-stories told round the frater fire during the dark alpine winters.

The emperor is now presented as larger than life in every way. He receives foreign embassies festooned in gold and jewels. He good-humouredly puts down self-important clerics, but fiercely punishes treachery, avarice and inhumanity. He has a gift for recognising and rewarding talent even in the humblest of men. This 'most energetic of all the bustling Franks' is incapable of resting idle. His every waking moment is filled with divine worship, law-making, war, diplomacy or grandiose building projects. In battle Charles is simply awesome. This is how Notker describes his paragon's advance on doomed Pavia:

> Then came in sight that man of iron, Charlemagne, topped with his iron helm, his fists in iron gloves, his iron chest and his Platonic shoulders clad in an iron cuirass. An iron spear raised high against the sky he gripped in his left hand, while in his right he held his still unconquered sword . . . His shield was all of iron. His horse gleamed iron-coloured and its very mettle was of iron . . . iron filled the fields and all the open spaces. The rays of the sun were thrown back by this battle-line of iron.[1]

In the following lines the heroic hyperbole reaches even greater heights. When the Pavians fail to throw open their gates to the invader, what does Charles do? Rather than spend the day in idleness, he sets his men to building a church! And not just any church:

> Between the fourth hour of the day and the twelfth, with the help of the leaders and the common soldiery, they had built such a cathedral, with walls and roofs, panelled ceilings and painted frescoes, that no one watching would have believed that it could have been achieved in a whole year.[2]

This is the stuff of bardic song rather than what we think of as 'history', but ninth-century readers did not make such clear-cut distinctions, nor did they think it necessary to do so. Our post-Enlightenment commitment to 'scientific' history would have seemed to Notker a pale and pointless thing. He would have agreed with Oliver Cromwell that what mattered was penetrating beneath the surface of human events to their eternal significance: 'those things whereof the life and power of them lay', the 'strong windings and turnings of providence'. Grant a real interaction between material and spiritual realities and anything is possible. Miracles become common currency and men become giants. Accept God's concern for his terrestrial creation, and divine activity ceases to be 'intervention'; it reveals itself as the very motor of human affairs. Charles the Great had seen himself as the chosen vehicle of God and it was Notker's purpose to demonstrate that this was so and that the Carolingian empire was the last and greatest of all the mighty empires raised up by the Creator:

> He who ordains the fate of kingdoms and the march of the centuries, the all-powerful Disposer of events, having destroyed one extraordinary image, that of the Romans ... then raised up, among the Franks, the golden head of a second image, equally remarkable, in the person of the illustrious Charlemagne.[3]

The Carolingian state, personified by Charlemagne, turned out *not* to be the ultimate in socio-political evolution. However, its collapse did not prevent it being revered as an ideal for future rulers to strive towards. The *imperium* of the 'Great Emperor' became a kind of template, taken out from time to time and applied by successor nations seeking a purpose, a meaning, an understanding of their place in the world. After several turbulent and chaotic decades the Carolingian dynasties in East and West came to an end. In what would become Germany, Henry I founded the Saxon ruling house in 919, and sixty years later Hugh Capet replaced the last ineffective Carolingian as king of 'France'. Neither event put an end to widespread lawlessness and sporadic warfare. The map of eleventh- and twelfth-century Europe resembled a stained-glass window that had been smashed and its fragments reassembled with no reference to the original design. It was a squirming mass of jostling and inconstant kingdoms and dukedoms. In what was essentially a martial society, rulers were frequently at war with each other and, when they were not, they devoted much of their efforts to enforcing the loyalty of their own magnates. Charlemagne's system of checks and balances scarcely survived him. Counts and *missi* who had once held land at the emperor's pleasure now regarded it as their outright possession, to be retained by main force. At local level, the dominant class was that of the 'chevalier', the descendant of Charlemagne's warrior-lord. He was far from being the 'verray parfit gentil knight' of Chaucer's poem, or the virtuous hero beloved of Sir Thomas Malory and later romanticists. In most cases he was nothing more than an uncouth, mounted thug, who wielded his sword for gain and ruthlessly exploited his social inferiors.

It was in the interest of kings and church leaders to counteract the tendency towards free-for-all, might-is-right anarchy. If unity, civilisation and the rule of law were to be defended, society needed guiding principles, ethical codes and an idealism that rose above the squalid pursuit of material gain. These were provided by, on the one hand, Christian morality, which held before men's eyes the sticks and carrots of divine law; and, on the other, feudalism, which bound overlords and vassals together with bands of mutual responsibility. Where these two overlapped there emerged the phenomenon of chivalry. And wherever preachers, poets and law-givers pointed men towards a better ordering of society, they claimed Charlemagne as their champion. The great emperor thus became not only a Herculean figure, but also a Protean one, able to assume numerous guises.

The eastern section of the empire witnessed a real, if brief, resurgence of the Charlemagne spirit in the second half of the tenth century. Otto I (the Great), the second emperor of the Saxon line, was determined to revive something of the magnificence of his renowned predecessor. He had himself proclaimed at Aachen in 936 and proceeded to bring the recalcitrant German dukes under centralised control. It was he who put an end to the Magyar threat, crushing the invaders in a mammoth, three-day battle on the Lechfeld plain south of Augsburg. Further wars strengthened his borders and added Bavaria to his empire. In 961, like his famous Frankish antecedent, he crossed the Alps at the behest of a beleaguered pope. The papacy was at its lowest moral ebb, and a later Catholic scholar dubbed the current regime the 'pornocracy'. The latest in a succession of licentious and villainous popes was the dissolute, twenty-year-old John XII, now accused by his opponents of cramming every human vice into his young life. Desperately in need of a protector, he offered to crown Otto as Roman Emperor in return for military aid against his pressing enemies. Otto accepted the investiture, but took the opportunity to confront the pope with his crimes, which included homicide, perjury, sacrilege, incest and invoking pagan gods. John responded by turning against his ally as soon as he left Rome. Otto deposed the pope and replaced him with his own nominee. The sudden death of John XII at the hands of a cuckolded husband did not end the faction-fighting. Over the next thirty-six years ten popes and antipopes squabbled over the chair of St Peter. This was the sequence of events that inaugurated the Holy Roman Empire! Having been drawn into the cesspit that was Rome, Otto and his successors were unable to extricate themselves. They shouldered the spiritual and moral leadership which they believed their status gave them and, like Charlemagne, they pledged themselves to reform.

Otto married his heir to a Byzantine princess, Theophano, as part of a treaty whereby his titles were accepted by the ruler in Constantinople. When his infant grandson, Otto III, succeeded to the imperial dignities, it seemed that the dream of twin states encompassing all Christian people might be approaching realisation. As soon as he came of age the young emperor gave evidence of his vision for the Christian empire by making a pilgrimage to Aachen, where he organised a search for the tomb of

Charlemagne. He probably intended to have his predecessor canonised, for strange stories about the 'discovery' were soon being circulated. Charles had been found, it was said, seated on a throne and in a remarkable state of preservation. His fingernails had continued to grow through the gauntlets he was wearing, and had to be trimmed. Otto took away one of the great emperor's teeth as a sacred relic and repaired the corpse's damaged nose with gold. It was not long before the new emperor was caught up in the sordid affairs of Rome, but he made a dramatic attempt to deal, once and for all, with this cancer in the body of the Church. He took influence out of the hands of the Roman nobility by appointing the first German pope (Gregory V) and, after the latter's death, installing the first French pope (Sylvester II). More than that, he transferred his own capital to Rome, building a fine palace on the Aventine and adopting the toga as his normal dress. How subsequent history would have changed, had the latterday Charlemagne survived to fulfil his early promise, we cannot know. Otto III died suddenly in January 1002 shortly before his twenty-second birthday. Poison was inevitably suspected – probably with good reason.

In the turbulent West (hereafter referred to by the convenient anachronism of 'France') no such powerful figures emerged who were potentially capable of re-creating something of Charlemagne's regime. Yet it was here that the one-time emperor appeared as a lead character in the heroic myth that emerged from the chrysalis of chronicled events to flaunt its multicoloured brilliance in the imaginations of the knightly class. A new architectural phenomenon had appeared in the land: the castle. In the great halls of these strongholds, which boldly blazoned ownership and defiance, greater and lesser lords held court – and frequently demanded to be entertained. Enter the *jongleur*, the itinerant minstrel who earned his living by telling stories, singing songs and reciting poems. He apostrophised love, indulged in bawdry and solemnly narrated moral tales. But what his audiences most wanted to hear during the long evenings when wintry draughts caught the smoke drifting up to the rafters was tales of heroism – tales that exalted the virtues of manliness and the obedience owed by knights to their overlords. These were the *chansons de geste*, 'songs of noble deeds', individual stories with stock characters that were told over and over again, but which were constantly being revised and augmented according to the changing tastes of the troubadour's patrons, and which eventually achieved written form as song cycles.

The earliest extant versions of the *chansons de geste* date from the late eleventh century, but they deal with events and personalities of three centuries earlier. What they present us with is multi-layered narrative. Beginning in the ninth century, the original stories were passed down in oral tradition by performers who were illiterate. At every stage they were adapted by the *jongleurs*, not only because they wanted, quite naturally, to please their clientele, but because their art demanded that the stories be given maximum dramatic impact. In the same way that Renaissance painters reset the Gospel stories in Flemish towns or against Italian landscapes, so the minstrels told their old stories in terms that their audiences would most easily understand.

The most famous, and one of the earliest, of these songs is the *Chanson de Roland*. It is set against Charles' Spanish campaign of 778, but that military foray provides a mere historical launch-pad for a fantasy adventure. It caught the imagination of early bards because it was the only war the mighty hero had waged against the infidel. The political fact that Charlemagne had simply taken the opportunity of rivalries within the Muslim world to strengthen his own borders was ignored. The poet tells us that the emperor received from the Angel Gabriel his instructions to go to the aid of beleaguered Christians in a foreign land. For the lyric writer, Charles was a Christian knight fighting under the Cross against the forces of Satan. That is precisely how Europeans viewed the followers of Islam by the turn of the millennium. The long-running conflict between the Christian kingdoms of Castile, Leon, Aragon and Navarre and the Umayyad caliphate was western Christendom's closest experience of the battle of the faiths and, over the years, many young adventurers seeking booty, fame and a reputation as champions of the Church crossed the Pyrenees to serve as mercenaries in the Christian armies. At the same time their Muslim counterparts from all round the Mediterranean were also drawn to Spain to pledge their swords in the name of Allah. What Asia Minor was to the Eastern Empire, Spain was to Latin Christendom. Soldiers were not the only travellers to Christian Iberia. The shrine of Santiago de Compostela (supposedly the tomb of St James) was well established as Europe's foremost pilgrimage site. The devout from far and wide trudged well-worn routes to offer their prayers and alms at the cathedral, built in 899. The razing of Santiago by al-Mansur in 997 outraged the whole of Christian Europe and provoked a fresh wave of anti-Muslim fervour. Thereafter, the shrine and the new cathedral, which was a-building from 1078 to 1211, drew into even sharper focus the fatal clash of cultures. So totally was Islam identified with ultimate evil that a *chanson* dealing with the Carolingian struggle against the Vikings claimed that the Northmen waged war in league with the Saracens. Nor was there any understanding of what Muslims actually believed; many of the songs assumed that, like other pagans, the Saracens were polytheistic. This is the highly emotional background to *Roland* and other *chansons*.

The event celebrated by the poem is the massacre of Charlemagne's rearguard at Roncesvalles. Roland of the Breton March is in charge of this section of the army, assisted by his friends, Oliver (a fictitious character) and Archbishop Turpin of Rheims. Before the return journey through the Pyrenean passes the rearguard has been betrayed by Roland's enemy, Ganelon, to the Saracen leader, Baligant. When the Christian knights realise that they have been caught in a trap and are confronted by five contingents of the enemy, the friends urgently review their tactical options. Oliver urges Roland to blow his ivory horn to summon Charlemagne and the main army to their aid, but the headstrong Roland refuses, determined to fulfil to the letter the task assigned to him. The heroic Franks account for four of the Muslim hosts before the horn is sounded. Charlemagne arrives, but too late to save his brave and loyal vassals. He does, however, avenge them. The traitor, Ganelon, is torn apart by being tied to wild stallions, and the emperor disposes of Baligant in fierce single combat.

Though Charlemagne's appearance in the *chanson* is brief, his personality dominates it. He provides the focal point of the two themes that underlie the story: the fight between good and evil and the stability of feudal society. Charles is the ruler chosen by God as defender of the Church and the leader against the forces of darkness. He is also the vassal-in-chief under God of all his people. The argument between Roland and Oliver is about how best to interpret loyalty to a man's overlord. Ganelon's horrific death underlines the heinousness of his crime, for what could be more vile than plotting against the king? The *Chanson de Roland* is all about the cohesion of Christian society, threatened from within and without. Charlemagne was the personification of this theme, a king who commanded the devotion of his warriors and who took the foremost of them into his councils. He was the model of ideal monarchy for medieval kings, just as the system he headed was the model for sustaining the ideal society.

It was not long before the mythical Charlemagne assumed a yet more elaborate and ambitious identity. This was enshrined, not in a song for the entertainment of its hearers, but in what purported to be a serious work of history for their instruction and inspiration. *The Story of Charlemagne and Roland*, better known as *The Chronicle of Pseudo-Turpin*, was a forgery of the late eleventh century, which fooled scholars for almost 300 years. It breathes the air of the cloister rather than the military camp; it is a churchman's version of the Spanish adventure. Supposedly written by the very Turpin who fell at Roncesvalles, this piece of ecclesiastical propaganda deliberately uses the popular Roland story as a hook and embellishes it to point a different moral. This monk's Charlemagne is above all a faithful son of mother Church, who invades Spain in obedience to a vision, in order to drive the Saracens out of Santiago, and then goes on to mount a fourteen-year crusade against the enemies of the Cross. A *jongleur* would simply have added these exploits to his repertoire, but for the chronicler things were not quite so simple. He had a major hurdle to overcome in his attempt to gain credibility: the absence of any reference in earlier annals to Charlemagne's lengthy commitment to the war in Spain. He deals in an almost casual way with this problem: 'These events', he says, 'took place a long way from where the annals were written and since the annalists had never been to Spain they knew nothing of what passed there.' His 'newly discovered' document, he blithely asserts, now fills the gap in the record. In fact, he was presenting a new message for a new age. It was a tract for the Church Militant.

The background to *Pseudo-Turpin* was the heightened Muslim–Christian conflict of the late eleventh and early twelfth centuries. The union of Aragon and Navarre in 1076 gave fresh impetus to the *reconquista* while, at the same time, the explosion of the Seljuk Turks into Asia Minor created a new crisis for the Eastern Empire. When the Byzantine emperor turned to Rome for aid, his appeal did not fall on deaf ears. The papacy had, at long last, dragged itself out of the moral slough and, under a succession of foreign popes not enslaved by local politics, had adopted fiercely interventionist attitudes in the wider Church and world. This new breed of pontiffs championed reform, and went onto the offensive against emperors and kings who had grown accustomed to exercising considerable power over the churches in their lands. Three landmark events indicate just how much had changed since Charlemagne's day. In 1053, Leo IX in person led an army against an invading Norman host instead of relying on the emperor to fight his battles for him. In 1076, Gregory VII excommunicated the emperor Henry IV, declared him deposed and obliged him to grovel for absolution. In 1095, Urban II proclaimed the First Crusade. Such activities by no means established without opposition that the pope was the leader of Latin Christendom in matters temporal, as well as spiritual, but they laid down very clear markers.

Hitherto the Church had, at least in theory, promoted peace and abhorred war. Now it was teaching that the sword not only could, but should, be wielded in the cause of faith. Urban was undoubtedly passionate about giving aid to fellow Christians in the East, but his call to arms also served his political aims. As a Frenchman he was particularly outraged by the corruption of the royal court and welcomed the opportunity to appeal over the head of Philip I, whom he excommunicated, to his military and ecclesiastical vassals. For the papacy to achieve what Urban believed to be its God-given position in society inevitably involved a challenge to feudalism.

The power struggle between clergy and lay rulers had become a defining element in medieval life, as the troubadours sang to their sympathetic knightly audiences:

> Once, kings and emperors,
> Dukes, counts and officers,
> Valiant knights of theirs,
> Governed the land.
> I see the clergy stand
> In the lords' places,
> Traitors and thieves
> Who have hypocrites' faces.

Urban cleverly chose Clermont in the Auvergne to launch his great initiative. It was a place not far off the pilgrimage route to Santiago and close to the spiritual power-house of the great abbey of Cluny. Here the homage owed by local rulers to the king meant very little. The pope chose an outdoor site and, addressing a large crowd comprising all sorts and conditions of men, he promised, 'whoever for devotion alone . . . shall set out to free the church of God at Jerusalem, that shall be counted to him for all penance' (in other words, all their sins would be forgiven and, if they died in the attempt, they would be in a state of grace). In an enthusiastic frenzy, men fell over themselves to enlist. The crusading movement was born. It would last for six or seven generations.

What the author of *Pseudo-Turpin* did was provide this movement with a super-hero. On campaign, miracles attend his progress, and at home he establishes a regime of justice and unity. Yet Charlemagne is not presented as a perfect human being. He has his faults. From among them the author singles out the emperor's incestuous relationship with his own sister, which results in the birth of Roland. The romantic hero is, thus, identified as Charles' illegitimate son. The moral here is that all men are sinners and stand in need of the ministrations of holy Church.

Yet it was in a different doctoring of the historical record that our unknown monk was to have the most fateful impact on the future. He appears to have had close connections with the royal abbey of Saint-Denis, where certain Charlemagne relics had long been housed, and where most of the kings since the seventh century were buried. He presented Charles as a thoroughly *French* hero. The fact that the ancient capital of Aachen did not lie within France's boundaries was dismissed by the simple expedient of claiming Paris as Charlemagne's real centre of government. Yet another forgery was brought forth to reinforce this claim. According to the *Donation of Charlemagne*, the kingdom had been granted to the abbey and commended to the protection of the nation's patron saint. The whole fiction was given magnificent, symbolic permanence by the reconstruction of the abbey church, the first expression of a new style, the Gothic. Abbot Suger, a friend of Louis VI, masterminded the new building, which spectacularly extended the existing Carolingian church, and work continued until well into the thirteenth century to create the building that would be the inspiration for Chartres and other great French cathedrals.

The author of *Pseudo-Turpin* sowed yet more seeds of nationalistic expansionism by identifying his subject as a *salvator mundi* whose posterity (that is, the French royal house) was divinely ordained to rule the world. At the time that *Pseudo-Turpin* was probably written, it would have seemed very unlikely that the French king could aspire to the conquests and achievements of his great predecessor. Philip I's writ scarcely ran outside the Île-de-France. However, over the next 115 years France experienced the rule of three long-lived and competent monarchs. During their reigns the Charlemagne myth came to be tightly woven into the ambitions of the Capetian dynasty. From the time of Louis VI, French kings associated themselves visually with the ancient hero by adopting the Oriflamme, a red and gold banner kept at Saint-Denis and purporting to be a standard given by the pope to Charlemagne. When the French army saw off an invasion attempt by the German Emperor, Henry V (1124), their success was piously attributed to their holy banner. Louis VII specifically associated himself with the growing volume of legend. He led the flower of French chivalry that set out on the Second Crusade in 1145 and, in later years, he made pilgrimages to Santiago and Canterbury. Philip II Augustus proudly claimed descent from Charlemagne on both sides of his family. When he went forth to the Third Crusade (1190) he had the Oriflamme borne before him. By this time *The Pilgrimage of Charlemagne to Constantinople and Jerusalem* had been written, further strengthening the link between the Charlemagne myth and the French royal house. The depiction of the emperor setting out with his bravely decked knights in attendance cannot fail to have stirred among the hearers memories of their own kings departing on similar holy missions. They may well have been more disposed to believe the inevitable wonder-stories that littered the text: the Franks' welcome in the fabulously wealthy Byzantine court; Oliver making love to the Greek emperor's daughter a hundred times in one night; the astonished veneration that Charles receives from the Patriarch of Jerusalem. *Pseudo-Turpin* and *The Pilgrimage of Charlemagne* projected the emperor onto an international stage, and *jongleurs* were not slow to add these new adventures to their stock in trade.

However, the French were not allowed to take sole possession of the legend. The German emperors made claims every bit as grandiose as those of their counterparts in Paris. For support they had their own extensive Charlemagne literature, including the *Rolandslied*, a version of the *Chanson de Roland*, and royal chronicles that traced succeeding imperial families back to the great Carolingian. More importantly, they had Aachen, and successive emperors continued to use Charlemagne's resting place to bolster their own authority. Unlike France, the eastern part of the old Frankish empire was not being brought gradually under the centralised rule of one hereditary family. Autonomous dukes and princes elected one of their number to be their leader, and the pope still asserted his right to crown the chosen candidate. Those who aspired to gain and hold the position of Holy Roman Emperor almost inevitably found their power challenged by their own peers and by Rome. Periodically their lives were also complicated by wars against France, involvement in the affairs of Italy and arguments over status with the *other* emperor in Constantinople. Asserting their supremacy involved military prowess, resisting papal encroachments on their authority and taking a lead in European affairs such as crusades. In all of these they appealed to Charlemagne as progenitor and model.

In the 1160s a major crisis threatened to split western Christendom permanently. The emperor Frederick I Barbarossa was the latest German ruler to find himself at loggerheads with the papacy. Frederick refused to recognise Pope Alexander III, and Pope Alexander III pronounced Frederick excommunicate. The pope sought protection in France. Frederick appointed a rival as Paschal III. No one was prepared to give way and the schism seemed set to continue indefinitely. However, some of the German princes were uneasy at the situation, and it was largely in order to secure his homeland base that the emperor made a spectacular appeal to the memory of Charlemagne. He had the legendary hero canonised by his own tame antipope. This action was never endorsed by any universally recognised pope, but to this day St Charlemagne is widely venerated throughout Europe. As part of the process of canonisation, a search was once again made for the saint's tomb. According to the official story, its location had been forgotten since the time of Otto III, but now a 'divine revelation' led the emperor to it. By these actions Frederick not only appealed to the patriotism of the German peoples and demonstrated that God was on his side in his conflict with Alexander; he also challenged the pretensions of Louis VII to be the true heir of Charles the Great. Two hundred years later the French, not to be outdone, elected Charlemagne as patron saint of the nation alongside the third-century martyr St Denis. When the Third Crusade was announced, Barbarossa took his place beside Philip Augustus and Richard I of England as joint leader.

Twenty-five years later it was his grandson, Frederick II, who found himself having to 'play the Charlemagne card'. He was nominated in infancy to succeed his father, Henry VI, but Henry's sudden death at the age of thirty-two effectively threw the German crown into the scrum and plunged the imperial lands into years of anarchy. Otto of Brunswick eventually emerged victorious, but still had many enemies and succeeded in alienating Pope Innocent III, who, true to form, excommunicated him. Frederick, meanwhile, had grown into a determined and charismatic teenager intent on recovering his birthright. At the age of seventeen he launched his challenge and, with the aid of Philip Augustus, overthrew his rival. At every stage of the campaign he needed to win over the princes and nobles of the various states, and it was with this in mind that he, too, chose Aachen as the setting for a dramatic gesture. He took the city in the summer of 1215. Shortly afterwards he made a ceremonial triumphant entry and the very next day had himself crowned there with all traditional pomp and ceremony. That was only the beginning. Frederick remained in the cathedral after the coronation to listen to a succession of sermons challenging him and his knights to take up the crusaders' cross. Afterwards, to emphasise his identification with Charlemagne, he had the bones of the dead emperor disturbed once more. Frederick had an ornate reliquary wrought in silver and gold and Charlemagne's remains were reverently placed in it. According to the chronicler, the young emperor laboured himself alongside the workmen hired to install the new shrine. Frederick understood the importance of PR.

The waging of war against Muslims, war between Christian rulers, the establishment of centralised royal power, the supremacy of emperor over pope, the supremacy of pope over emperor, the importance of pilgrimage, the undergirding of feudalism – the Charlemagne myth was pressed into service to justify all these. So powerful was the abiding fame of the Carolingian monarch that politicians and propagandists of all stamps used it to support whatever policies and actions they wished to implement. Just as followers of various orthodoxies and heresies pulled proof texts out of the Bible, so Europe's temporal and spiritual leaders dipped into the growing corpus of Charlemagne legend to find reasons and excuses for what they had already decided to do.

Yet there was one area of medieval thought that was closely in touch with the genuine ideals of the Frankish emperor. One might almost say that Charles' shade stood as guardian over the conscience of the age in this particular aspect of its life. His concerns and proscriptions were foundational to what became the code of knightly behaviour – chivalry. Among the numerous virtues for which he was venerated was that of being a wise law-giver. In the capitularies that poured from his chancellery, Charlemagne not only sought to create a just and stable society, but attempted to encase Christian morality within a framework of law. Many were the exhortations that his *missi* toured the empire delivering to the local counts and dukes. Perhaps they might all be summed up in words from a capitulary of 802, in which the emperor ordained that every man should strive 'to maintain himself in God's holy service, according to God's command and his own promise'.[4] The unity and cohesion of society for which Charles strove throughout his reign was to be based on a system of mutual interdependence in which imperial officials, magnates, churchmen, minor landholders and peasants were tied together by bonds of allegiance and support. The emperor extracted oaths from all his subjects and laid out in some detail what was expected of each rank.

Aristocrats and all members of the warrior caste had particularly heavy responsibilities because of the sheer power they wielded and because of the code they inherited based on dynastic pride and territorial rivalry. The ruler's dilemma was that he needed the military prowess of these men, and the contingents of armed followers they contributed to his campaigns, but their capacity for destructive private warfare and their tendency to exploit underlings made them a dangerously destabilising element in society. The rules that Charles issued over and again set down standards of behaviour, but also tried to instil some ethical principles into the thinking of the warrior community. They were to maintain their vows to the emperor and their feudal overlords. They were to avoid blood-feuds. They were to administer justice impartially. They were to support the Church and be ready to take the field against unbelievers. They were to protect widows and orphans. This was a mix of pragmatism and idealism, and its effectiveness in motivating the secular leaders of society was decidedly limited. The disintegration of Charles' empire into numerous petty, feuding states is sufficient indication that appeal to higher ideals failed to make much impression on the underlying aggressive ethos of the warrior class.

No less than kings and emperors, popes found it difficult to deal with the military element in society. Christianity is a religion of peace, and men who devoted their lives to war were theoretically regarded as thugs. The only way a warrior could be sure of salvation was to renounce his profession and enter the cloister to atone for his sins. In reality the Church could not afford to maintain this high moral tone. Popes, bishops and abbots frequently needed the men of war. For centuries theologians grappled with theories about the 'just war', but, at the same time, the ecclesiastical hierarchy quietly got on with the business of having their cake and eating it. Officially they stuck to their founder's principles while, at the same time, employing armies to defend their rights and property.

It was the emergence of a more militant Christianity in the eleventh century, and the stretching of doctrine to cover it, that changed the official status of the knight. When popes competed with emperors for the leadership of Christianity, and when bishops began to lead their own military contingents to war, distinctions became blurred. Now churchmen insisted that the duties of the *milites christiani* included offensive action against pagans and heretics:

> In our time God has instituted holy warfare so that the knightly order and the unsettled populace, who used to be engaged like the pagans of old in slaughtering one another, should find a new way of deserving salvation. No longer are they obliged to leave the world and choose a monastic way of life . . . but in their accustomed liberty and habit, by performing their own office, they may in some measure achieve the grace of God.[5]

So wrote Abbot Guibert of Nogent in 1108 and, as we have seen, the sanctification of the profession of arms was reflected not only in the call to the crusades, but also in the character of the *chansons*, which – as well as lauding the feudal virtues of duty, sacrifice and loyalty to one's lord – advocated religious war against the unspeakable evil of Islam. Horace's dictum, *dulce et decorum est pro patria mori*, may be the 'old lie', but it has always exerted enormous power over men. In every age some such mantra has been offered to those who need justification for giving free rein to their aggressive instincts. 'King and country', 'hearth and home', 'freedom' – all these have been taken up as battle cries by those setting out to massacre their fellow men. In the Middle Ages the excuse was the defence of the faith.

The way was now open for chivalry, the code of the mounted warrior, to develop a semi-mystical character. Orders of knighthood were founded, beginning with the crusading fraternities, the Templars and Hospitallers. These had very clear functions in protecting pilgrims and maintaining access for Christians to the Holy Land, but over the next couple of centuries the idea of the knightly order took on an increasingly fantastic character and became intimately bound up with royal prestige. Kings and princes vied with each other to found exclusive orders – the Garter, the Golden Fleece, the Star, the Sword, etc. – hedged about with arcane ritual (a sort of medieval Freemasonry). At root the chivalric ideal involved submission to God. Just as a king, going on crusade, metaphorically laid his realm at the foot of the Cross, so all knights devoted themselves to the Almighty, renouncing worldly diversions. They were called to holiness of living, were to attend mass daily, fast on Fridays, show themselves honourable towards women and set a good example to their social inferiors. The ceremonies of initiation to knighthood became ever more dramatic and elaborate. Those to be admitted took a bath, to symbolise the washing away of the old life, their hair and beards were trimmed, then they held an all-night vigil in church or chapel. The following day they attended mass, swore solemn oaths and were ceremonially invested with sword, spurs and robes. That, at least, was the ideal.

In reality it proved impossible wholly to sanctify the bloody business of war or to disinvest it of the spurious glamour that has always been part of the soldier's life. Hitherto the warrior class had been a self-conscious, self-regarding elite, but now the development of the art of mounted warfare – with its attendant heraldic splendours and elaborate rituals – produced an arrogant, gang culture, which revelled in its own machismo and paid only lip-service to cultural refinement and spiritual values. A young man being received into the knightly corps might fulfil all the attendant holy rites, but he was also excited at being admitted to a privileged brother-hood of celebrities and this could well outweigh the solemnity of the occasion. When two·royal princes were knighted in 1389 at the abbey of Saint-Denis, the monks found the proceedings far from edifying:

> The lords, in making day of night and giving themselves up to all excesses of the table, were driven by drunkenness to all such disor-ders, that, without respect of the king's presence, several of them sullied the sanctity of the religious house, and abandoned themselves to libertinage and adultery.[6]

Such behaviour was as nothing compared with what the armies of Christ did, once they were unleashed on their enemies. The crusades are a long horror story of human savagery; of atrocities not only against the armies of Islam, but also against Christian cities; of ports and garrisons put to the sword; of allies turning against each other; of national rivalries being fought out in distant lands. An estimated 70,000 defenceless citizens perished in the first onslaught on Jerusalem. The earliest European pogrom was perpetrated in 1096 when 7,000 Jews were massacred in the Rhineland. In 1203, when the leaders of the Fourth Crusade were deflected from their declared objec-tive of liberating the Holy Land settlements and turned their fury on Constantinople, the looting went on for years. The eastern capital was stripped of everything beautiful or valuable. Churches and palaces alike were looted and their contents carried back to the West. Reliquaries and statues were broken up and melted down for the sake of their precious metals and gems. These and a thousand other obscenities were condemned, not just by later historians, but also by outraged contemporaries. As the survivors straggled home with their stories of the horrors they had witnessed, it became obvious to anyone not blinkered by insane bravado that the chivalric ideal had been prostituted in the interests of the baser instincts of the participants.

Were any lessons learned?

> The crusaders of 1396 started out with a strategic purpose in the expulsion of the Turks from Europe, but their minds were on something else. The young men . . . born since the Black Death . . . and the nadir of French fortunes harked back to pursuit of those strange bewitchments, honour and glory. They thought only of being in the vanguard, to the exclusion of reconnaissance, tactical plan and common sense, and for that their heads were to roll in the blood-soaked sand at the Sultan's feet.[7]

Such was Barbara Tuchman's verdict on the Nicopolis Crusade, virtually the last expedition that could be called a crusade. For more than 300 years, and even overarching the Black Death, which changed so many perceptions in Europe, chivalric notions remained a prominent strand in the motivation of knights who set out eastwards in search of military adventure.

And Charlemagne's place in the bellicose propaganda of holy war? It was central. By the mid-twelfth century no one doubted that the holy emperor had been the prototype crusader who had fought the infidel in Spain and marched beneath the Oriflamme to the very portals of Jerusalem. The legend outlived the collapse of the crusader states in the Holy Land, because the loss of the last Christian fortresses in 1291 did not put an end to the conflict. The Seljuk state collapsed, but only to be replaced by the Ottoman Empire, which began its expansion into Anatolia and the Balkans in the fourteenth century. As long as Christendom had an alien and potentially aggressive eastern neighbour there would be periodic alliances of European rulers to deal with the threat. Opinion-framers continued to appeal to the memory of a supposed golden age when a great Christian monarch had ruled Europe and wielded his victorious sword against the Islamic hordes. From the early fourteenth century Charlemagne had a place among the so-called 'Nine Worthies' of history. This list of legendary heroes included the Old Testament leaders, David, Joshua and Judas Maccabaeus; the classical champions, Hector, Alexander and Caesar; and the Christians, Arthur, Charlemagne and Godfrey of Bouillon. One of the first printed books in Burgundy was *Chroniques et Conquestes de Charlemagne*. Published in 1478, it was an immediate best-seller. During the next century it went through twenty-six editions.

Notes

1 *Einhard and Notker*, pp.163–4
2 Ibid., p.164
3 Ibid., p.93
4 R. Collins, *Charlemagne*, 2000, p.155
5 See C. Morris, *The Papal Monarchy, the Western Church from 1050 to 1250*, Oxford, 1989, p.337
6 See R. Barber, *The Knight and Chivalry*, 1970, p.47
7 B. W. Tuchman, *A Distant Mirror*, 1979, p.563

11

Imperial Fantasies

On 7 April 1498 the twenty-eight-year-old King Charles VIII of France was taken with a fit of apoplexy and expired on a pile of urine-soaked straw. It was a humiliating end for a young exotic who had seen himself as a reincarnated Charlemagne. Veneration for the national saint had coloured Charles' upbringing. His father, Louis XI, had instituted a holy day in Charlemagne's honour and ordered its observance on pain of death. This was part of the old king's programme of political reform, the final subjection of the semi-autonomous nobles and the establishment of a strong monarchy with almost unrestrained powers. Louis, a cunning ruler widely known as the 'Spider', took every opportunity to appeal to ordinary Frenchmen over the heads of the aristocracy and call upon their patriotism. In his propaganda he made full use of the well-known legends. Thus, when his heir was married to Anne of Britanny, in 1492, cheering crowds were treated to the spectacle of the bride being received at the gates of Paris by a mounted figure representing Charlemagne, who brought in his train an elephant and other exotic beasts. Everyone would have recognised the allusion to the animals presented to the emperor by Harun al-Raschid. When the royal couple had a son, he was baptised 'Charles-Roland'.

As a part of his political reform Louis enhanced the power of the *parlement de Paris*. He provided it with suitably impressive accommodation, and pride of place in the debating chamber was given to a large triptych, painted earlier as an altarpiece, and now relocated to impress the representatives of the people. This *Retable du Parlement* was loaded with symbolism. Beneath the crucifixion scene sat the enthroned Louis XI. The two outer panels were occupied by a company of saints. On the extreme right stood Charlemagne, next to the decapitated St Denis, blood gushing from his neck. Despite his location at one side of the composition, the emperor seemed to dominate it. Sumptuously robed, he carried the orb and the sword of justice and stared straight out of the painting, as though presiding over the proceedings of the *parlement*.

Charles VIII was, to put it politely, intellectually challenged. He was a sickly and unprepossessing young man, but he believed it was his destiny to make a major mark on history, to be another Charlemagne. He had grandiose plans for a new crusade to the Holy Land and, as a first stage, he marched into Italy, preceded by the Oriflamme, to conquer the Kingdom of Naples, currently ruled by the house of Aragon. The connection may seem tenuous to us, but to Charles the issue was straightforward enough. He claimed to be the fulfilment of an ancient prophecy that the saviour of Italy would come from the French royal house and that this champion would go on to 'rule the world'. Not only did Charles have a dynastic claim to the kingdom, which embraced the whole of southern Italy, but one of the titles still claimed by the King of Naples was King of Jerusalem. Furthermore, for his own political reasons, Pope Alexander VI (the notorious Rodrigo Borgia) welcomed the French king's intervention, so that Charles could claim that he was crossing the Alps as protector of the Church. A more significant element of his propaganda was that he came as the descendant of that great champion who had delivered Italy from 'Germanic barbarism' (that is, the Lombards). If the challenge to the Holy Roman Emperor was not blatant, it was certainly implicit.

Having borrowed heavily to furnish his grandiose expedition, Charles set out on his great adventure in the autumn of 1494. Italian allies, eager to shrug off the Spanish yoke, hurried to join him, and the 'saviour of Italy' marched unopposed into Naples the following February. However, defeat rose swiftly from the ashes of victory. The appalling behaviour of the French sickened those who had thrown open their gates to them, and Charles had utterly failed to take the measure of his wily allies. The leaders of the northern Italian states were skilled quick-change artists. As soon as the French king set off for home, they banded against him and entered a league with Ferdinand of Aragon. In little more than a year the Spanish had resumed control of their territory and the great enterprise had ended as a bloody shambles. Charles' glorious ambition, however, seems to have been undimmed by its encounter with the harsh realities of war and politics. He was planning more ventures when sudden death intervened a year later.

Charles VIII's expedition might have been regarded as an irrelevant folly, were it not seen in relation to two events that were to shape the history of Europe for centuries. In 1452 the pope crowned the first Holy Roman Emperor of the house of Habsburg. The next year the Turks overran Constantinople. What followed was an intensification of both internal and external tension. The rivalry between France and the empire reached new heights as the houses of Habsburg and Valois wrestled for leadership of Europe. Meanwhile, the eastern borders of Europe once more assumed the nature of marchland as the Ottomans forced their way through the Balkans and Hungary up to the very gates of Vienna (1529). Once again Christendom was under threat from forces without and within.

It is not surprising that people took comfort from apocalyptic prophecies that spoke of new saviours who would arise to lead one last crusade against the infidel, and that rival kings should identify themselves with such messianic visions. The popular myths looked both backward and forward. They spoke of a Charlemagne or a Frederick Barbarossa who were but sleeping until the divine trumpet call summoned them once more to lead Christendom in that final battle that should usher in the last days. More disturbing was the tone of fanatical nationalism that characterised the millenarian tracts which circulated in increasing numbers after the establishment of the first printing presses. The chosen one could only emerge from the chosen people, who were either German or French, depending on where the text in question originated. Thus, the *Book of a Hundred Chapters* spoke of an emperor who would emerge from the Black Forest and establish a thousand-year reich. He would:

> Come on a white horse and will have a bow in his hand and a crown shall be given him by God so that he shall have power to compel the whole world; he will have a great sword in his hand and will strike many down.

The enemies singled out for annihilation by this sanguinary champion are not merely unbelievers. They are all those whom the author finds particularly objectionable: usurious moneylenders, corrupt officials, luxury-loving nobles, lazy monks and nuns and, above all, the clergy. The writer draws on the hatred of Rome that had become common in many German lands. He envisages that the all-purging emperor will cut down 2,300 clerics every day for four and a half years and establish his own purified church independent of Rome.[1]

The projectors of these terrifying visions did not invariably appeal to the Charlemagne legends, but the once-and-future emperor was part and parcel of the popular apocalyptic expectation. He certainly loomed large in the thinking of those who coveted the imperial crown. Frederick, the first Habsburg emperor, craved a historic role. He was scarcely less cast in the historic mould than Charles VIII, being fat, scholarly and, according to one source, 'cold, phlegmatic and parsimonious'. Yet he was determined to build the greatness of his house and of Christian Europe. His wide reading set his feet firmly on a mystic path. He devoted much time to a quest for the philosopher's stone and no less endeavour to its political counterpart, the spiritual power that would unite Christendom and transmute the whole world into the kingdom of God.

We must not underestimate the power of this vision, which persisted at all levels of society until well into the second half of the sixteenth century. It had an impeccable pedigree. Jesus himself had declared that the Gospel must be 'preached through all the world for a witness to all mankind and then the end will come' (Matthew 24.14). For one and a half millennia Christians had longed for the fulfilment of this prophecy and worked for it by spreading the message through proclamation and holy living, but, as we have seen, the Church had been seduced by apparent shortcuts. By alliance with Christian rulers it had looked to widen its bounds by sword-point conversions and draconian laws. A corrupt hierarchy had laboured for expansion and internal unity by crusade, inquisition, thought control and priestly 'magic'. But the concept of a united, militant Christendom was increasingly being strained at the seams. Not only did the behaviour of the knights of the Cross make a mockery of Christian ethics, the rivalries of kings and magnates tarnish the image of Christian brotherhood, and the spectacle of competing popes create a continuing Christian scandal, but the very spiritual intensity on which church leaders relied spawned a growing number of heretical sects. On the eve of the Reformation, Europe was experiencing not a rejection of traditional faith, but an upsurge of religious zeal that traditional devotional disciplines could no longer contain. The appeal of old myths, which were mixes of biblical truth, romantic legend and national pride, was never stronger.

Early in his life Frederick III went on pilgrimage to the Holy Land. In preparation for his imperial coronation in 1440 he made a thorough study of all the ancient rites, and the resulting ceremony at Aachen was the most elaborate that had been seen there in centuries. Frederick ordered impressive new robes and jewels and insisted on all the church's holy relics being brought out. Most significantly, he donned the crown of Charlemagne, a precious artefact that had rarely been worn since the ninth century. Twelve years later, when he travelled to Rome for a second coronation, Frederick took the crown of Charlemagne with him for the solemn ritual. This imperial coronation, the last to be held in Rome, thus harked back to the first such event, six and a half centuries before. Frederick III never lived up to the standard he had set himself, but he did, by a clever system of marriage alliances, establish the territorial power of the Habsburgs and hand on to his son, Maximilian, a secure political base upon which he could build yet more exotic messianic fantasies.

It might be thought that in the age of the Renaissance, which reached back across the medieval 'void' to the supposed sophistication and harmony of the classical world, there would be no room for post-Roman myths and superstitions. Many medieval concepts and thought processes were, indeed, jettisoned by the intelligentsia of the New Learning. As we shall see, Renaissance scholarship was soon employed in demythologising the Charlemagne story. However, the more vigorous elements of common culture survived. Because innovative technologies and techniques were, in themselves, neutral, they could be used to give expression to any ideas. Given a patron or an assured market, the manufacturers of paintings, sculptures, books, pamphlets and engravings would deliver whatever their customers wanted. And the Habsburg and Valois courts wanted powerful propaganda to enhance the standing and ambitions of their princes.

The cult of chivalry did not survive the sixteenth century, but it went out in a blaze of glory as Europe's competing monarchs employed writers, artists and the impresarios of ever more elaborate knightly tournaments for diplomatic and public-relations purposes. Kings employed 'genealogists' to trace their ancestry through all the 'greats' of history – Charlemagne, Arthur and Constantine and so on right back to the heroes of the Trojan War:

> From the very roots of Arthurian romance to the deeds of Maximilian
> I disguised in fictional form, the borderline between the romantic
> dream world and the military reality was always indistinct: history
> was subject to the vagaries of imagination, and the chivalric figments
> of the mind posed as sober truth.[2]

Fortunes were spent on magnificent suits of gilded, damascened armour. Whole national treasuries were emptied to provide for the theatricalities of war. Taxpayers were further burdened so that their sovereigns could preen themselves in stunning displays of dynastic *gloire* such as the Field of Cloth of Gold (1520), at which Francis I and Henry VIII of England strove mightily to outdo one another in conspicuous consumption.

In German lands newly discovered classical documents provided Renaissance scholars with more ammunition to assert the superiority of their own culture. In the 1470s the *Annals* and *Germania* of the first–second century historian, Tacitus, were published and excited Germans could read for the first time how their ancestors had humiliated the Roman legions. Conrad Celtis, crowned as the first native poet laureate of the empire in 1487, used such reappraisals of history to stir up a pan-Germanism which would unite the numerous petty states into which the eastern part of Charlemagne's empire had become divided:

> Behold the frontiers of Germany: gather together her torn and shat-
> tered lands! Let us feel shame, yes, shame, I say have to let our nation
> assume the yoke of slavery.[3]

Other scholars took up the banner of German national identity which was to become a rallying point for many who denounced the interfer-ence of a decadent papacy in their affairs. In 1495 Hans von Hermansgrün published *Somnium*, the account of a dream in which Charlemagne, Otto I and Frederick Barbarossa met together to urge their descendants to throw off the humiliation of having lost lands to France and influence to Rome. In his *Chronicles of Memorable Things of Every Age and All Peoples* (1516) Johannes Nauclerus asserted that Charlemagne's coronation signified God's removal of imperial power from the Byzantines to the Germans who were, thus, destined to rule Europe.

But the most influential publication was the *Prognosticatio* of Johann Lichtenberger. This almanac of prophecies first appeared in 1488 and was reprinted every year for almost half a century, nor is it difficult to see why it was so popular. Its forecasting of future events was couched in lurid prose and it fascinated thousands of readers just as Nostradamus' *Centuries* and *Old Moore's Almanac* would in future centuries. As is the manner of such semi-mystic productions, the *Prognosticatio* was couched in vague, ambiguous language. Readers interpreted it according to their own fancies. However, when the author referred to the imminent arrival of a great German leader who would be a second Charlemagne the iden-tification with the next Holy Roman Emperor, Maximilian I, was fairly obvious.

Maximilian, who was crowned King of the Romans (heir to the empire) at Aachen in 1486 and succeeded his father in 1493, was a *Wunderkind*. Impressive of bearing, intelligent, a skilled military tactician, affable, a master of several languages, a generous patron of artists – here, surely, was the new Charlemagne, the great emperor of the last age. Thus many of his subjects believed and thus Maximilian himself was convinced. He was only thirty-four when he assumed sole rule of the Habsburg lands and leadership of the German people but he had already – by marriage, inheritance and war – added Burgundy, the Netherlands and the Tyrol to his dominions, as well as securing the reversion of Hungary and Bohemia on the death of the existing incumbent. He had twice bested France in major engagements. Maximilian dazzled Europe with his achievements and the brilliance of his court but he was determined to make an even greater impression on his contemporaries and on posterity.

The emperor well understood that image is everything, especially in a land most of whose population was illiterate. He intended that everyone should recognise him, his achievements, his ancestry and his destiny as *salvator mundi*, so he commissioned paintings, sculptures, coins and medals – any artefact that would aid the ubiquity of the imperial presence. But the most bizarre and original works he ordered were the *Triumphal Arch* and the *Triumphal Procession*. Everyone was familiar with the concept of these elements of public celebration. Royal visits, marriages and anniversaries featured elaborate processions through streets lined with bunting and marked by elaborate timber and canvas constructions in honour of the dignitaries being welcomed. Maximilian took these familiar things and had them represented in the most familiar popular art form, the woodcut engraving. He employed the leading craftsmen of the day, including Albrecht Dürer, Albrecht Altdorfer and Hans Burgkmaier to produce hundreds of printed sheets, which could then be pasted together to form the largest engravings ever made. The *Procession* was never completed, but the *Arch* was made up of 192 separate woodcuts which, when amalgamated, covered ten square metres with elaborate and intricate designs glorifying the emperor and presenting him to the beholders as a latterday Charlemagne.

As well as building an impressive territorial base, Maximilian emulated his illustrious predecessor in his relations with the Church. He extended imperial control over the ecclesiastical hierarchy in Habsburg dominions. He called for the convening of a general council to redress the creeping corruption spreading outwards from Rome. In 1511, when Julius II fell seriously ill, he even considered putting himself forward for election as the next pope. Finally, lest anyone should doubt his multi-faceted genius, Maximilian planned a three-volume book – part-autobiography, part-romantic fantasy – that would ensure his continuing fame.

Where the emperor led, those seeking favour followed. The city fathers of Nuremberg ordered from Dürer two larger-than-life figures of the emperors Charlemagne and Sigismund to adorn the relic chamber of the Schopper House in the market place. All the imperial coronation regalia, including Charlemagne's crown, were kept in Nuremberg's Hospital of the Holy Spirit, but once a year, by Maximilian's decree, they were brought under armed guard to the Schopper House so that the public could come and marvel at these impressive historical symbols of their emperor's authority. As they did so, they now came under the formidable gaze of the empire's presiding saint.

Other cultural centres also boasted Renaissance representations of Charles the Great. The Vatican was just as adept as the imperial court at employing the new generation of artists for propaganda purposes. In 1516 Leo X commissioned a fresco from the studio of Raphael. Its subject was to be the *Coronation of Charlemagne* and it was to remind a generation of temporal rulers intent on establishing national churches and loosening their ties with Rome just where their authority came from. But the painting had a much more immediate political point to make. Two contemporary portraits appeared within the composition: Leo X had himself displayed in the guise of his predecessor, Leo III, and the face of 'Charlemagne' was actually that of Francis I. The Italian states were, as we have seen, highly vulnerable to the dislocation brought about by Franco–Spanish rivalry, and Leo had, somehow, to steer the papacy through the increasingly turbulent waters of European diplomacy. In fact, although he could not know (or chose not to acknowledge) it, the Roman Church approached the brink of its biggest ever crisis between 1515 and 1521. The papacy had not freed itself from the stench of worldliness and corruption given off by the Borgias and it was becoming increasingly difficult to ignore the clamour for a reforming council, which, among other things, would limit the power of the pope. It was Leo's refusal to address himself to ecclesiastical abuses that, in 1517, provoked an obscure university lecturer, named Martin Luther, to issue that challenge which ushered in the Reformation. In 1515 the young, ambitious and highly volatile Francis I became King of France. He had his sights on the imperial crown and his agents were soon wooing the German electoral princes in anticipation of Maximilian's demise. The Habsburg candidate was Charles (subsequently elected as Charles V) who, by inheriting the crowns of both Aragon and Castile, was master of Spain and Naples. Leo did not relish the thought of either of these superpowers gaining the upper hand in Europe. For the moment, however, France seemed the better bet. Leo reached an agreement with Francis, known as the Concordat of Bologna, which in effect ceded to the king the right to appoint all senior ecclesiastics in his territory, and it was in honour of this new alliance that Leo commissioned the *Coronation of Charlemagne*. Part of the pope's grand strategy was to deflect Europe's powerful rulers from their own feuds and persuade them to unite in a war against the Turk.

The forces ranged against him (including his own arrogance and lack of political foresight) proved too strong. When he died suddenly in 1521 he left western Christendom in a state of turmoil that would change it (and subsequently the world) beyond recognition. Viewed from one angle, the Reformation was the last expression of the three-way struggle between the papacy and the two halves of Charlemagne's empire. The man who became the Emperor Charles V was the most powerful monarch Europe had seen since his ninth-century namesake. Indeed, when we take into consideration Spain's recent conquests in the bullion-rich New World, he and his family were potentially even more influential:

> You know that I am born of the most Christian emperors of the noble German nation, of the Catholic kings of Spain, the archdukes of Austria, the dukes of Burgundy, who were all to the death true sons of the Roman church, defenders of the Catholic faith, of the sacred customs, decrees and usages of its worship, who have bequeathed all this to me as my heritage and according to whose example I have hitherto lived . . . Therefore I am determined to set my kingdoms and dominions, my friends, my body, my blood, my life, my soul upon [the unity of the Church and the purity of the faith].[4]

So Charles staunchly affirmed at the Diet of Worms in 1521 after he had, without reference to the pope, proclaimed on his own imperial authority that Martin Luther was a heretic. If anyone could have made good his boast to be the leader of a resurgent Christendom, it should have been this shrewd and iron-willed young man. His overseas empire stretched from the Philippines to Peru, and his European dominions (ruled either directly or through other Habsburgs as regents) incorporated Spain, the Balearics, Sardinia, Sicily, southern Italy and a swathe of central Europe from Flanders to Hungary and from the Baltic to the Aegean.

In fact it was the very extent of his inheritance that was a major reason for Charles' failure. The conglomeration of nations was difficult and expensive to administer. Subject peoples, especially those of the Netherlands, resented rule by a distant and alien monarch. Habsburg territory completely ringed France, so it was inevitable that Charles and Francis would become locked in conflict. In fact, the two monarchs exhausted their territories in a series of five wars, and the wealth of the Indies proved quite inadequate to meet the needs of an imperial government faced with these and other major expenditures. But the supreme irony was that, at the very time when a Christian empire appeared that bore some territorial relationship to Charlemagne's, the unity of the Christian West was finally shattered by Martin Luther and the rainbow-hewed company of reformers who appeared in his wake.

But the Protestant rebels were not members of an anarchic conspiracy that appeared suddenly and from nowhere intent on rending the seamless robe of Christendom. The idea, the vision of a church militant, united under the leadership of emperor and pope to wage war on the unspeakable evil of Islam, had enjoyed wide popular support for more than seven centuries but, as we have seen, it had never been firmly grounded in reality. Heresies, anti-clericalism and nationalistic resentment of Rome had always plagued the Church, but protest had become a growing problem since the emergence of the Cathari in around AD 1000. At the same time that Rome had embraced militarism in the struggle with the Saracens, it had also turned to violence in its attempts to suppress all unorthodox Christian beliefs. The holy inquisition was set up in 1231 and, if one were to judge by recantation statistics, a policy based on torture, paid informers and intimidating public autos-da-fé would appear to have been, in broad terms, successful. Ecclesiastical authorities could usually rely on their secular counterparts, for kings and princes were as anxious as bishops and abbots about any threat to public order. But force and the fear of force have seldom been effective in purging minds and hearts of deep-seated convictions and resentments, and by the early sixteenth century an ardent spirituality that could not find expression within conventional forms was threatening to burst the seams of traditional doctrine and devotional practice. Scholars were questioning old dogmas, and fiery preachers were challenging the unlearned to dare to think new thoughts. Printing presses were disseminating radical texts and satirical woodcuts. No longer did individuals with troubled consciences, and groups who met clandestinely to read banned books, feel themselves isolated. They were part of a movement, a movement that was bent on reform from the bottom up.

The literati who were part of what would become a revolution were for the most part reluctant revolutionaries. In their excitement with their discoveries, many of them did not realise where those discoveries would lead — to the final rejection of the overarching myth of Christian unity and the emergence of nation states with their own churches. They were disciples of reason. In the universities, and in the courts and salons where intellectuals met to discuss new thoughts and new ways of thinking, all forms of conventional wisdom were put under the spotlight in the quest for truth. *Ad fontes*, 'back to the sources', was the watchword of the new generation of scholars. They re-evaluated documents long accepted as genuine and authoritative and rejected many of them. The problem with exposing old errors, half-truths and downright lies was that it had a devastating impact on those beloved institutions and respected beliefs that had been built upon them. Many hens now came home to roost. Documents that had boosted papal authority or supported territorial claims made by acquisitive abbeys were now exposed for the forgeries they were. Teachings that had been imposed upon the faithful on pain of prosecution for heresy were now seen to have no foundation in Scripture or the Fathers. The results were overwhelming, not least for those whose researches were doing the damage. Many were the theologians and philosophers who watched with dismay the crumbling edifice of Catholic Europe as they picked away at the ancient mortar. They found their loyalty to truth conflicting with their loyalty to the Church and the Crown.

The problem was the same for those who committed themselves to a rewriting of national history. This involved casting critical eyes over the Charlemagne legends. While humanists enjoyed the old stories and approved the sacred principles that those stories had been designed to support, their intellectual honesty obliged them to reject large parts of the Charlemagne corpus as fable – and absurd fable at that. They poured scorn on *Pseudo-Turpin* and the myth of Charles as the great crusader. They peeled away the layers of miracle and chivalric idealism of the *chansons*. Then they looked mournfully on what was left – and began a work of reinterpretation. We should not think of them as 'scientific' historians, writing history for history's sake. They had royal and noble patrons to please and they still looked to the past as the repository of virtuous characters and noble deeds that could inform the present. The dilemma reveals itself in the work of the leading Parisian humanist at the turn of the sixteenth century, the general of the Trinitarian order, Robert Gaguin. He was also a diplomat, a royal servant and a dedicated monarchist. He wrote for Charles VIII a life of Charlemagne (now lost) and incorporated his fresh thinking about the emperor in a larger book, *De origine et gestis Francorum Compendium*. Gaguin's work fed the king's obsession with *la gloire*, and Charlemagne's military exploits were certainly stressed, but the hero who emerged from Gaguin's version of ninth-century history was essentially a *cultural* prodigy, a scholar and a generous patron of scholars. This Renaissance writer looked back to that earlier flowering of learning and the arts and claimed that Charlemagne always regarded his prime function as the civilising of his people. He even suggested that it was France's patron saint who had founded the University of Paris (which did not, in fact, come into being until 1150). It was this aspect of Charlemagne's reign that made him, in Gaguin's view, the perfect prince upon whom the French king should model himself.

All this was part and parcel of that change of focus made by an age that rediscovered and celebrated the glories of the classical world. Now Charlemagne was presented as a member of the great pantheon of heroes of Greece and Rome. Any suggestion that he came of barbarian stock was rejected. On the contrary, he was fêted as the hammer of the pagan Saxons, and as the warrior who had delivered Italy from the uncouth Germanic hordes. Far from quietly drawing a veil over an ancestor whose identity had become obscured under embarrassing accretions of nonsensical myth, France's intelligentsia was using him to craft a new identity for the monarchy and the nation – that of world cultural leadership.

Yet this was not the only reinterpretation of the life and accomplishments of the great emperor that was in vogue. It seems that almost every individual and faction with a political or religious programme to advance wanted the endorsement of the Frankish hero. Thanks to the printing press they could reissue old texts and use them to advance their cause or attack the cause of their opponents. Luther, good Saxon that he was, scorned the unholy Rome–Aachen axis and denigrated Charlemagne for accepting his crown from the pope. John Calvin, the leader of the Geneva reform, on the other hand, found Charles a useful ally in his war on the veneration of images and quoted approvingly from the recently republished *Libri Carolini*, Charlemagne's reaction to the Iconoclastic Controversy. Pius V, who was elected pope in 1566, took little time to conclude that Charlemagne was an embarrassment to the cause of extirpating heresy. This most zealous of pontiffs, who is particularly remembered in Britain for excommunicating Elizabeth I, gave the Inquisition sharper teeth and set up the Congregation of the Index to oversee the burning of banned books and the prosecution of printers suspected of encouraging free thinking. In 1568 he removed Charlemagne's name from the official list of saints. This made as much impact in France and Germany as did the pope's prohibition of bull fighting in Spain. Yet it was an acknowledgement that the legend of the Carolingian ruler was still a powerful influence, which could effectively be called upon to validate a wide range of beliefs and convictions.

However, all this lay in the realm of ideas. Power remained in the hands of kings and they used ideas only when it suited them. Scholars might try to impart new relevance to old legends, but the realities of sixteenth-century power politics mocked them. With a rejuvenated Islam making great strides in the East and across the Mediterranean, and Europe torn by dynastic rivalries and religious strife, kings and emperors had pressing issues to confront. They made use of imaginative interpretations of history for their own propaganda purposes, but were just as ready cynically to disregard the moral claims of the past. In 1526 Francis I strengthened his position by making an alliance with the Turks. The following year Charles V underpinned his power by sending troops to sack Rome and make the pope his prisoner.

Notes

1 See N. Cohn, *The Pursuit of the Millennium*, 1970, pp.119ff.
2 Barber, op. cit., pp.146–7
3 See A. G. Dickens, *The German Nation and Martin Luther*, 1974, p.35
4 See A. Wheatcroft, *The Habsburgs; Embodying Empire*, 1995, pp.117–18

12

New Absolutisms for Old

'Null, void, invalid, iniquitous, unjust, damnable, reprobate, inane, and devoid of meaning for all time.' So, in 1648, Pope Innocent X condemned the Peace of Westphalia, which put an end to the appalling suffering of central Europe after a century of vicious warfare. Technically, the treaty marked the conclusion of the Thirty Years War. In retrospect it may be seen as signalling the emergence from a 'dark age' of political and religious strife. The century just passed was the most devastating in the history of Europe before 1914. It had cost millions of lives, destroyed commerce, rendered vast tracts of farmland unproductive and brought about the breakdown of social order throughout the German empire. The Habsburg–Valois conflicts of the sixteenth century had been followed by the French wars of religion and merged with the long-drawn-out Dutch war of independence and the Thirty Years War, which began as a struggle between the emperor and the German princes and ended by sucking in all the nations of Europe. Confessional rivalries were intricately interwoven with issues of political power and served to make those issues all the more bitter.

Why, then, was the pope violently opposed to the treaty that put a merciful end to so much suffering and allowed the peoples of Europe, who had known nothing but war, to hope for a future in which life might become tolerable? It was because the delegates who gathered in Osnabrück and Münster to sign the various documents which constituted the treaty agreed that 'citizens whose religion differs from that of their sovereign are to have equal rights with his other citizens'. The toleration implied in this declaration was not universally applied by the countries signing up to the treaty, but a revolutionary principle had been stated and acknowledged that struck at the cultural unity of Europe and the position of the pope as spiritual leader of Christendom. Indeed, 'Christendom' was now a dead idea. Henceforth people spoke rather of 'Europe' and no longer looked, even theoretically, to the Church as the arbiter in international affairs. Roughly speaking, the region became what it had been struggling to become ever since Luther nailed his 95 Theses to the door of the castle church in Wittenberg: a Catholic federation in the south and a Protestant federation in the north. Princes had not been alone in resenting the influence of Rome in their affairs. Clergy and their flocks were rarely enthusiastic about being taxed to support a distant and often corrupt papal establishment. Heresy had often taken on a nationalistic identity and attracted those who were motivated more by animosity to Rome than by attraction to novel theologies. And behind all these complaints lay a fundamental cultural distinctiveness between the peoples living on either side of the barrier extending from the Pyrenees to the Carpathians. Seventeeth-century Europe sundered along old fault lines.

None of the contending parties had bothered to ask Innocent X to mediate in their disputes. No one took any notice of his outraged anathema. This was partly because the man himself attracted little respect. He was so notoriously under the thumb of a certain lady who wielded power in his name that men referred to his reign as the 'pontificate of Donna Olympia'. In Florence a medal was struck that showed on one side the lady in question resplendent in papal robes and, on the obverse, Innocent attired as a woman at her spinning wheel. But the snubbing of the pope went beyond issues of personality. The office itself no longer carried the authority it had always claimed and sometimes exercised. In northern Europe it had lost its organisational structure. Of the 620 surviving Catholic dioceses in 1600, fewer than sixty remained north of the Alps. Protestant countries had developed their own vernacular liturgies, thus denying Catholicism the uniformity once provided by the Latin mass. The internal reform, revival of preaching and more vigorous discipline that were the marks of the Counter-Reformation made little impression beyond Italy and Spain. In the recent war Rome had even lost the support of its old ally, France. Realpolitik had so far come to dominate the conflict that Catholic France had allied itself with Protestant Sweden against the forces of the Catholic empire. Never again would the pope be acknowledged as one of the twin foci of Christian civilisation.

Nor would the emperor. By 1648 the Habsburgs had failed in their attempt to provide political leadership for Christian Europe. They had failed in their trial of strength with the Valois and Bourbon kings of France. And they had failed to overawe the princes and princelings of Germany.

It was symbolic of the emperor's weakening control of his hereditary lands that, after the death of Ferdinand I in 1564, no further coronations were held in Aachen. Charlemagne's city was by then too far from the centre of imperial power. It lay surrounded by the lands of the Spanish Habsburgs, with whom their Austrian relatives were frequently at loggerheads, and it was too close for comfort to France. Several territories had slipped from the emperor's grasp, including the United Netherlands and Switzerland – now thriving, prosperous republics. Germany was no more than a mosaic of around 300 principalities, duchies, free cities and bishoprics, of which the most powerful – Saxony, Brandenburg-Prussia and Bavaria – were often able to challenge the will of their overlord. The Austrian Habsburgs' hereditary lands lay to the east in Silesia, Bohemia, Moravia, Austria, Styria, Carinthia and the Tyrol, but even here there was little centralised control. The empire still had common institutions, predominantly the Diet or *Reichstag*, which met in Regensburg, but this was little more than an ineffective talking shop.

'For the person of the emperor to be subjected to the will of an insolent people and to the dictates of an elected diet which considers itself the equal, or even the superior, of its master is beyond measure unwise.'[1] So wrote a horrified French visitor to the Hungarian Diet. What he observed was in startling contrast to the political system of his own country. The one nation that had emerged strongly from a catastrophic century was France. It had survived the succession of two royal minors (Louis XIII, 1610–17, and Louis XIV, 1643–61) largely due to the endeavours of the powerful ministers Cardinal Richelieu and Cardinal Mazarin and a group of talented battlefield generals; and when Louis XIV took up the reins of government in 1661, France was poised to take advantage of the weakness of its neighbours. However, there was no inevitability about the expansionist policies on which the young king embarked. These had their origin entirely in his own passionately held convictions. He believed himself to have a divine mission to impose order, civilisation and Catholicism on his own people and all those whom God added to his empire. Louis was determined to be absolute master in his own realm – and in Europe. If that sounds familiar to those who are acquainted with the policies of Charlemagne, the similarity is far from coincidental.

Three emotions formed the character of the man who would become known as the 'Sun King' – fear, piety and the thirst for glory. No sooner had the Thirty Years War come to an end than a dislocated society turned in on itself. France had been plunged into civil conflict. The 'Frondes', which erupted when Louis was only ten, devastated the country. There were 'peasant revolts and urban anarchy, military occupation and religious persecution, treason here and treachery there, baronial bandits at one end of the social scale and looters of city shops at the other'.[2] Louis would remember till the end of his days being harried from his own capital and suffering months of privation while his humiliated ministers were obliged to treat with the rebels. Nor was it only France that was afflicted in this way. Portugal, Naples and Catalonia had their own uprisings, while in England Parliament had risen against the king and cut off his head. The lesson Louis learned from this was ruthlessness. To be king in anything more than name he must impose his will on all sections of French society by personal application, supported by an extensive bureaucracy and a large standing army.

If he was to become just such an autocrat he had to believe that he was, indeed, God's deputy. Without conviction of a divine destiny and responsibility, Louis would have been nothing but the world's most complete egotist. He was genuinely religious, but his piety was the piety of kings – that is to say, the moral sanctions he acknowledged were not those that were binding on ordinary mortals. Just as monarchs are called upon to inflict death and suffering by waging war, and may justify deceit, imprisonment and even assassination by claiming to protect the state, so they may express that virility which is essential to strong government in whatever amorous adventures they choose to indulge. The future king had been well trained in childhood for the role of absolute monarch. His mother, Anne of Austria, and her lover, Cardinal Mazarin, had overseen his education and were determined that he should be truly master of his realm. From his earliest days Louis was surrounded by priests, and their influence over him increased with the passing of the years. He accepted without question his solemn responsibility for the unity and purity of the French Church. This showed itself most dramatically in his treatment of the nation's million or so Protestants. Vicious systematic persecution built up over two decades and culminated in the revocation of the Edict of Nantes (1685), which, at a stroke, removed the religious and civil rights that the nation's Huguenots had enjoyed for eighty-seven years. More long-lasting was the campaign against Jansenism, a reformist and rigorist movement within the Catholic Church, which upset the ecclesiastical hierarchy. When the sect was finally abolished in 1713 and its buildings and cemetery razed, the tombs of its two most celebrated figures, Jean Racine and Blaise Pascal, had to be rescued from the hands of a desecrating mob.

Louis's obsession with *gloire* was centred on the projection of his own image. He was both the impresario and the lead player in a glittering state production that ran for fifty-four years, most of the performances being staged at that marvel of the age, the Palace of Versailles. The king had the advantage of a naturally overpowering personality and he consciously built on this to strike awe, wonder and terror into all who came before him. It was political calculation that demanded that all the aristocratic families should dance personal attendance on him. If they were at court, they could not be away at their distant estates hatching subversive plots. Once held virtual prisoners at Versailles, they were obliged to play their parts in a highly elaborate daily ritual, knowing that their prosperity and even their survival depended on the impression they created for their royal master. A smile, a frown, a nod from the king could make or break fortunes. This influence radiated out from the court through the bureaucracy largely created by Mazarin to the far corners of France. A century later, Montesquieu had Louis XIV very much in mind when he wrote:

> As virtue is necessary in a republic, and honour in a monarchy, so fear is necessary in despotic government . . . In a despotism people capable of setting a value on themselves would be likely to create disturbances. Fear must therefore depress their spirits and extinguish even the least sense of ambition.[3]

At about the same time, the posthumously published *Mémoires* of Saint-Simon described Louis as 'a prince who was more a master than any other whom one can remember, even by recourse to books, who was such for a long time abroad as he was at home and whose aura of terror persists'.

Nor was it just in politics that Louis XIV was the dominant force of his day. So exuberant was the Bourbon court, so strong a magnet for every kind of literary, artistic and scholarly talent, that its cultural supremacy throughout Europe was inevitable. The names of those who were the darlings of the court and the salons of the fashionable include Racine, Corneille, Molière, La Fontaine, Rameau, Lully, Couperin, Claude Lorraine and Watteau, while Le Vau, Le Nôtre and Le Brun created the baroque splendour of Versailles, to which others monarchs could only distantly aspire. This was the era that saw the establishment of the Académie française and the Comédie-Française, the Paris Opera and the dance craze that swept Europe, the minuet. Among the international *haut monde* French taste was all. No other nation could contest France's claim to be the leader of the civilised world.

But it was in the exercise of military might that Louis imposed himself most dramatically on Europe. He buttressed his power with a massive standing army, which was reorganised and provided with the most up-to-date weapons and equipment. Military academies were established to supply a cadre of officers selected by merit rather than noble birth. The engineering genius,

Vauban, protected France's borders with 160 new fortresses. Louis more than tripled the size of the French navy and thereby laid the foundation of the country's overseas expansion. Thus resourced, the *Roi Soleil* launched and sometimes led a succession of wars against his neighbours. It matters not for our purposes that he failed in some of his military and diplomatic objectives; or that he bankrupted his country; or that his excesses provoked frequent bloody revolts; or that — beneath the dazzling surface — royal power in the provinces was never complete; or even that Louis's experiment in absolutism powerfully demonstrated its unacceptability. What is important is that Louis XIV was the wonder of his age, just as Charlemagne had been the wonder of his.

The parallels are striking. Both rulers were absolutists who held power in the final analysis by the force of their personality. Both went to war over and again basically to establish and strengthen their borders. Both developed political systems whose aim was to keep the aristocracy under close supervision. Both were intensely religious after their fashion. Both were sexually promiscuous. Both were determined to control the Church in their dominions. Both could with some justification make the claim, '*l'état c'est moi*'. We can be even more specific in making comparisons. For Aachen read Versailles. For Charlemagne's itinerant royal *missi* read Louis's *intendants*. For the evil pagans against whom the Carolingian emperor resolutely set his face read the harried French Huguenots. For Charles' annual campaigns read Louis's four major wars. For the Carolingian renaissance read the flowering of art and letters in the land of the Sun King.

How consciously did Louis XIV follow the pattern of his ancestor? By the time the young king was growing up, Charlemagne's position in the history syllabus that formed part of royal child's education was ineradicable. He was the essential link between the heroes of Greece and Rome and the saintly, martial kings of France. And it was 'heroism' that was the operative word in the patriotic historiography of the seventeenth century. Just as the Victorian schoolboy was fed on stories of Drake and Marlborough, Agincourt and Trafalgar, so Louis and his contemporaries were brought up on the legends of Charlemagne and kings such as Philip Augustus and Louis IX (St Louis), who consolidated the power of the monarchy. Many of the books in the child-king's classroom freely mixed together fact and fantasy. Louis seems to have been aware that the received tradition did not altogether carry conviction. In later years he appointed as official historian of France a Jesuit scholar by the name of Gabriel David. In his *Histoire de France depuis l'établissement de la monarchie française* David to some extent managed to divide the sheep and goats of verifiable fact and patriotic myth, but he could not altogether distance himself from the miraculous element in the national story. His primary tasks (which doubt-less agreed with his own convictions) were to glorify the monarchy and especially his own royal patron and to demonstrate that the French were God's chosen people. His account of Charlemagne's reign left plenty of room for divine intervention and, since he was at pains to point out that Charles and Louis XIV were the two greatest kings ever to occupy the throne of France, the message was clear: Louis, too, enjoyed the blessing of Providence.

However, it was not only dry history books that drew this comparison. Louis commanded a ceaseless round of court entertainments. Balls, masques, plays, ballets, musical extravaganzas, waterborne pageants – any and every diversion that poets, costumiers and the engineers of elaborate scenic effects could devise was staged for the pleasure of the Sun King and the sophisticates who revolved around him like heavenly bodies, reflecting his effulgence. Naturally these performances had a political purpose – to proclaim the splendour of the regime. Heroes of fable, of antiquity and of French history were paraded across the stage while hyperbolic eulogies compared them with the present paragon occupying the throne:

> Behold the fine flower of chivalry, who far exceeds the champions
> of fable in gallantry and noble deeds. In the veins of this awe-inspiring
> prince, who brings Love and Glory in his train, flows the pure blood
> of Charlemagne.[4]

Some pieces made their point more subtly. The first theatrical spectacle of the reign in which Louis himself appeared was *Les Plaisirs de l'Île Enchanté*. Among its themes was that of the loyalty due from nobles to their king. In it the part of Roland was given to the son of the Prince de Condé, one of the erstwhile Frondeurs. In the *chansons* Charlemagne's nephew had often been the focus of debate about obedience to a man's liege lord. The symbolism of repentance and restitution would not have been lost on the audience.

There was a conspiracy between hopeful protégés and their royal patron to present the king in what seem to us outrageously exaggerated propa-gandist terms. The poet Nicholas Courtin in his *Charlemagne, ou le Rétablissement de l'Empire romain* looked forward confidently to Louis estab-lishing an empire as extensive as that of his great ancestor. Yet it was not sufficient to present 'Louis the Great' as a reincarnated Charlemagne; what poets, philosophers and dramatists were trying to arrive at was a sense of France's national destiny. What was emerging from the retelling of history with its admixture of myth was a saga that would establish France's leading role in the divine plan for humanity.[5] That heroic destiny would first be called into question, and then receive a new impetus, in the century following the death of the Sun King in 1715.

Louis XIV has not gone on record as claiming complete identity with his imperial ancestor in as many words, but Napoleon Bonaparte was not as reticent. 'Take a good look at me,' he told papal representatives in 1809. 'In me you see Charlemagne. *Je suis Charlemagne, MOI! Oui, je suis Charlemagne!*'[6] He had more than a little justification for the boast. He ruled, directly or through satellites, a continental empire that stretched from the Straits of Gibraltar to the River Niemen, a swathe of territory far greater than anything his Carolingian predecessor had controlled – and his ambition was not at an end. It was one indication of Napoleon's political genius that he exploited the Charlemagne connection to the full. Far more than any previous rulers, he associated himself with the varied qualities of the ancient hero: conqueror, law-giver, preserver of his people's liberties, protector of the Church, forger of a united Europe.

There were many reasons for assuming the mantle of France's founder-hero, but one was particularly pressing. Napoleon took into his own hands more personal power than any Valois or Bourbon king had ever wielded, but he had to avoid being tarred with the absolutist brush. He posed as the saviour of the revolution, the political messiah who would safeguard the rights and freedoms of French citizens and extend them to all the other peoples who came under his beneficent rule. The new emperor presented himself as the enemy of the *ancien régime* whose creed was summarised by Alexander I, Tsar of all the Russias, when he met Napoleon at Tilsit in 1807: 'We are Europe,' he said, and by 'Europe' he meant the crowned heads of the leading nations – Russia, Austria, Prussia and perhaps he would have included Britain. The continental monarchs were every whit as absolutist in intent as Louis XIV. In Austria the Holy Roman Emperors still entertained pretensions of power, though they were obliged to concentrate most of their activities on their eastern lands. Within their domains they behaved with the same detached, autocratic extravagance and disdain as their French counterparts. Leopold I (ruled 1658–1705), Joseph I (1705–11) and Charles VI (1711–40) harried Protestant communities out of existence, taxed their subjects heavily to pay for magnificent baroque palaces, combined morbid religiosity with moral decadence, bolstered the wealth and power of the Roman Church and, in the words of one historian, attempted to 'restore the union between the Empire and the Kingdom of God'.[7] They used their position to make a virtue of eccentricity. Charles, for example, spent lavishly to build a palace-monastery complex outside

Vienna that took its inspiration from Philip II's Escorial while, at the same time, ordering fifteen hogsheads of the best wine per year to be set aside for bathing the imperial parrots.

What all Europe's absolute monarchs feared most was the common people who must, at all costs, be kept in their place. Dangerous free thinkers who considered themselves 'enlightened' must also be carefully watched. Jean Jacques Rousseau and Voltaire were only the more celebrated radical philosophers who were forced into exile or suffered imprisonment under the *ancien régime*. It was at his haven in Geneva that Voltaire wrote *Le Siècle de Louis XIV*. He had the audacity not only to criticise the exercise of royal government, but to strike at the hallowed name and reputation of St Charlemagne. For Voltaire, the old hero, taken as a model by so many kings and their sycophantic supporters, had been nothing more than an illiterate, barbarian mass-murderer who cloaked his monstrous regime in religion and had been hailed down the centuries by the Roman Church for its own purposes. In fact, the well-established legend would prove too strong to be consumed by the blast of Voltaire's vituperative indignation. Some Enlightenment thinkers even revered Charlemagne as a man of the people. They saw a ruler who sat loose to the imperial dignity, propounded wise laws and whose power always rested on the support of his subjects, on whose shields he had been raised to kingship. Obviously, Charlemagne was still capable of being all things to all men and he remained an icon for those who regarded Europe as the most civilised part of the world, and France as the most civilised part of Europe. What Napoleon needed to do was tap into this nationalistic use of history while detaching it from royalist tradition.

Bonaparte was neither the first nor last frustrated general to stage a political coup with the objectives of purging the civil administration of incompetents and imparting discipline and a sense of purpose to his country. However, he was, arguably, the most brilliant. He understood how the common people felt and he sensed intuitively the most effective ways to appeal to their hearts. His steps to ultimate power were decisive but cautious. In 1799, by the coup of Brumaire, he overthrew the Directory and established the Consulate, of which he was one member. The following year he became First Consul and, in 1802, Consul for life. It only remained to make his position hereditary, and the empire was proclaimed in May 1804. These developments had been watched with growing anxiety by observers inside and outside France. To many, the creation of a new dynasty looked like a return to the bad old days of Bourbon repression. Napoleon was well aware of these misgivings. He therefore prepared for his coronation with elaborate care. In September he made a nine-day visit (one might almost say a pilgrimage) to Aachen. There he paid his respects at the tomb, was shown all the famous relics and attended a solemn Te Deum. These (what we would now call) 'photo-opportunities' were, of course, well covered in the government press and their significance pointed out. The Holy Roman Empire was no more (see page 187). Its legitimate successor was the French Empire.

When it came to the actual coronation, which took place in Notre Dame on 2 December, Napoleon was faced with a problem similar to that which had confronted Charlemagne a millennium before – the relationship between the emperor and the pope. Napoleon had recently concluded a concordat with Rome, which had given the government control of ecclesiastical appointments in return for freedom of worship guaranteed by law, an arrangement similar to that which Charles the Great had had with Leo III, though for Napoleon the Church was the servant of the state and not vice versa. Yet there still remained some unfinished business. All those centuries before, Leo had crowned Charlemagne and from that simple act had stemmed generations of acrimonious debate about where ultimate authority lay. Napoleon needed to have Pius VII at his coronation in order to give added legitimacy to the event, but who was to preside at the ceremony and who should perform the act of crowning? When the pregnant moment arrived, the new emperor solved the problem by taking the crown from Pius and placing it on his own head. If, as seems likely, the action took the pope by surprise, the wheel may be said to have come full circle since Christmas 800. There were other pointers to that earlier ceremony. Charlemagne's sword and associated relics were used in the ritual, and Napoleon had a replica of Charlemagne's crown made for the event. He was also presented with a sceptre surmounted by a figure of the Carolingian emperor, which had been fashioned for King Charles V. As the official propaganda pointed out, the spectacular coronation of 1804 looked both backwards and forwards:

> The long minority of the human race lasted until the reign of Charlemagne. By conquest and by law that prince established a vast empire and by employing the building blocks of religion he brought Europe into being . . . Diverse peoples were no longer strangers to each other . . . Europe emerged as one great family made up of different nations which . . . found themselves united by religion, science and custom . . .

That process, begun a thousand years before, had now been brought to glorious completion by the only man worthy to wear Charlemagne's crown.[8] As an adulatory letter to a Paris newspaper put it, 'Sire, you have brought back to life the Empire of the Franks and the throne of Charlemagne, buried beneath the ruins of ten centuries.'[9] This response was prompted by the crowning of Napoleon as King of the Romans in Milan Cathedral in May 1805.

In 1806 the Holy Roman Empire, which had been comatose for years, finally died. The emperors Napoleon I and Francis II together switched off its life-support system. Both dictators were committed to forging a new Europe and were equally ruthless about jettisoning outmoded ideas. But, whereas Napoleon adopted the Charlemagne mythology and tried to weave it into the fabric of a new, essentially secular, state, Francis simply took a pair of scissors to those aspects of the past that did not fit his dynastic vision for the future. He was an autocrat by principle and a pragmatist by nature. He loathed the political contagion spreading out from France and was determined, by the use of draconian laws, informers and secret police, to restrict the epidemic in his own dominions. But it did not take defeats in war and the progressive loss of territory to make him realise that France and some of her client states were possessed of a vigour and administrative efficiency that the creaking Habsburg government machine could not match. Francis was not afraid to think new thoughts and try new methods, but they were all geared to preserving his own autocratic power. From 1792 France had been encroaching on German lands, and Napoleon had won allies by allotting confiscated territory to the larger political entities, principally Prussia, Bavaria and Württemberg. Francis countered by concentrating on measures designed to glorify the Habsburg dynasty and strengthen his position in his own heartland.

One necessary ingredient in this process was the rewriting of history. Francis set his own scholars to produce an approved version of Austria's past. Joseph Hofmayr was appointed imperial historiographer and his *Handbook for a National History* and the twenty-volume *Austrian Plutarch* intermeshed history and myth to create a new national identity tightly bound up with the house of Habsburg. Charlemagne still had his part in this saga, but it was a shadowy one. The hero selected to be the real founder of the nation was Rudolf I. Crowned King of the Germans at Aachen in 1273, Rudolf was a formidable warrior who carved out a territorial 'empire' that became the nucleus of the Habsburg patrimony. Legends clustered round this patriarch, who was revered by later generations as a ruler fearless in battle, wise in government and devout in his service of the Church. Children were told the story of the king who gave his horse to a priest who was taking the sacred host to a dying man, and who afterwards refused to receive the animal back because he would not sit astride a beast that had carried his saviour. In later generations the feast of Corpus Christi was given a special place in the Austrian calendar, and a major element in the increasingly elaborate ceremonies was the sight of the emperor walking bareheaded behind the clergy carrying the holy vessels. Francis now made these and other elements of the imperial cult the golden thread of Austria's life. He performed breathtaking acts of renunciation, which associated him more firmly with his illustrious ancestor and indicated the new thrust of his own policy. Rudolf I, for all his fine qualities, had never received the crown of the Holy Roman Empire from the hands of the pope. Francis' reaction to the proclamation of the French Empire in 1804 was to restyle himself Emperor of Austria and defender of the German people. Napoleon continued to extend his sphere of influence into those lands west of the Elbe where the Habsburgs traditionally claimed the loyalty of local rulers. In 1806 several of those rulers combined to form the Confederation of the Rhine, a political entity under the patronage of Napoleon, which carried within it the seeds of real German unity. This time Francis' response was simply to declare the Holy Roman Empire at an end. He regarded this not as an abject abdication, but rather as the casting aside of a threadbare coat of which he, as Germany's champion, the new Rudolf, had no need.

In fact, the significance of the event was far greater. When the Holy Roman Empire was finally interred, what went into the tomb with it was the idea of Christendom. To be sure, the concept of 'one Europe, one Church' had been dealt its mortal wound by the Reformation, but it had been a long time dying because the Catholic powers had fought strenuously against the disruptive forces of nationalism and 'heresy'. Religion had been a major factor in the breakaway of the Netherlands and the Swiss cantons from control by the monoliths of Europe, but the demand for freedom of worship led, inevitably, to the emergence of the secular state. The American and French Revolutions laid down the right of citizens to believe anything – or nothing. 'No man shall be compelled to frequent or support any religious worship, place or ministry whatsoever.' So ran the Statute of Religious Liberty introduced into the Virginia legislature by Thomas Jefferson. Napoleon's concordat with Rome had recognised that most Frenchmen wanted to remain Catholic, but it, too, had established the freedom of the individual to hold any religious conviction, or none. Thus, after a thousand years, the ideological *raison d'être* for Charlemagne's empire was formally and finally discarded.

This does not mean that, in seeking to re-establish it, Napoleon was motivated totally by national aggrandisement, or that he espoused no principles or ideals. He often spoke, with a measure of sincerity, of establishing a brotherhood of nations and, towards the end of his life, he regretted his failure to create a polity that would have provided opportunities:

> to bring everywhere unity of laws, of principles, of opinions, senti-ments, views and interests. Then, perhaps, it would have been possible to dream for the great European family of a political model such as that of the American Congress or of the Amphictyons of Greece.[10]

This vision of a 'United States of Europe' was shared not only by the emperor's own agents, but by enthusiastic radicals in conquered lands who welcomed French republican ideals. Disillusionment came when those ideals were betrayed by political reality. 'Liberating' armies perpetrated acts of violence and plunder. 'Enlightened' statesmen used lands and peoples as bargaining counters, just as their *ancien régime* predecessors had done.

Yet, briefly, Napoleon had given Europe a glimpse of what a united, liberal, secular Europe might be like. He ruled, directly or indirectly, over 40 per cent of its population and he began to give that population new ways of thinking about themselves in relation to government. The reform of civil law enshrined in the *Code Napoléon* guaranteed individual liberties and tidied up regulations governing property and employment. Napoleon reformed the French education system. He created a well-trained, efficiently officered army that remained invincible for more than a decade. He gave France an improved bureaucracy at both central and local levels. And over-arching all these changes was the revolution's Declaration of Rights, which might, in the fullness of time, have become for all subjects of the empire a surrogate religion. In all these ways Napoleon mirrored Charlemagne (one of his new Parisian schools was even named the Lycée Charlemagne). He faced the same problems in administering his empire that the great Carolingian had faced, and he set about solving them in similar ways.

But there were basic dissimilarities between the two emperors, dissim-ilarities that made the difference between success and failure. Napoleon was finally defeated at Waterloo, but his experiment came to nothing because the imperial and revolutionary ideals were incompatible. Imperial subjects were being encouraged to throw off old tyrannies in the interests of 'liberty' while, at the same time, rendering obedience to a remote auto-crat for whom many of them felt little or no loyalty.

In any comparison between the Napoleonic and Charlemagnic regimes, two facts stand out that account for the failure of one and the success of the other. Charlemagne gave his peoples two things that Napoleon took away. The first was God. The dynamic of the Frankish empire was essen-tially a *religious* dynamic. Charles could, and did, appeal to something greater than himself, which legitimated conquest and provided the rationale for educational and cultural change. He regarded himself as the servant of a higher power with a responsibility to rule wisely and justly here and prepare his subjects for eternity. Hence his constant emphasis on preaching and teaching. In this 'mission' he had the support of the Church, which, through its parochial and monastic organisations, reinforced the government message in the localities on a day-to-day basis. As new tribes were brought into the empire by battle and baptism, they understood that they were becoming part of 'Christendom', something distinct from the worlds of heathendom and Islam, something they could identify with, something their monks risked martyrdom to promote in pagan lands, something their warriors were prepared to fight and die for.

The second thing Charlemagne offered people, which Napoleon denied them, was a considerable degree of regional autonomy. Alongside the loyalty to the Christian empire that Charlemagne demanded went a respect for local and tribal custom. The Celtic missionaries had for a couple of centuries developed ways of achieving this. While unleashing their righteous zeal against pagan shrines and ritual sacrifice, wherever possible they were content to put a Christian gloss on traditional practices and to hallow old worship sites by building churches on them. Charlemagne's passion for unity left room for the expression of local loyalties. He allowed considerable autonomy to the nobles who wielded power in the regions. In fact, he had little choice if he was to hold together a heterogeneous empire, ragged at the edges, in which local ancestral loyalties were strong. That said, Charles had a genuine respect for the old ways. He showed this by conferring with the leading men at the annual *campus maii*. He sent contingents of warriors to war under their own leaders. He ordered the customary law of different communities to be written down so that people would be judged by precepts to which they and their forebears had consented. He did not try to turn Saxons or Bavarians into Franks.

Napoleon well understood that religion could be a useful unifying factor, but that was not at all the same thing as allowing a vigorous Christianity to provide the force that powered the imperial machine. As head of a secular state, he had nothing but his own personality to offer as a standard around which men could rally and behind which they could march to war. That personality was very potent. Millions of Frenchmen were devoted to their emperor, and his soldiers regarded him almost as a father figure. But when distance or time intervened between the ruler and his subjects, there was nothing else to inspire their loyalty or sacrifice. When faith in the man faltered, the 'empire' was scarcely a tangible or convincing entity for them to believe in and identify with. Matters were made worse by Napoleon's attempts to impose uniformity throughout his dominions. He appointed relatives and members of his own entourage as rulers in the regions of the empire. He conscripted annually more and more soldiers into his armies. Everywhere local interests were subordinated to the needs of his regime. For example, in an attempt at commercial warfare against Britain, Napoleon imposed the Continental System throughout the empire. This forbade all trade with the enemy, irrespective of the impact on local economies. Such activities provoked mounting criticism even in France. Benjamin Constant, novelist and pamphleteer, was just one of many critics who took himself into exile in order to express his disgust at the way the revolution had been betrayed:

> While patriotism exists only by a vivid attachment to the interests, the way of life, the customs of some locality, our so-called patriots have declared war on all these. They have dried up the natural source of patriotism and have sought to replace it by a fictitious passion for an abstract being, a general idea stripped of all that can engage the imagination . . .[11]

The Napoleonic empire followed the Holy Roman Empire into the trash can of failed ideas. Over the next century they would be joined by Europe's remaining absolutist states. That did not mean that other dictators would not appear from time to time offering to 'liberate' neighbouring states, or claiming *Lebensraum*, but henceforth all such would find themselves confronted by the clamorous hordes demanding 'freedoms' – freedom to express national identity, freedom of religious belief, freedom to make their own laws, freedom to choose systems of government, freedom to elect political representatives. Europe would become a hotchpotch of independent states, and Europeans would be united, in the words of François Guizot, only 'in their shared capacity for being different'.

Yet all this did not mean that Europe had finished with Charlemagne, or that Charlemagne had finished with Europe.

Notes

1 J. Berenger, 'La Hongrie des Habsburgs au XVIIe siècle', *Revue Historique*, 1967, p.77
2 E. N. Williams, *The Ancien Régime in Europe*, 1970, p.138
3 *Oeuvres Complètes de Montesquieu*, 1799, 1, p.9
4 C. I. Silin, *Benserade and his Ballets de Cour*, Baltimore, 1940, p.282 (my translation)

5 For an extensive discussion of the Charlemagne literature of the seventeenth century, see R. Morrissey, *L'Empereur à la Barbe Fleurie: Charlemagne dans la Mythologie et l'Histoire de France*, Paris, 1997, pp.205ff.

6 Ibid., p.362

7 F. Heer, *The Holy Roman Empire,* 1967, p.236

8 Morrissey, op. cit., p.360 (my translation)

9 Ibid., p.349

10 B. Fontana, 'The Napoleonic Empire and the Europe of Nations', in Pagden (ed.), op. cit., p.123

11 B. Constant, *De l'esprit de conquête* . . . in *The Political Writings of Benjamin Constant* (ed. B. Fontana), Cambridge, 1988, pp.73–4

13

Past Tense and Future Conditional

I see no reason why, if the German and French peoples overcome their mutual grievances and the intrigues of foreigners, they should not end up uniting together. In effect, this would be to rebuild on modern foundations – economic, social, strategic and cultural – the achievements of Charlemagne.[1]

Those words were spoken by Charles de Gaulle, the French prime minister, in 1950 after a period of seventy years during which his country had been invaded by Germany no fewer than three times. The wartime hero and ultra-nationalist politician well understood that collaboration between long-standing enemies was the only hope for European – and probably worldwide – peace. Yet the mention of Charlemagne suggests that there was another item on the general's agenda for the future world order. If the Second World War had humiliated France, it had also undermined the concept of Europe as leader of the free world. Not only had the nations who mastered vast tracts of the planet's surface via their colonial possessions been exposed as squabbling neighbours who could not peacefully regulate their own affairs, but the conflict had left them too exhausted to resist the demands for independence from their overseas possessions. As if loss of empire was not enough, they also experienced steadily declining influence. Culturally, economically, politically and militarily their role was being taken over by the USA and the USSR. De Gaulle could never reconcile himself to France's diminished status in international affairs, hence his appeal to that mystic entity comprising the heartland of continental Europe from which, he firmly believed, everything that was wholesome, enterprising and civilised had come. By bringing together once more the fragments of Charlemagne's empire, the French leader hoped to create a strong Europe – with himself at the centre. He was reviving a dream declared by several visionaries since 1815.

Napoleon's deliberate, and perhaps cynical, evocation of France's patron saint had debased the old emperor's currency. In nineteenth-century Europe, Charlemagne could no longer be a useful political role model. To reactionaries he would always be tarred with the Napoleonic brush. At the Congress of Vienna (1814–15), which was convened to sort out the political, diplomatic and territorial mess produced by a quarter of a century of revolution and war, the preoccupation of the delegates was the restitution of 'legitimate' governments, by which they meant traditional monarchies. They were determined to have no truck with dangerous progressive ideas. Their violent antipathy to anything that smacked of democracy was given eloquent voice by the Austrian chancellor, Prince Metternich. He characterised (or caricatured) it as 'the disease which must be cured, the volcano which must be extinguished, the gangrene which must be burned out with a hot iron, the hydra with jaws open to swallow up the social order'. In France, Louis XVIII was restored to the throne of his ancestors. Elsewhere liberal constitutions that had been granted were rescinded. The map of Europe was redrawn, with the more powerful states granting themselves swathes of territory in recompense for their losses, without reference to the clamour of patriots for self-determination. The crowned and coroneted heads gathered in Vienna seriously believed that they could restore the *status quo ante*. Many of them also believed, more credulously, that, by a system of alliances and solemnly sworn sacred oaths, they could maintain peaceful coexistence among themselves and police Europe in such a way as to prevent the eruption of any new *casus belli*. Their vision of the future categorically excluded ambitious empire-builders who might seek justification in the supposedly beneficent rule of ancient tyrants.

As far as progressives were concerned, Charlemagne was simply associated with despotic government. The brave new thinkers of the age were pursuing the chimera of 'freedom' in all its personal and nationalistic guises. For them history offered nothing but warnings of what to avoid. Salvation lay in a future blessed with all the exciting scientific discoveries and technical innovations which the genius of man was producing in abundance. Henri de Saint-Simon, an aristocrat who survived the Terror and became one of the leading liberal ideologues of the new century, observed in his last political work, *Nouveau Christianisme* (1825), 'The Golden Age, which a blind tradition has hitherto located in the past, is ahead of us.'

What men of good will of all political hues desired was peace. The Congress System, resting on the twin pillars of the balance of power and the suppression of political radicalism, barely survived for a decade, but it did attempt to address the vital question of how Europe might avoid the appalling convulsions (based on tribal, national, regional, religious and dynastic loyalties) that had shaken it for centuries. It was the liberal Saint-Simon who actually appeared at the Congress of Vienna with a paper whose ponderous title was 'The Reorganisation of European Society; or the Need and the Means to Unite the Peoples of Europe in a Single Body Politic while Preserving their Several National Identities'. The idealistic reformer based his argument on a pan-Europeanism that was by no means new. Indeed, it was an ideal to which most political activists subscribed. Rousseau and Voltaire had insisted that Europe was simply, in the words of the latter, 'one great republic divided into several states, all with common religious bases, all with the same legal and political principles unknown in other parts of the world'. Saint-Simon thought it absurd that nations with a shared religious and cultural heritage, and a common language of diplomatic intercourse (French), should continue to confront each other on bloody battlefields. Even the most reactionary monarch understood that he had common interests with his brother sovereigns. Yet if peace and harmony were the characteristics of the destination that most men desired to reach, how were they to get there? They might have mused ruefully on the old Irishman's reply when being asked the way to Dublin: 'Well, if it was me, I wouldn't start from here.'

The next 130 years would show just how tortuous and landslip-prone was the route to European peace and stability. Revolutions broke out in 1820, 1830 and 1848, each followed by a period of repression. France, fluctuating between monarchical and republican rule, experienced no fewer than five changes of constitution between 1815 and 1870. The German peoples, who had been given a taste of unity in 1815 when the pre-Napoleonic plethora of political units was reduced to a confederation of thirty-nine states, were reaching for a new national identity. What form 'Germany' might take would be decided by which of the two major powers, Prussia and Austria, achieved the leadership of the new entity. This issue was resolved by the 'Iron Chancellor' of Prussia, Otto von Bismarck. By diplomatic bullying and a series of lightning wars between 1863 and 1870 he imposed his will on the whole of Europe. Austria and France were humiliated and, for the first time since the medieval heyday of the Holy Roman Empire, there came into being a German Empire based on military might. Shouldered aside from the German heartland, the Habsburgs realigned their state as the Dual Monarchy of Austria-Hungary. This was Europe's last remaining multi-national empire. In it a Germanic minority held sway over a sprawling and diverse territory in which there were seventeen official languages. On its Balkan border the once-mighty Ottoman Empire had become the 'sick man of Europe', bequeathing to its neighbours a power vacuum, prime cause of the infamous 'eastern question'.

Mounting tension between the two major powers of western Europe led to the Franco-Prussian (or more accurately Franco-German) War of 1870–1). The result was total humiliation for the French. Their emperor, Napoleon III, was captured and obliged to go into exile in England, while their capital city was battered and starved into submission. It is not fanciful to see this as a triumph of the German Charlemagne over the French Charlemagne. Mutual Franco-German antagonism was in the genes and had its ultimate cause in the division of the Carolingian Empire. It was inevitable that the new, exhilarating sense of national identity, fed by poets and historians (see page 198) and given tangible form by Bismarck, should direct itself against the nation across the Rhine that had occupied its land between 1805 and 1815 under the leadership of a pseudo-Charlemagne. When the Prussian king, William I, was crowned as German emperor, the triumphalist symbolism of the event could not have been plainer: the ceremony took place in the Palace of Versailles.

By the century's end there was scarcely a country from one end of Europe to the other in which political activists did not harbour jealousies, resentments and frustrated ambitions. Yet there was a further element to be added to the equation: colonial rivalry. Throughout the century Britain, less preoccupied with political and constitutional contretemps, had become the envy of its neighbours. Radicals admired the Westminster pattern of parliamentary democracy, while businessmen and tax-gatherers were impressed by the island's development of heavy industry and overseas commerce. Much of Britain's wealth, as was obvious to all, was derived from colonial trade, from which other nations were, to some extent, debarred. When, from the 1870s, the 'dark continent' of Africa was opened up for exploitation, the leading continental states were determined that Britain should not have a free hand. France, Germany, Spain, Portugal, Italy (newly emerged as one united nation) and Belgium all wanted a slice of the action and took part in 'the scramble for Africa'. To become a major colonial power was as much a matter of national pride as of calculated commercial advantage. New disputes were, thus, added to the list of potential European conflicts as were new locales for staging those disputes.

However, we must pause briefly at this juncture to point out that it was not just their rivalries that Europeans transported to other parts of the world; they also, largely subconsciously, took with them a commodity they all shared. This was a sense of cultural superiority. None of the mission-aries, explorers, governors, entrepreneurs or colonial secretaries doubted for a moment that there was such a thing as *European* culture, that it was superior to any other culture in the world or that it was capable of being adopted, to their advantage, by any people, anywhere. These were the core doctrines of the 'white man's religion' and there was nothing new about them. They had inspired bold, foolhardy, zealous, power-hungry and avari-cious adventurers ever since Columbus. In 1793 the Marquis de Condorcet, one of France's more liberal aristocrats, observed that hitherto deprived peoples around the world 'seem to be waiting only to be civilised and to receive from us the means to be so, and find brothers among the Europeans, to become their friends and disciples'.[2] Here, again, we can see the influ-ence of Charlemagne, who harnessed the state to the universal mission of the Christian Church and helped to confirm in his contemporaries, and those who came after him, that the religion of the Galilean and all the legal, political and cultural accoutrements attaching to his teaching should be proffered to all God's children. Paradoxically, at the very time that Europe's peoples were fragmenting into nation states that were frequently hostile to each other, they were also becoming more familiar with the inhabitants of a wider world and, therefore with beliefs, values and atti-tudes that were distinctively 'European'.

But to return to the 1870s and those 'neighbours from hell', France and Germany. In political terms neither now looked for inspiration to their common ancestor. French leaders of the Third Republic had had their fill of imperial dreams, which had promised *gloire* and given *déshonneur*. In 1878 the creators of a large equestrian statue of Charlemagne were trying to find a buyer for it. They approached the Paris city council, suggesting that the impressive bronze sculpture would be an adornment to the city if displayed in the environs of Notre Dame, and would serve to remind citizens and visitors of the great founding father of the nation. The response was not encouraging: 'The figure of Charlemagne has only limited interest for the people of Paris. The great Emperor of the West was not a Parisian, nor even a Gaul.'[3]

For ardent republicans the Carolingian ruler had become almost a hate-figure. Not only was he seen as the patron saint of absolutism, but he was identified with the barbarous *bosche* from beyond the Rhine. What particu-larly annoyed some of the councillors was the fact that a recent request for a statue of Voltaire had been turned down. Under these circumstances, they argued, how could a memorial to an ancient tyrant even be contemplated? The problem was eventually solved with a Gallic compromise: two statues were erected, one to Charlemagne and one to Voltaire – the philosopher who had so roundly denounced the ninth-century emperor.

However, the fact that Charles was identified by the framers of French public opinion with Germany does not mean that the German leaders readopted him as a political legend. This was only in part because they refused to be associated with Napoleon's model hero. It was also because those charged with building foundation myths for the new empire – philosophers, historians, poets and collectors of folk legends – were looking for unambiguously German heroes, and Charlemagne no longer belonged to that category. The nineteenth century was passionate about history. Everywhere students were seeking out ancient documents, while national and regional authorities were setting up public archives. Historians of different schools advocated various reasons for studying the past and proposed distinctive rules for their discipline. There were in Germany those obsessed with unearthing the origins of the *Volk*. Historians and teachers of allied 'sciences', such as anthropology, philology and even phrenology, believed that understanding where the Germans came from would tell them who they really 'were'. It was, for example, mid-nineteenth-century scholars who produced the concept of Aryanism. Having located the origins of Teutonic languages in ancient Indo-European, they deduced the existence of a noble North European race who spoke this language and whose descendants could be distinguished by such characteristics as blond hair, blue eyes and above-average height. It was but a short step from this nationalistically inspired theory to the assertion that the inhabitants of Bismarck's empire were intellectually and physically superior to their neighbours. Manifestly, Charlemagne did not belong to this master race. Another passion of the historians was *facts*. Leopold von Ranke spoke of recording the past 'as it really happened' and he was just one historian among many who believed in the myth of 'scientific history'. Accuracy was the goal; thoroughness and precision the means of achieving it. It followed that myth and legend were to be ruthlessly expunged from the record. This boded ill for much of the received Charlemagne literature, with its exaggerations and devout fables. It also meant that discreditable incidents in the record, such as the bloodbath at Verden in 782, had to be unflinchingly set down. The emperor who emerged from the early records would now be for many Germans the 'butcher of the Saxons'. In the quest for folk heroes, a more likely candidate was Widukind, who for so many years had kept up a brave resistance to the Frankish invaders. Yet even the Germans needed inspiring stories of romance and mystery. While turning their backs on the great Christian emperor, they enthusiastically embraced a sequence of tales from the *mythistoire* of fifth-century pagan Burgundy. The *Nibelungenlied* was an epic poem of the thirteenth century, based on earlier troubadour songs, which freely mixed the exploits of the historical Burgundian kings, the Nibelungs, with later strands of Christian chivalry. At about the same time that the Paris city fathers were arguing about Charlemagne's statue, Richard Wagner's *Ring of the Nibelung* was given its première at Bayreuth.

What saved Charles the Great from being assigned to the lumber room of history was the growing internationalism of some of Europe's leading thinkers. They regarded him as having contributed to the development of society in three essential areas – civilisation, unity and peace. In 1828, three years after Saint-Simon's death, François Guizot, Professor of History at the Sorbonne, published a series of lectures under the title *Histoire générale de la civilisation en Europe*. Like several other historians of the period, he regarded the human saga as a progress from barbarism to 'civilisation', which he defined as 'the amelioration of society by means of the [moral] amelioration of the individual'.[4] Guizot lifted his gaze above nationalistic interests in his quest for those countries and individuals that had contributed most to the improvement of the human condition. For example, he extolled the British political system, which he believed provided a balance between the major socio-political elements of monarchy, aristocracy, church, common people and government institutions at central and local levels. He argued that Britain had avoided the more extreme constitutional swings and roundabouts of its neighbours because, even at times of dramatic change, none of these essential elements had wholly perished or been wholly triumphant.

For Guizot, Charlemagne stood out as a trail-blazer for European civilisation. His experiment did not last, but it contained all the elements that later leaders should copy. In warfare the emperor set his face against barbarism: the Muslims on one border and pagan tribes on others. As ruler over a vast and heterogeneous domain, 'he felt indignant at seeing all things incoherent, anarchical and rude, and desired to alter their hideous condition'. Guizot approved of Charlemagne's passion for law, his collaboration with nobles and churchmen in propounding law, and his employment of *missi* to enforce the law. 'Under whatever point of view you consider the reign of Charlemagne,' Guizot concluded:

> You will always find in it the same character, namely, warfare against the barbarous state, the spirit of civilisation; this is what appears in his eagerness to establish schools, in his taste for learned men, in the favour with which he regarded ecclesiastical influence, and in all that he thought proper to do, whether as regarded the entire society or individual man.[5]

Any thesis about the 'spread of civilisation' has to face a fundamental problem: how can such a benign objective be squared with the use of naked force to accomplish it? Guizot finds the answer to this conundrum in motive. He cites the example of France under the *Roi Soleil*. It was, beyond doubt, the leading nation in seventeenth-century Europe in terms of both power and culture, but the impulse behind all its accomplishments was the establishment of royal absolutism. This Guizot totally condemns. There is nothing worse, he declares, than 'the danger, the evil and the insurmountable vice of absolute power, whatever form, whatever name it may bear, and towards whatever aim it may direct itself'.[6] It violates one of the twin objectives in Guizot's definition of civilisation, that of advancing the moral progress of the individual. However, in denouncing the politics of power and genuflecting towards Charlemagne as a standard bearer of civilisation, Guizot avoids the question of religion. As a serious-minded Protestant, he believed in the outworking of divine Providence. His theology compelled him to recognise the special destiny of European civilisation: 'it progresses according to the intentions of God. This is the rational account of its superiority.'[7] But he avoided what would seem to be the logical conclusion of this argument: the distinctively *religious* mission of the Christian state. Charles saw himself as a viceroy in the Kingdom of God, dedicated to extending the boundaries of that kingdom both territorially and in the hearts of men. In a secular state what can replace the spiritual imperative?

In the middle years of the century Romantic poets and radical politicians grappled with this question and thought they had found the answer in secular humanism. The central tenet of this faith was the progress of the indomitable spirit of mankind. It had its own type of apocalyptic, but these progressives looked forward to a *telos* vastly different from the Christian hope. Not for them some cataclysmic divine intervention that would wind up human history and usher in the rule of the saints. They looked forward to the establishment of some form of *earthly* paradise, the evolution (a buzz-word before the appearance of Darwin's *Origin of Species* in 1859) of *homo sapiens* to his full potential, the apogee of civilisation in both its individual and social aspects. Augustine's *City of God*, Charlemagne's favourite text, had claimed that the only perfect society would exist in heaven. It was a goal to which believers must strive – unattainable in this world, but a goal nevertheless. Nineteenth-century idealists begged to differ. All their energies were bent towards creating a better world here and now. Of course, their visions of earthly bliss varied widely. For some it was the achievement of nationhood; for others the freedom of the individual; for Karl Marx it was the rule of the proletariat.

One problem posed for mid-century thinkers by social utopianism was the role of great men in the march of human progress. A scholar like Jean-Jacques Ampère regarded it as axiomatic that history could be told in terms of outstanding individuals. In his *Histoire littéraire de la France avant le douzième siècle* (1839–40) he ranked Charlemagne alongside Alexander the Great, not because they were both great conquerors, but because – unlike other military leaders – they had been motivated by the desire to spread civilisation. But it was the towering literary figure of the age, Victor Hugo, who most dramatically wrestled with the issue of the individual versus the collective. It was for him a very personal conflict. As a member of the legislative assembly he supported the election of Louis Napoleon as President of the Republic after the overthrow, in 1848, of the last Bourbon, Louis-Philippe, and his prime minister – none other than François Guizot, whose ideas of a balance of political elements under a constitutional monarchy had become increasingly unpopular with the idealists of the Left. Hugo's disillusionment with the new people's champion was rapid. Napoleon's rule became increasingly autocratic and, when the Second Empire was declared in 1851, the poet went into voluntary exile, where he remained for most of the next two decades. As a Romantic poet, Hugo fell under the spell of Charlemagne. During a visit to Aachen, in around 1840, he had an almost mystic experience. Confronted by the cathedral with its confusion of architectural vogues and the vulgar commercialisation directed at the tourist market, he seemed to see through, beyond and above it the resplendent figure of the emperor in his coronation robes: a once-and-future king whose work, like the building that housed his tomb, was both incomplete and embraced a variety of peoples, symbolised by the melange of constructional styles in the church. Charlemagne impressed Hugo as the very personification of European civilisation. But, as he reflected on this experience, Hugo the politician demanded caution of Hugo the poet. Hero worship was manifestly fraught with danger:

> It might well be necessary to redo the work of Charlemagne and Napoleon but without either Napoleon or Charlemagne. Those great men have, perhaps, become obstacles in that they too precisely personify ideas and arouse by their very beings . . . national jealousies. From this there might emerge mutual contempt and the peoples [of France and Germany] might come to believe that they serve a man and not a cause, the ambition of an individual and not the common civilisation.[8]

For Victor Hugo, as for other liberals, any flowering of European civilisation was bound up with unity. Progressives saw themselves as belonging to a universal brotherhood, a fraternity occasionally strengthened by shared exile (notably in Britain, which became a haven for men as diverse as François Guizot, Karl Marx, Victor Hugo and Napoleon III). As we have seen, there was nothing new in this European cosmopolitanism. For a century or more it had been a commonplace of thinkers such as Rousseau, Voltaire, Kant and Saint-Simon. The bonding together of the European states was seen as the only certain way of taming national rivalries, advancing liberalism, enabling the countries of continental Europe to compete more effectively in world markets and pursuing its civilising mission. In 1849 Hugo expressed his vision in an impassioned speech to an international conference in Paris:

> The day will come when you Russia, you France, you England, and you Germany, when all the nations of the continent, without forfeiting your distinctive characteristics or your individual splendours, will bind yourselves tightly together into a single, superior entity, and come to constitute a European brotherhood, as complete as Brittany, Burgundy and Alsace are now bound together as parts of France.[9]

Such rousing rhetoric was all very well, but how were noble aspirations to be provided with any kind of political structure? At the 1849 conference, Saint-Simon's idea of a United States of Europe resurfaced, but, in so far as it had any coherence, it was largely confined to issues of free trade and economic cooperation. In 1860 Giuseppe Mazzini, the hero of Italian unification, proposed something much more radical: the transformation of Europe into a federation of republics. Set alongside such grandiose schemes Victor Hugo's own proposal was modest in the extreme – though none the less impractical. In order to defuse Franco-German conflict over Rhineland territories, why should the two nations not come together in a grand central-European state, a re-formation of the Carolingian Empire? This would ensure peace between the neighbouring nations and, in terms of current power politics, would form a bloc able to withstand the pressures of the existing alliance between Britain and Russia.

Peace was the overriding concern of all men of good will. The only way the chancelleries of Europe could conceive of preventing major conflict was by preserving the balance of power by means of defensive alliances. It is interesting that even Victor Hugo conceded to this international realpolitik in his proposal for a union of France and Germany. The events of 1870–1 cruelly revealed the futility of any such dream. Not only did they reveal the hideous power of nationalism, but they tore open all the old half-healed wounds between the two parts of Charlemagne's ancient empire. Henceforth Germany would maintain its contempt for the 'effete' nation so easily overthrown in the war, and France would never rest content until full revenge had been visited on its 'barbaric' neighbour. There would be no possibility of rapprochement until both nations had totally exhausted themselves and could only gaze upon each other across the rubble of ruined towns and cities. There was no room for idealism in the harsh political world of post-1871 Europe. In order to protect themselves from each other, the two countries resorted to the old political stratagem of forming defensive leagues. Before the new century was out of its cradle the Triple Alliance of Germany, Austria-Hungary and Italy glared defiantly at the Triple Entente of France, Britain and Russia. The security that Bismarck had aimed to give his new creation had vanished. Germany found itself hemmed in by powerful potential aggressors. Europe had seen it all before; the France of Francis I and of Napoleon I had been in the same unenviable position. The result on both occasions had been prolonged, bitter warfare. History was about to repeat itself. But with two terrifyingly significant differences. One was the development of appalling weapons of total war. The other was the dragging of nations far and near into the conflict. There were, of course, other reasons, deep and complex, for the outbreak of the world's two worst military clashes, but the strongest roots ran deep into the soil of European nationalism. What we call the First and Second World Wars were in reality phases of the same hate-driven confrontation. The unfinished business of 1871 was thrashed out in 1914–18, and the unfinished business of 1919 was put back on the agenda in 1939–45.

It was Adolf Hitler who found a use for the Charlemagne mythology during the second phase of the twentieth-century conflict. Into the philosophical ragbag that he gathered to explain and justify his aggression went any elements of history and folklore that could be of service. This now included the great Carolingian warrior-king. He rescued the reputation of the old emperor, which had sunk to an all-time low, by the simple expedient of forbidding anyone to traduce Charles' name. Specifically, he outlawed any reference to the 'butcher of the Saxons'. This was because he had come up with a resounding title for the empire he was building. The grand idea with which he harangued the marshalled crowds at the spectacular Nazi rallies was the 'Third Reich'. Like Bismarck's, his state would unite all Germans under one *führer*. Like Charlemagne's, his state would sweep invincibly onward, bringing the advantages of master-race rule to all Europe's peoples (he claimed to have no ambitions beyond mainland Europe and was genuinely aggrieved that Britain was not prepared to enter a pact guaranteeing its own overseas empire while allowing him a free hand on the mainland). Unlike the previous German empires, however, the Third Reich was destined, as he claimed, to last for a thousand years. The old Francophobia was deeply lodged in Hitler's psyche. Most of us are familiar with the old newsreel footage that shows the Nazi leader gloating with uncontrollable joy on his first visit to conquered Paris. He rubbed the old foe's nose in its defeat by making it sign an armistice in the very place where the German surrender had been signed in 1918. And when, in 1944, he formed an SS division of Frenchmen who had come over to the side of the victors, what did he call it? The 'Charlemagne' division.

After 1945 would there be any place left for Charlemagne in a Europe that had battered and frightened itself into peace? Its major states were no longer the lead players in international affairs. A new political drama, in which they only had bit parts, was being played out between two superpowers. One could, in fact, no longer speak of 'Europe' in political terms, for Churchill's celebrated 'iron curtain' now divided it into 'East' and 'West', two entities committed to competing ideologies. In fact, it was the Soviet threat that forced the countries of 'free' Europe to look to their shared past and rediscover a common identity. When the leader of wartime Britain made a speech in Zurich in 1946 he expressed something that, for him, was more than an opportunity, more than a pious hope; it was an imperative:

> If the European countries succeed in uniting, their 300 to 400 million inhabitants would know, by the fruit of their common heritage, a prosperity, a glory, a happiness that no boundary, no border could contain . . . We must construct such a thing as the United States of Europe.[10]

Dedicated student of history that he was, Churchill understood that western Europe had to emerge from the flames of war as a phoenix, commercially strong and politically united, if it was to continue to have a significant role in the world. He also took it as axiomatic that there was such a thing as European civilisation. That civilisation might be as difficult to define as it always had been. Whatever 'Europe' was had to do with a common religious foundation; with a reverence for law, individual freedom and responsibility to society; with a shared inheritance of art, music and literature; with a sense of belonging to something bigger than the nation, yet holding on to national identity; with the desire (even the compulsion) to export its beliefs, culture, legal systems and political institutions to other lands. If the quarrelsome neighbours of Europe could not learn to live and work together as never before, they stood the risk of being swamped by Soviet totalitarianism or American globalisation. Moreover, the world would lose that unique contribution to its well-being that only Europe could offer. It really was a question of 'unite or die'.

Charles de Gaulle, Churchill's wartime ally and peacetime opponent, also understood this. Yet for him there was another problem. In any postwar settlement, a crushed France that had had to be rescued by British and US forces stood the risk of being relegated to the sidelines. His vision for a new Europe was one in which France would take the lead. When he spoke, in 1950, of his country and Germany 'uniting together', he knew that he had the old enemy at a disadvantage. The new, liberal regime in Germany was desperate for help in rebuilding its shattered economy and was equally desperate to slough off the image of aggressive nationalism. In the new Europe that emerged over the next few decades, governments in Bonn always declared themselves in favour of moves towards federalism. They were dependent on French support, and de Gaulle intended to use this to control the agenda of the European community that was being created. At the conference table he bullied, threatened and sulked to such good effect that the ground rules of the European Economic Community were almost entirely framed in France's interest. The EEC came into being with the Treaties of Rome in 1957. It was not entirely coincidental that the six nations comprising the European Economic Community – France, Germany, Italy, the Netherlands, Belgium and Luxembourg – covered territory almost completely coterminous with Charlemagne's empire. These were the successor nations of Carolingian Francia. For more than a millennium, through war and peace, social catastrophe and commercial expansion, internal feuds and the threat of external aggression, they had shared a common culture. They were 'family'.

Britain had always been a more distant relation – in recent decades a kind of patronising rich uncle, if that does not stretch the analogy too far. This country now made de Gaulle's task easier by remaining aloof from the EEC. When, in 1965, Britain had second thoughts and applied for membership, de Gaulle enjoyed his moment of triumph. He vetoed Britain's entry. It would be 1973 before the UK gained admittance to the European 'club'. Since then that club has undergone dramatic change and growth. The EEC became the European Community and then the European Union. Its membership has grown from six to twenty-five. It has survived, almost nonchalantly, the reunification of Germany, the collapse of the Soviet bloc and the application of former Communist states to join its ranks. Throughout most of its history the Franco-German entente has been at the heart of the new Europe, setting the pace economically and politically. Other members have often grumbled about a 'two-tier' Europe, but mature reflection suggests that there are distinct advantages about a situation in which these two traditional belligerents, the heirs of Charlemagne's divided empire, are committed to working together. In any case, the bigger the union, the more diluted will become the dominance of the two states at the geographical centre.

The world constantly changes. No one in 1957, at the peak of the Cold War, could have foreseen how vastly different the international scene would appear half a century later, when the chilling blasts from the Communist East had ceased to blow and the 'free world' had to look to the Middle East for its enemies. Europe has tried to respond to the dynamics of change. Not unnaturally, opinions vary as to how effective such responses have been. EU citizens frequently grumble about 'Brussels bureaucracy', the almost incomprehensible organisational structure of the Union, the threat to national sovereignty, and centrally agreed policies that seem to be quite divorced from regional reality. Beyond doubt, enthusiasm for the EU is greater among the politicians who operate it than among the peoples they represent. It may be a long time before many of us can say, 'Europe with all thy faults I love thee still.' Yet it is worthwhile contemplating the alternatives: a Europe of nation states thrashing out their problems in time-honoured ways; an international situation dominated by a single superpower claiming leadership of the 'free world' and bent on commercial and ideological domination (backed up by force when necessary); a marginalised collection of European countries with an ancient culture and centuries of political experience no longer able to bring their collective expertise to bear upon the problems of the planet. At the peak of the Iraq crisis in 2003, when the USA was not getting everything its own way in preparation for the forthcoming war, a spokesman for the Bush administration referred contemptuously to the caveats raised by some of the leaders of 'Old Europe'. The phrase should strike a warning note about what could happen in a world where a united Europe no longer had a strong presence.

I subtitled this book 'The Great Adventure' and I suppose the time has come to justify that description. That Charles the Great was an adventurer is beyond doubt. He was a leader of vision, commitment and energy, remarkable by the standards of any age. To secure the territory he inherited and to bring other peoples into the Christian fold, he pushed his boundaries ever outwards. He was successful in war more often than not. He made a reasonable fist of administering his multi-ethnic empire. That Greater Francia did not survive was not his fault, and the adventure did not end either with his death or with the demise of his empire. What lived on was the 'idea' of Europe. Something came into being between 771 and 814 that had not existed before – a community of peoples and tribes, united by religion, respect for classical culture, commitment to the rule of law and a sense of belonging to something larger than their own political units. From that point on the adventure story became the narrative of the successes and failures of an idea. 'Europe' advanced and retreated territorially and conceptually, now fragmenting, now coalescing, now turning in on itself, now venturing to the farthest regions of the globe. This is one of the great adventure stories in the history of the world, even though it is not focused on the deeds of a single champion. Unless that champion be Charlemagne. Time and again the memory of the great emperor was revived in a variety of guises – conqueror, law-giver, saint, crusader, patron of scholars, educational reformer. The man and the myth – inseparable even in the most rational of ages – became all things to all men, inspiring crusaders, tyrants and liberal politicians alike. Through all the ups and downs of a millennium, Charlemagne personified for all sorts and conditions of men what it meant to be French or German.

Latterly his name has been linked to Europeanism, because that concept seems to many who live in the lands where once his writ ran to be an important contribution to human progress in the twenty-first century. In 1950 the city fathers of Aachen decided to institute an annual Charlemagne Prize. It is awarded to that statesman who has, in the opinion of the judges, done most to further the cause of European unity. Whether or not Europeanism is something to be encouraged, the reader must decide for himself or herself. What, I believe, is beyond dispute is that without Charlemagne – man, monarch and myth – there would be no debate. 'Europe', if it existed at all, would be something very different. For that reason alone the latest version of the Charlemagne legend has validity. He was what the eighth-century poet said he was: 'the King and Father of Europe'.

Notes

1 See Morrissey, op. cit., p.415
2 See Pagden., op. cit., p.53
3 See Morrissey, op. cit., p.409
4 Guizot, op. cit., p.20
5 Ibid., pp.60–1
6 Ibid., p.244

7 Ibid., p.32
8 See Morrissey, op. cit., p.388
9 V. Hugo, *Douze discours: Oeuvres complètes*, Paris, 1882, VI, p.127
10 See A. C. d'Appollonia, 'European Nationalism and European Union', in Pagden, op. cit., p.178

Select Bibliography

There is a vast literature on Charlemagne and his influence, much of it in French and German. In the following highly selective summary I have concentrated on works written in English or available in translation. The exceptions are standard works that are widely accepted as authoritative, indispensable studies. The place of publication is London unless otherwise indicated.

Primary sources
Allott, S., *Alcuin of York*, 1974
Carolingian Chronicles: Royal Frankish Annals and Nithard's Histories (trs. B. W. Scholtz with B. Rogers), Michigan, 1970
Chanson de Roland, La (trs. D. Sayers), 1957
Charlemagne: Translated sources (trs. P. D. King), Lancaster, 1987
Einhard and Notker the Stammerer; Two Lives of Charlemagne (trs. L. Thorpe), 1969
Guizot, F., *The History of Civilization in Europe* (trs. K. W. Hazlitt), 1997
Journey of Charlemagne to Jerusalem and Constantinople, The (trs. J.-L. G. Picherit), 1984
Monumenta Germaniae Historica: Epistolae Karolini aevi, Hanover, 1826–
Oeuvres de Claude-Henri de Saint-Simon, Geneva, 1977
Pèlerinage de Charlemagne (ed. G. S. Burgess), 1998
Reign of Charlemagne, The: Documents on Carolingian government and administration (ed. H. R. Loyn and J. Percival), 1975
Textes de Charlemagne, Eginhard, Alcuin, Hincmar (ed. G. Tessier), Paris, 1967

Secondary sources

Alcuin of York – Papers of the Germanic Latina Conference, 1998

Almedingen, E. M., *Charlemagne*, 1968

Baker, G. P., *Charlemagne and the United States of Europe*, 1932

Barber, R., *The Knight and Chivalry*, 1970

Barraclough, G., *The Crucible of Europe, The Ninth and Tenth Centuries in European History*, 1976

Bartlett, R., *The Making of Europe: Conquest, Colonization and Cultural Change, 950–1350*, Princeton, 1993

Becher, M., *Charlemagne*, New Haven, 2003

Bordonove, G., *Charlemagne, empereur et roi*, 1989

Boussard, J., *Civilisation of Charlemagne* (trs. F. Partridge), 1968

Braunfells, W., *Karl der Grosse, Lebenswerk und Nachleben*, Aachen, 1965

Brown, P. R. L., *The Rise of Western Christendom: Triumph and Diversity AD 200–1000*, Oxford, 1996

Bullough, D. A., *The Age of Charlemagne*, 1973

Bullough, D. A., *Caroline Renewal*, Manchester, 1991

Butzer, P. and Kerne, M., *Charlemagne and his Heritage: 1200 years of civilization and science in Europe*, 1997

Chamberlin, E. R., *Charlemagne, Emperor of the Western World*, 2003

Collins, R., *Charlemagne*, 2000

Cusack, C. M., *The Rise of Christianity in Northern Europe, 800–1000*, 1998

Delanty, G., *Inventing Europe: Idea, Identity, Reality*, 1995

Duckett, E. S., *Alcuin, Friend of Charlemagne, His World and His Work*, 1951

Fichtenau, H., *The Carolingian Empire* (trs. P. Munz), Toronto, 1978

Fletcher, R. M., *The Conversion of Europe: From Paganism to Christianity, 371–1386 A.D.*, 1997

Folz, R., *Le Souvenir et la légende de Charlemagne dans l'empire germanique médiéval*, Paris, 1950

Ganshof, F.-L., *The Imperial Coronation of Charlemagne: Theories and Facts*, Glasgow, 1949

Ganshof, F.-L., *Frankish Institutions under Charlemagne* (trs. B. and M. Lyon), New York, 1968

Gibbon, E., *History of the Decline and Fall of the Roman Empire*, 1983 edn

Godman, P., *Poets and Emperors: Frankish Politics and Carolingian Poetry*, Oxford, 1987

Godman, P. and Collins, R. (eds), *Charlemagne's Heir, New Perspectives on the Reign of Louis the Pious (814–840)*, Oxford, 1990

Heer, F., *Charlemagne and His World*, 1975

Jones, G., *The History of the Vikings*, Oxford, 1968

King, P. D., *Charlemagne*, 1986

Select Bibliography

McKitterick, R., *The Frankish Church and the Carolingian Reforms 789–895*, 1977

McKitterick, R., *The Frankish Kingdoms under the Carolingians, 751–987*, 1983

McKitterick, R., *The Carolingians and the Written Word*, Cambridge, 1989

Morris, C., *The Papal Monarchy, the Western Church from 1050 to 1250*, Oxford, 1989

Morrissey, R., *L'Empereur à la barbe fleurie: Charlemagne dans la mythologie et l'histoire de France*, Paris, 1997

Munz, P., *Life in the Age of Charlemagne,* 1969

Nelson, J., *The Frankish World, 750–900*, 1996

Norwich, J. J., *Byzantium, the Early Centuries*, 1989

Norwich, J. J., *Byzantium, the Apogee*, 1991

Pagden, A. (ed)., *The Idea of Europe from Antiquity to the European Union*, Cambridge, 2002

Political Writings of Benjamin Constant, The (ed. B. Fontana), Cambridge, 1988

Pratt, K. (ed.), *Roland and Charlemagne in Europe: Essays on the reception and transformation of a legend*, 1996

Riché, P., *Daily Life in the World of Charlemagne* (trs. J. A. McNamara), Liverpool, 1978

Riché, P., *The Carolingians: A Family who Forged Europe* (trs. M. I. Allen), Philadelphia, 1993

Runciman, S., *A History of the Crusades*, Cambridge, 1951

Sawyer, P. H., *The Age of the Vikings*, 1977

Steward, R. J., *Charlemagne and the Carolingian Empire* (trs. G. de Nie), Oxford, 1977

Sullivan, R. E., *Aix-La-Chapelle in the Age of Charlemagne*, 1963

Ullmann, W., *The Carolingian Renaissance and the Idea of Kingship*, 1969

Vasiliev, A. A., *History of the Byzantine Empire, 324–1453,* Wisconsin, 1952

Wallace-Hadrill, J. M., *The Frankish Church*, Oxford, 1983

Wallace-Hadrill, J. M., *The Barbarian West, 400–1000*, Oxford, 1996

Wallach, L., *Alcuin and Charlemagne: Studies in Carolingian History and Literature*, Ithaca, 1959

Wallach, L., *Alcuin and Charlemagne*, Ithaca, 1968

Werner, K. F., *Karl der Grosse oder Charlemagne?*, Munich, 1995

Wood, I., *The Missionary Life: Saints and the Evangelisation of Europe, 400–1050,* 2001

Index